Understanding Health
Inequalities

Understanding Health Inequalities

EDITED BY
Hilary Graham

Open University Press
Buckingham · Philadelphia

Open University Press
Celtic Court
22 Ballmoor
Buckingham
MK18 1XW

email: enquiries@openup.co.uk
world wide web: www.openup.co.uk

and
325 Chestnut Street
Philadelphia, PA 19106, USA

First Published 2000
Reprinted 2001

A catalogue record of this book is available from the British Library

ISBN 0 335 20553 4 (pbk)   0 335 20554 2 (hbk)

Library of Congress Cataloging-in-Publication Data available

Typeset by Type Study, Scarborough
Printed in Great Britain by St Edmundsbury Press, Bury St Edmunds, Suffolk

Contents

List of contributors

Waqar Ahmad, Professor of Primary Care Research, Centre for Research in Primary Care, University of Leeds.

Mel Bartley, Principal Research Fellow, Department of Epidemiology and Public Health, University College London.

Sharon Bennett, Research Fellow, Institute for Public Health Research and Policy, University of Salford.

Michaela Benzeval, Senior Lecturer, Department of Geography, Queen Mary and Westfield College, University of London.

Lee Berney, Research Assistant, LSE Health, London School of Economics and Political Science.

David Blane, Reader, Division of Neuroscience, Imperial College of Science, Technology and Medicine.

Lisa Bostock, Researcher, Department of Applied Social Science, Lancaster University.

Nicola Brimblecombe, Information Officer, Maternity Alliance, London.

Sylvie Briscoe, Research Assistant in Psychology, School of Psychology, University of St Andrews.

Bo Burström, Senior Research Fellow, Department of Public Health Sciences, Karolinska Institute, Stockholm.

Katharine Charsley, Researcher, Department of Social Medicine, University of Bristol.

George Davey Smith, Professor of Clinical Epidemiology, Department of Social Medicine, University of Bristol.

Chris Dibben, Researcher, Department of Applied Social Studies and Social Research, University of Oxford.

Finn Diderichsen, Professor of Social Epidemiology and Health Policy Research, Department of Public Health Sciences, Karolinska Institute, Stockholm.

Andrew Dilnot, Director, Institute for Fiscal Studies, London.

Danny Dorling, Professor of Quantitative Human Geography, School of Geography, University of Leeds.

Anne Ellaway, Researcher, MRC Social and Public Health Sciences Unit, University of Glasgow.

Carol Emslie, Research Associate MRC Social and Public Health Sciences Unit, University of Glasgow.

Steve Fenton, Senior Lecturer, Department of Sociology, University of Bristol.

David Firth, Senior Fellow in Statistics for the Social Sciences, Nuffield College, University of Oxford.

Ray Fitzpatrick, Professor of Public Health and Primary Care, Institute of Health Sciences, University of Oxford.

Anthony Gatrell, Professor and Director of Institute for Health Research, Lancaster University.

Simon Gleave, Lecturer, Sociology Department, City University and Centre for Longitudinal Studies, Institute of Education, London University.

Elspeth Graham, Senior Lecturer in Human Geography, School of Geography and Geosciences, University of St Andrews.

Hilary Graham, Professor of Social Policy, Department of Applied Social Science, Lancaster University.

Rosemary Hiscock, Research Associate, MRC Social and Public Health Sciences Unit, University of Glasgow.

Paula Holland, Research Fellow, Department of Public Health, University of Liverpool.

Kate Hunt, Senior Research Scientist, MRC Social and Public Health Sciences Unit, University of Glasgow.

Marie Johnston, Professor in Health Psychology, School of Psychology, University of St Andrews.

Heather Joshi, Professor and Deputy Director, Centre for Longitudinal Studies, Institute of Education, London University.

Ken Judge, Professor of Health Promotion Policy, Department of Public Health, University of Glasgow.

Saffron Karlsen, Research Fellow, Department of Epidemiology and Public Health, University College London.

Ade Kearns, Professor and Head of Department, Department of Urban Studies, University of Glasgow.

Helen Lambert, Senior Lecturer in Medical Anthropology, London School of Hygiene and Tropical Medicine.

Kevin Lynch, Computing Research Officer, Centre for Longitudinal Studies, Institute of Education, London University.

Sally Macintyre, Professor and Director, MRC Social and Public Health Sciences Unit, University of Glasgow.

Malcolm MacLeod, Lecturer in Social and Forensic Psychology, School of Psychology, University of St Andrews.

Richard Mitchell, Researcher, Department of Geography, University of Leeds.

Irene Morgan, Clinical Psychology Assistant, Astley Ainslie Hospital, Edinburgh.

James Y. Nazroo, Senior Lecturer in Sociology, Department of Epidemiology and Public Health, University College London.

Sheila Paul, Research Fellow, Centre for Research in Primary Care, University of Leeds.

Jennie Popay, Professor of Sociology and Health Policy, Nuffield Institute for Health Policy, University of Leeds.

Amanda Sacker, Senior Research Fellow, Department of Epidemiology and Public Health, University College London.

Said Shahtahmasebi, Consultant Statistician, ICIS Technology Ltd, Harrogate.

Mary Shaw, ESRC Research Fellow, School of Geographical Sciences, University of Bristol.

Jayne Taylor, Senior Research Economist, Institute for Fiscal Studies, London.

Carol Thomas, Senior Lecturer, Department of Applied Social Science, Lancaster University.

Graham Watt, Professor of General Practice, Department of General Practice, University of Glasgow.

Margaret Whitehead, Professor of Public Health, Department of Public Health, University of Liverpool.

Richard D. Wiggins, Reader, Department of Sociology, City University, London.

Gareth Williams, Professorial Fellow in the Social Sciences, School of Social Sciences, Cardiff University.

Acknowledgements

The chapters of this book all draw on research funded under the Health Variations Programme by the Economic and Social Research Council (ESRC), the major funder of social science research in the UK. We would also like to acknowledge the help of Caroline Osander of Lancaster University, and Jonathan Ingoldby of Open University Press with production of the manuscript.

Introduction

1 The challenge of health inequalities

Hilary Graham

Introduction

This book turns the spotlight on the link between social inequality and individual health. It does so by focusing on socio-economic inequality: on the fact that how well and how long one lives is powerfully shaped by one's place in the hierarchies built around occupation, education and income.

The chapters draw on new research from the UK which sheds light on the mechanisms which link socio-economic status (SES) to health. Some of the chapters are concerned with lifecourse pathways: with how exposure to disadvantage takes its toll on health through childhood and across adult life. Others explore whether and how our place of residence – our home and neighbourhood, local area and wider region – influences our chances of leading a long and healthy life. Framing the chapters is a concern with how SES connects with other axes of inequality, like ethnicity and gender, in making a difference to health.

These themes are explored through analyses of existing surveys and through new empirical studies. The chapters draw both on quantitative data, using established measures of SES and health, and on qualitative data, where people talk in their own terms about the influence of biography and place on their lives. The research forms part of the Health Variations Programme, funded by the Economic and Social Research Council (ESRC). The programme was set up in 1996 to shed light on the causes of health inequalities in the UK.

The UK provides an illuminating case study. On the one hand, it exhibits trends evident in other older industrial societies, where greater prosperity and better health for the population as a whole has not brought about a narrowing of inequalities in income and mortality. Instead, rising living standards and increasing life expectancy have been achieved at the cost of widening inequalities in these two fundamental dimensions of human welfare. On the other hand, the UK has a new public health strategy which aims to reduce health inequalities by addressing broader inequalities in life chances and living standards. As the government put it, 'tackling inequalities generally is the best way of tackling health inequalities in particular' (Secretary of State for Health 1998: 12).

Measuring socio-economic inequality

The long tradition of health inequalities research in the UK makes it well placed to unravel the links between inequalities generally and health inequalities in particular. However, as elsewhere, research has been resourced by data on individuals: from medical records and vital registrations, from cross-sectional studies, where individuals are surveyed at one point in time, and from longitudinal studies, where individuals are followed up over time. These individual data have enabled researchers to trace the influences on health back through intermediate factors, like living and working conditions, to individual SES. Only rarely does the search for causes extend beyond the individual to the underlying structures of inequality. As a result, much less is known about the macro determinants of socio-economic inequality than about the lives and lifestyles of individuals. Lives and lifestyles are mediated by other dimensions of inequality, including ethnicity and gender. Again, these are typically treated as personal attributes (Asian man; White woman), an approach which obscures the structures of disadvantage and discrimination which make them important influences on health.

UK studies have relied on occupation-based measures, like the registrar general's classification, to measure individual SES (see Table 1.1). The classification was developed 100 years ago to capture the pecking order of power, property and prestige among men; a pecking order in which women and children earned their place indirectly, through the occupation of the 'man of the house'. Recognizing the limitations of this schema, other measures of SES are increasingly used alongside occupation, including parental social class, education, income, housing tenure and car ownership. There are, of course, strong associations between these measures. Family background is a powerful predictor of educational attainment, while staying on at school and gaining qualifications anticipates a well-paid career, which in turn provides the income needed to buy a home and own a car. As these associations suggest, socio-economic inequality is made up of an intricate web of hierarchies which individuals negotiate as they journey from childhood through adolescence and into adult life. Focusing on one thread in this web – on current

Table 1.1 Examples of occupations in their social class groupings

	Social class	Occupations
I	Professional	Accountant, doctor, lawyer
II	Managerial and technical/ intermediate	Sales manager, teacher, journalist, nurse
IIIN	Skilled non-manual	Secretary, shop assistant, cashier
IIIM	Skilled manual	Joiner, bus driver, cook
IV	Partly skilled manual	Security guard, machine tool operator, farm worker
V	Unskilled manual	Building labourer, cleaner, laundry worker

occupation, for example – can obscure how health is shaped by a broader range of influences which run back to the early years of life. A key research task is to unravel these dimensions of SES and map their health effects.

Measures of SES have been developed from and for the White population. However, ethnicity mediates access to the domains which these measures are designed to capture. For example, people from minority ethnic groups face higher rates of unemployment and of employment in low-skilled jobs than similarly qualified Whites (Modood 1998). As this suggests, measures of SES may have a variable – rather than consistent – relationship to life chances and living standards in different ethnic groups. A second important research task is therefore to develop ways of measuring SES and ethnicity which are sensitive to how these core dimensions of identity are experienced.

Part 1 of the book tackles these two research tasks. George Davey Smith and colleagues explore the ways in which ethnicity and SES intersect in the lives of minority ethnic groups. Their chapter describes how an individual's opportunities with respect to employment, occupation and housing are disrupted by migration and constrained by racism. It notes how social networks, and the exchange of material and social resources, further influence living standards.

Saffron Karlsen and James Nazroo focus on ethnicity as identity. They highlight five dimensions of identity in minority ethnic groups, including self-description and experience of racism, and examine the associations between ethnic identity, SES and health. They conclude that the experiences of racism and socio-economic disadvantage are strongly associated with poor health for minority ethnic groups in Britain.

Focusing on women, Mel Bartley's team explore how different dimensions of inequality – like employment conditions and material living standards – have different roles to play in health inequalities. Their analysis suggests that material disadvantage has the greatest effect on health. The task of unpacking

Table 1.2 Average age of death by social class and area of residence, 1838–41

District	Gentry and professional	Farmers and tradesmen	Labourers and artisans
Rutland	52	41	38
Bath	55	37	25
Leeds	44	27	19
Bethnal Green	45	26	16
Manchester	38	20	17
Liverpool	35	22	15

Source: Whitehead (1997) adapted from Lancet 1843, Office for National Statistics © Crown Copyright 1997.

SES is continued in other chapters, through an examination of the contribution of income (Chapter 6) and housing tenure (Chapter 8).

Health inequalities: patterns and trends

Evidence of an association between socio-economic position and health dates back to ancient China, Greece and Egypt and is apparent today in societies for which data are available (Krieger 1997; Whitehead 1997). Table 1.2 captures this association in mid-nineteenth-century England. It highlights, too, how the scale of these socio-economic differences varied across the country. In Liverpool, for example, the average age of death for labourers was 15, less than half that recorded for gentry in the city (35 years) and for labourers in rural Rutland (38 years).

Mid-nineteenth-century England was a rapidly industrializing society in which infectious diseases of childhood and early adulthood kept life expectancy low. Since then, death rates have fallen by half and it is the chronic diseases of later life, like coronary heart disease (CHD) and cancer, which dominate the mortality statistics. Despite these changes, the distribution of ill-health continues to follow the contours of disadvantage.

The map of regional mortality still marks out the poorer industrial and rural areas of northern UK from the richer rural and suburban areas of the south (see Figure 1.1). The spatial patterning of health is repeated at area level. For example, the prevalence of limiting long-standing illness varies from under 10 per cent in areas of the country characterized by growth and prosperity to over 20 per cent in the coalfields and industrial ports (Wiggins et al. 1998).

Inequalities between places are matched by inequalities between individuals. Each step down the class ladder brings an increased risk of premature death (see Figure 1.2). The gradient is less steep for women but, as for men, higher SES protects against premature death. Major causes of

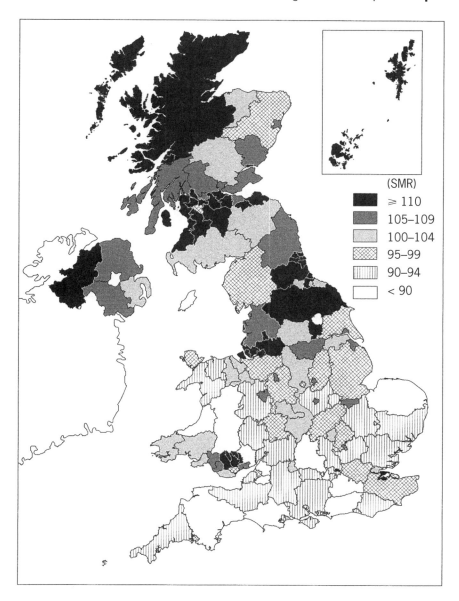

Figure 1.1 Standardized mortality ratios (SMRs) in the UK by county and unitary authorities, 1997
Source: 'Regional Trends 34', Office for National Statistics © Crown Copyright 1999.

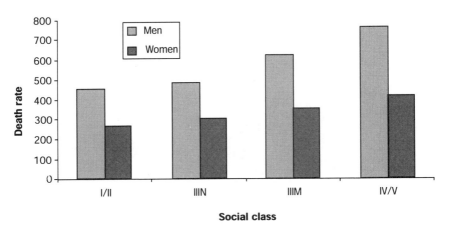

Figure 1.2 Age standardized death rates per 100,000 people by social class, men and women aged 35–64, England and Wales, 1980–92
Note: Women are classified by partner's occupational details or, if absent, by their own.
Source: Harding *et al.* (1997), Office for National Statistics © Crown Copyright 1997.

death also display strong socio-economic gradients. CHD, the focus of three chapters in this book, is the leading single cause of death in the UK. Among men, death rates from CHD are about 40 per cent higher among manual workers than among non-manual workers; the death rate for wives of manual workers is about twice the rate for wives of non-manual workers (Marmot 1998). Like mortality, morbidity from CHD also displays a socio-economic gradient, with angina and heart attacks (myocardial infarction – MI) more common among manual than non-manual groups. Less is known about recovery from myocardial infarction and whether socio-economic disadvantage slows the recovery process, an issue addressed in Chapter 11.

Statistics on disease and death provide a negative picture of the health of the population. Subjective measures, where individuals are invited to assess their physical and psychosocial health, again reveal a socio-economic gradient. While self-rated health has been regarded as a less accurate measure of health, it predicts mortality and is associated with other clinically-based measures of disease (Power *et al.* 1998).

The inequalities captured in Figures 1.1 and 1.2 are widening. Life expectancy has continued to rise for men and women in all socio-economic economic groups, but the differential has become more pronounced. Between 1972 and 1996, life expectancy for men in social class 1 increased by 5.7 years: among men in social class 5, the gain was 1.7 years (Hattersley 1999). Mortality rates tell a similar story. While death rates have fallen, the decline has been greater in higher socio-economic groups. Figure 1.3 captures the trend among men of working age using standardized mortality

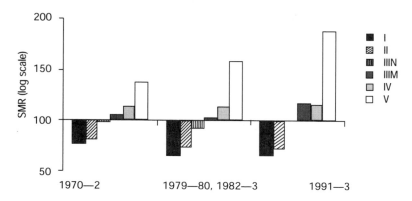

Figure 1.3 SMRs by social class (based on occupation), males, England and Wales 1970–2, 1979–80, 1982–3 and 1991–3, all causes
Source: Drever *et al.* (1996), Office for National Statistics © Crown Copyright 1996.

ratios (SMRs) which take account of differences in the size and age composition of different classes. If there were no class inequalities, men in each social class would have an SMR of 100. An SMR below the line indicates a lower than average death rate; one above the line reflects a greater than average death rate. In recent decades, class differences in mortality have widened. In the 1970s, death rates were twice as high among unskilled manual workers as among professionals; by the 1990s, the death rate was three times higher. Underlying this widening class divide are widening differentials in major causes of premature death, including coronary heart disease, stroke and lung cancer. Among children, falling mortality rates have again been associated with widening inequalities in major causes of mortality, including accidents (Roberts and Power 1996).

Spatial inequalities in health are also increasing, as the poorer areas of Britain are left behind in the general improvement in health. Poorer areas which had mortality rates 20 per cent above the national average in the 1950s, like Oldham, Salford and Greenock, had mortality rates 30 per cent above the national rate by the 1990s (Shaw *et al.* 1998). The result is a concentration of premature deaths in areas of high (and often increasing) deprivation. Danny Dorling and colleagues extend their analysis of this polarization of mortality in Chapter 12. Geographical inequalities in health in Britain, they conclude, 'now stand at the highest levels ever recorded'.

Socio-economic inequalities: patterns and trends

This book sets its analyses of health inequalities – between individuals and between areas – against the backdrop of broader economic and social change. Again, trends in the UK capture patterns evident in other older industrial societies.

The economic base has shifted away from the traditional manufacturing industries which provided full-time manual jobs for men, to the service industries which have opened up part-time work for women. The result has been a sharp rise in unemployment among men in unskilled manual groups (to 20 per cent in the late 1990s compared with 1 per cent in professional households) and a continuing rise in women's employment. Seventy per cent of women are now in paid work, but their hourly wages are 25 per cent lower than men's (ONS 1998; Harkness and Waldfogel 1999). Gaining entry to this changing labour market increasingly turns on educational qualifications. Those with qualifications are more likely to be employed in a well-paid job, while lack of qualifications is linked to unemployment and low-paid work. Although overall levels of educational attainment are improving, the gap between the highest and lowest attaining pupils widened through the 1990s (Sparkes 1999).

While education is increasingly determining access to employment, employment is increasingly determining access to housing. Since the 1970s, there has been a rapid rise in owner occupation and a sharp decline in the availability of social housing (homes to rent from local authorities and housing associations). The result is that housing tenure, and the neighbourhoods in which tenants and owner-occupiers live, are increasingly patterned by SES. In the owner-occupied sector, eight in ten heads of household are in paid employment; in the social housing sector, six in ten are economically inactive (ONS 1998). Polarization in the housing market has been associated with an increase in the number of households excluded from it, in a sharp rise in homelessness and in households in temporary accommodation (see Chapter 12).

Changes in the labour and housing markets are fuelling a spatial polarization of poverty and wealth. The industrial conurbations, like Greater Manchester, Merseyside and Tyne and Wear, have seen their populations fall as the manual jobs on which working-class men relied have been lost, with those left behind concentrated in local authority housing (Power 1998).

Changes in access to employment and to housing have coincided with changes in family structure. In the 1950s and 1960s, social class made little difference to the domestic pathways which women and men negotiated as they moved through their adult lives. Across the class spectrum, the vast majority of men and women married in their early twenties, had their first baby within three years of marriage and remained married until separated by death (Kiernan 1989). Today, this uniform progression through marriage and parenthood has given way to domestic trajectories which are strongly patterned both by social class and by gender. Young people who grow up in non-manual families and out of poverty are deferring – perhaps indefinitely – both marriage and parenthood, while it is those exposed to disadvantage

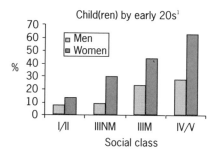
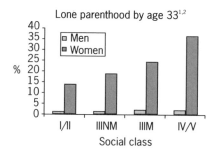

Figure 1.4 Domestic pathways by social class at age 23
Notes:
1 p < 0.001
2 ever been a lone parent (greater than 1 month).
Source: unpublished analysis of data from the National Child Development Study by Sharon Matthews, Institute of Child Health.

in childhood who are most likely to marry and have children before their mid-twenties (Ferri and Smith 1997; Harding *et al.* 1999). These divergent socio-economic pathways take a gendered form, with early parenthood and lone parenthood marking out the trajectories of working-class women. Figure 1.4, based on the 1958 birth cohort study, describes the domestic circumstances of young adults by their social class at the age of 23 (in 1981). Among men in the highest social class, less than one in ten are fathers by the age of 23; among women in the lowest social class, more than six in ten are mothers. Single parenthood shows even more pronounced gender and class differences. Few men in any social class are lone fathers by the age of 33; the proportions are significantly higher among women and are finely graded by social class. Among women in social classes IV and V, nearly four in ten are lone mothers by the age of 33.

Changes in people's working and domestic lives are fuelling a redistribution of employment between households. Through the 1980s and 1990s there was a rapid shift away from households containing a mix of employed and non-employed adults and a corresponding increase in two-earner and no-earner households (Gregg and Wadsworth 1996). The growth in single adult and single parent households explains some of the growth in no-earner households. Figure 1.5 is therefore restricted to two-adult (male/female) households, which make up about 60 per cent of all households in Britain. As it indicates, male earner households are being replaced by two-earner and no-earner households.

The changing distribution of work is changing the distribution of income. The clumping of households on incomes in the middle of the income range is giving away, as the incomes of working households rise and non-working households struggle to make ends meet. The result is an increase in poverty

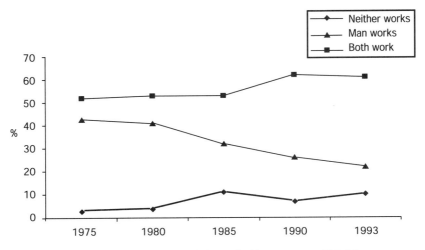

Figure 1.5 Employment in two-adult households, Britain, 1975–93
Source: Gregg and Wadsworth (1996).

and income inequality. Figure 1.6 plots the proportion of the UK population below the European Union (EU) poverty line, a line represented by a household income below half the average for all households, adjusted for size and composition. In the mid-1970s, less than one in ten (7 per cent) were in poverty: by the mid-1990s one in four (25 per cent) were. The increase in poverty has impacted disproportionately on households with children. One in three children (35 per cent) live in poverty, a rate which dwarfs those elsewhere in the EU. In France, for example, less than one in six children live in poverty (HM Treasury 1999).

Income inequality has been identified as an important determinant of health in richer societies. A series of studies have found that population health is related less to how wealthy a society is and more to how equally or unequally this wealth is distributed. Life expectancy is higher in more equal societies: the USA, for example, has a gross domestic product per capita which is over twice as high as that of Greece, yet life expectancy is higher in Greece than in the USA (Wilkinson 1999).

An increase in poverty and income inequality is not the inevitable consequence of social and economic change. A key factor is the extent to which the living standards of households are dependent on the labour market position of their adult members (as they are in the UK). In countries with redistributive fiscal and social policies – for example, with progressive taxation and social security benefits pegged to average incomes – poverty and income inequality have not increased inexorably with the rise in unemployment.

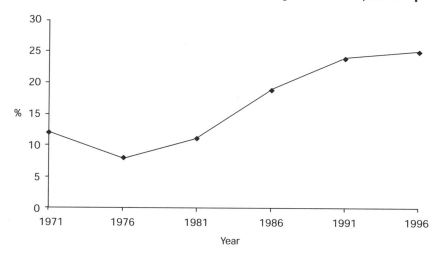

Figure 1.6 Proportion of the population below 50% of average income (after housing costs), 1971–96/7, UK
Source: Goodman and Webb (1994); Department of Social Security (1998). (Crown copyright is reproduced with the permission of the Controller of Her Majesty's Stationery Office.)

In Finland, for example, unemployment climbed from 3 per cent in 1990 to 18 per cent in 1993, but direct taxation curbed the incomes of high-earner households while social security benefits protected the incomes of no-earner households (Keskimaki *et al.* 1999). The result has been a relatively modest increase in income inequality. By the mid-1990s, only Sweden and Denmark had smaller income inequalities than Finland among older industrial countries. Sweden provides another instructive example. While low SES in the UK is synonymous with poverty, Sweden's tax and welfare system keeps poverty levels low in all socio-economic groups. In the 1990s, the prevalence of poverty among men ranged from 2.3 per cent in the higher non-manual group to 3.6 per cent in the unqualified manual group. Among women, the poverty rate increased from 1.8 per cent in the highest socio-economic group to 4.1 per cent in the lowest socio-economic group (Burström and Diderichsen 1999).

Understanding health inequalities

How can the enduring association between SES and health be understood?

In seeking answers to this question, researchers have been aware that the association may be a statistical artefact: an illusion resulting from flaws in the measurement of SES and in the statistical techniques through which its health effects are calculated. It is now accepted that such statistical inaccuracies are insufficient to account for the consistency and scale of the gradient (Davey Smith *et al*. 1994). Researchers have been mindful, too, that an individual's health is a determinant as well as an outcome of their socio-economic circumstances. Those in better health are more likely to move up the occupational ladder, amplifying the health advantages associated with higher socio-economic status. Conversely, the downward mobility of those in poorer health is likely to increase the rates of morbidity and mortality in lower socio-economic groups. While health selection is contributing to the socio-economic gradient, its contribution is modest (Power *et al*. 1996).

With neither statistical errors nor health-related mobility providing the answer, attention has turned to the pathways through which SES might exert an influence on health. A single pathway would, of course, simplify the explanatory task and provide a 'clear steer' to policymakers seeking to reduce health inequalities. However, the evidence points to multiple chains of risk, running from the broader social structure through living and working conditions to health-related habits like cigarette smoking and exercise. Different factors are likely to combine in different ways for different health outcomes. For example, health-related habits are known to play a larger part in the socio-economic differentials in lung cancer and CHD than in accidents, where environmental hazards, and exposure to road traffic in particular, are major causes.

The chains of risk have been uncovered primarily through surveys of individuals. However, a small seam of research is beginning to locate individuals in the places in which they live and to suggest that both individual factors and area influences have their part to play in the aetiology of health inequalities.

Factors at the individual level

The search for causes has focused on factors whose distribution varies in line with socio-economic position and which have proven or plausible health effects. These factors are typically grouped under three broad headings: material, behavioural and psychosocial, although it is recognized that many health influences fall between and across these categories.

Material factors include the physical environment of the home, neighbourhood and workplace, together with living standards secured through earnings, benefits and other income. Behavioural factors are the health-related routines and habits which display a strong socio-economic gradient, like cigarette smoking (see Figure 1.7), leisure-time exercise and diet. While these lifestyle factors have been a major focus of national strategies to improve health, they make a relatively small contribution to health inequalities. Recent estimates suggest that between 10 and 30 per cent of the socio-economic

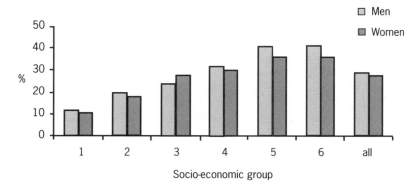

Figure 1.7 Cigarette smoking among adults by sex and socio-economic group, Britain 1996
Source: Office for National Statistics (1998), © Crown Copyright 1996.

gradient may be explained by socio-economic differentials in health-related behaviour (Lantz *et al.* 1998).

Alongside these material and behavioural determinants, research is uncovering the psychosocial costs of living in an unequal society. For example, perceiving oneself to be worse off relative to others may carry a health penalty, in terms of increased stress and risk-taking behaviour (see Chapters 4 and 11). Attention has also focused on the health effects of the work environment and particularly on the control that individuals exercise over the pace and content of work (Marmot *et al.* 1997).

Material, behavioural and psychosocial factors cluster together: those in lower socio-economic groups are likely to be exposed to risks in all three domains. Health-damaging factors also accumulate together: children born into poorer circumstances clock up more by way of material, behavioural and psychosocial risks as they grow up and grow older. For example, girls and boys born into social classes 4 and 5 are more likely than those in higher social classes to grow up in overcrowded homes, to develop health-damaging habits like smoking and to be exposed to stressful life events and work environments (Power *et al.* 1998).

Such analyses lend weight to what has become known as the 'lifecourse perspective'. This perspective suggests that health inequalities are the outcome of cumulative differential exposure to adverse material conditions and to behavioural and psychosocial risks. Longitudinal studies are uncovering how the socio-economic structure becomes inscribed in the biographies and bodies of individuals. The emphasis in these quantitative studies is on how individuals are shaped by class-related 'exposures' and 'insults'. Qualitative studies focus less on the exposures and more on the experiences of those who endure them. They explore how people act against, as well as within, their class circumstances. Rather than plotting lifecourses, these studies record people's life narratives: the biographical accounts through which we thread together understandings of the influence of the past and the impact of the present. This biographical approach is also uncovering how class relationships and class identities are expressed through health habits.

Lifecourse and biography are the focus of Part 2 of this book. Lee Berney and colleagues map the lifecourse influences on health in early age. They describe how, for some dimensions of health, influences accumulate across the whole of a person's life; for other dimensions, childhood influences are more important. Michaela Benzeval's team focus on the role played by income, examining how financial circumstances in childhood and adulthood are related to adult health. While childhood experiences are important, their analysis indicates that recent financial circumstances also have a significant effect on adult health. Policies to tackle poverty and inequality are reviewed in the light of this evidence.

Kate Hunt and colleagues draw on qualitative research to explore people's understandings of how their family history influences their risk of ill-health. Focusing on CHD, they found that traits attributed to heredity and, as one respondent put it, 'how people have been brought up in their family' figured prominently in people's assessment of whether they were at risk.

Area influences

Statistical advances, like multi-level modelling, are enabling researchers to locate individuals in the areas in which they live and to measure the contribution which people and places make to health inequalities. These new analyses confirm that poorer people in poorer health raise the rates of morbidity and mortality in poorer areas, while richer people in better health keep rates below average in more prosperous areas. However, while individual factors are the primary cause of spatial inequalities in health, areas also have an effect. In other words, poorer people may have poor health in part because they have to live in places which are health damaging (Macintyre 1997).

How can places damage health? Both material and psychosocial pathways have been suggested. For example, the areas populated by poorer people score higher on material hazards, like environmental pollution, traffic volume and rates of road traffic accidents (Independent Inquiry into Inequalities in Health 1998). These areas are also less well-resourced in terms of shops, recreational facilities, public transport and primary healthcare services than those serving better-off neighbourhoods (Macintyre 1997).

With respect to psychosocial pathways, research has focused particularly on the ways in which communities operate to resource and support the well-being of residents. Community support is typically measured by aggregating data from individuals – on their involvement in voluntary organizations and with neighbours, for example, or their feelings of trust in those who live around them – but it is seen to operate independently of the individuals whose lives are influenced by it (Lochner *et al.* 1999). The concept of social capital has gained particular currency in research concerned with these social dimensions of areas. The concept was popularized by Putnam (1993), in his study of people's engagement in community life in different regions of Italy. His finding that income inequality is associated with lower levels of social capital has prompted research on the contribution that it may make to health in richer societies (Wilkinson 1996).

The influence of home and place is discussed in Part 3 of the book. Sally Macintyre's team is concerned with why and how housing tenure (owning or renting one's home) is related to health. They confirm that renters are both poorer and in poorer health than owners. Renters also live in homes and neighbourhoods which contain more health hazards (noise, disrepair) and fewer health resources (gardens, safe play spaces).

Heather Joshi and colleagues use multi-level modelling to test for area effects. They confirm that, while area differences in health are mainly attributable to the socio-economic backgrounds of residents, where people live also matters. They explore the contribution of economic decline and low social cohesion, concluding that these factors are not the only reason why poor people in poor areas are at a health disadvantage.

Anthony Gatrell and colleagues shed further light on how where one lives contributes to how well one feels. Combining quantitative and qualitative data, they demonstrate how access to local facilities and participation in local networks have positive health effects. Elspeth Graham and colleagues focus on recovery from MI to highlight some of the complex pathways through which areas may influence health, including how wealthy an individual is relative to others in the area, the area's social mix and its level of morbidity.

Completing Part 3, Danny Dorling's team focuses on the increasing spatial inequalities in mortality. They consider whether differential migration – the movement of richer and healthier people into low mortality areas and of poorer and less healthy people into high mortality areas – may be contributing to these inequalities. They conclude that it may play a role, and focus on housing and homelessness to highlight the processes involved.

Research into policy

Reducing health inequalities is moving up the policy agenda of national governments and international agencies. Older industrial countries like the

UK are seeking 'to improve the health of the worst off and to narrow the health gap' (Secretary of State for Health 1999) and are looking to research to guide the development of new public health strategies. An appreciation of both lifecourse and area influences is evident in the flagship policies of the New Labour government.

A lifecourse perspective frames a raft of interventions designed to lift those heading for a lifetime of disadvantage onto more advantaged trajectories. The New Deal programme is seeking to provide a ladder out of dependency on social security benefits and into paid work for disadvantaged young people and adults (see Chapter 6). On a smaller scale, Sure Start, an area-based intervention targeted at children aged 0 to 3 in disadvantaged areas, is designed to improve their health and development in the run-up to school and provide a springboard into better health and higher SES in adulthood. Other area-based interventions to tackle health inequalities and social exclusion include the New Deal for Communities and a range of 'zoned' interventions like Health Action Zones. These area interventions typically operate within the framework of universal services – like education, health, policing and housing – to enforce basic standards of provision and to provide additional resources designed to improve the social and physical fabric of disadvantaged areas.

The effectiveness of these policies is likely to turn on the extent to which their positive impact is blunted by trends which are increasing poverty and income inequality, like the continuing collapse of demand for low-skilled workers and the continuing fall in the living standards of claimant households. Further, the targeted nature of many of the interventions limits their reach and impact: while there are areas with high and increasing levels of disadvantage, most poor people do not live in disadvantaged areas (see Chapter 9).

Assessing the impact of policy is the focus of the final part and chapter of this book. Margaret Whitehead and colleagues present an innovative conceptual framework and methodology through which to undertake health inequalities impact assessment. They then use this approach to analyse the impact of welfare policies on the health and socio-economic circumstances of lone mothers in two contrasting countries: the UK and Sweden. Their analysis suggests that around 50 per cent of the health disadvantage of lone mothers in the UK is accounted for by poverty and joblessness, compared with under 15 per cent in Sweden where universal welfare services have resulted in higher levels of employment and higher levels of benefits for lone mothers.

Together, the chapters provide powerful evidence that social inequalities are embodied in individual health: in our physical functioning, psychosocial well-being and vulnerability to disease and disability. While these embodied inequalities are found in all societies, it is clear that their scale varies over time and between countries. As this suggests, health inequalities are not immutable: policies can and do make a difference.

Acknowledgements

This chapter draws on research funded by the ESRC under the Health Variations Programme (L128341002) and on analyses presented in Graham (2000). We are grateful for permission to reproduce data from the Office of National Statistics (Table 1.2, Figures 1.1, 1.2, 1.3, 1.7); Cambridge University Press (Figure 1.5, taken from J. Hills, ed., *New Inequalities*, 1996); the Institute for Fiscal Studies and Her Majesty's Stationery Office (Figure 1.6); unpublished analyses by Sharon Matthews from the National Child Development Study (Figure 1.4); and from regional mortality data by Mary Shaw (Figure 1.1).

References

Burström, B. and Diderichsen, F. (1999) Income-related policies in Sweden, in J.P. Mackenbach and M. Droomers (eds) *Interventions and Policies to Reduce Socio-economic Inequalities in Health*. Rotterdam: Department of Public Health, Erasmus University, Rotterdam.

Davey Smith, G., Blane, D. and Bartley, M. (1994) Explanations for socio-economic differentials in mortality, *European Journal of Public Health*, 4: 131–44.

Department of Social Security (DSS) (1998) *Households Below Average Income, 1979 to 1996/97*. Leeds: DSS.

Drever, F., Whitehead, M. and Roden, M. (1996) Current patterns and trends in male mortality by social class (based on occupation), *Population Trends*, 86: 15–20.

Ferri, E. and Smith, K. (1997) Where you are and who you live with, in J. Bynner, E. Ferrie and P. Shepherd (eds) *Twenty Something in the 1990s*. Aldershot: Ashgate.

Goodman, A. and Webb, S. (1994) *For Richer, For Poorer: the Changing Distribution of Income in the United Kingdom*. London: Institute of Fiscal Studies.

Graham, H. (2000) Socio-economic change and inequalities in men and women's health in the UK, in K. Hunt and E. Annandale (eds) *Gender Inequalities in Health*. Buckingham: Open University Press.

Gregg, P. and Wadsworth, J. (1996) More work in fewer households, in J. Hills (ed.) *New Inequalities: the Changing Distribution of Income and Wealth in the United Kingdom*. Cambridge: Cambridge University Press.

HM Treasury (1999) *The Modernisation of Britain's Tax and Benefit System: No. 4, Tackling Poverty and Social Exclusion*. London: HM Treasury.

Harding, S., Bethune, A., Maxwell, R. and Brown, J. (1997) Mortality trends using the longitudinal study, in F. Drever and M. Whitehead (eds) *Health Inequalities* (Series DS No. 15). London: The Stationery Office.

Harding, S., Brown, J., Rosato, M. and Hattersley, L. (1999) Socio-economic differentials in health: illustrations from Office for National Statistics Longitudinal Study, *Health Statistics Quarterly*, 1: 5–11.

Harkness, S. and Waldfogel, J. (1999) *The Family Gap in Pay: Evidence From Seven Industrialised Countries* (Casepaper 30). London: London School of Economics.

Hattersley, L. (1999) Trends in life expectancy by social class – an update, *Health Statistics Quarterly*, 2: 16–24.

Independent Inquiry into Inequalities in Health (1998) *Independent Inquiry into Inequalities in Health Report* (the Acheson Report). London: The Stationery Office.

Keskimäki, I., Lahelma, E., Koskinen, S. and Valkonen, T. (1999) Policy changes related to income distribution and income differences in health in Finland in the 1990s, in J.P. Mackenbach and M. Droomers (eds) *Interventions and Policies to Reduce Socio-economic Inequalities in Health*. Rotterdam: Department of Public Health, Erasmus University, Rotterdam.

Kiernan, K. (1989) The family: formation and fission, in H. Joshi (ed.) *The Changing Population of Britain*. Oxford: Blackwell.

Krieger, N. (1997) Measuring social class in US public health research, *Annual Review of Public Health*, 18: 341–78.

Lantz, P.M., House, J.S., Lepkowski, J.M. *et al.* (1998) Socio-economic factors, health behaviours and mortality, *JAMA*, 279(21): 1703–8.

Lochner, K., Kawachi, I. and Kennedy, B.P. (1999) Social capital: a guide to its measurement, *Health and Place*, 5: 259–70.

Macintyre, S. (1997) What are spatial effects and how can we measure them? in A. Dale (ed.) *Exploiting National Survey and Census Data: the Role of Locality and Spatial Effects* (CCSR occasional paper 12). Manchester: University of Manchester.

Marmot, M. (1998) The magnitude of social inequalities in coronary heart disease: possible explanations, in I. Sharp (ed.) *Social Inequalities in Coronary Heart Disease*. London: The Stationery Office.

Marmot, M.G., Bosma, H., Hemingway, H., Brunner, E. and Stansfeld, S. (1997) Contribution of job control and other risk factors to social variations in coronary heart disease incidence, *Lancet*, 350: 235–9.

Matheson, J. and Holding, A. (1999) *Regional Trends, 34*. London: The Stationery Office.

Modood, J. (1998) Employment, in J. Modood and R. Berthoud (eds) *Ethnic Minorities in Britain: Diversity and Disadvantage*. London: Policy Studies Institute.

ONS (Office for National Statistics) (1998) *Living in Britain: Results from the 1996 General Household Survey*. London: The Stationery Office.

Power, A. (1998) The relationship between inequality and area deprivation, in Centre for Analysis of Social Exclusion *Persistent Poverty and Lifetime Inequality: The Evidence*. London: HM Treasury.

Power, C., Matthews, S. and Manor, O. (1996) Inequalities in self-rated health in the 1958 birth cohort: life time social circumstances or social mobility? *British Medical Journal*, 313: 449–53.

Power, C., Matthews, S. and Manor, O. (1998) Inequalities in self-rated health: explanations from different stages of life, *Lancet*, 351: 1009–14.

Putnam, R.D. (1993) *Making Democracy Work: Civic Traditions in Modern Italy*. Princeton, NJ: Princeton University.

Roberts, I. and Power, C. (1996) Does the decline in child injury vary by social class? A comparison of class specific mortality in 1981 and 1991, *British Medical Journal*, 313: 784–6.

Secretary of State for Health (1998) *Our Healthier Nation: A Contract for Health*, Cm 3852. London: The Stationery Office.

Secretary of State for Health (1999) *Saving Lives: Our Healthier Nation*, Cm 4386. London: The Stationery Office.

Shaw, M., Dorling, D. and Brimblecombe, N. (1998) Changing the map: health in Britain 1951–91, in M. Bartley, D. Blane and G. Davey Smith (eds) *The Sociology of Health Inequalities*. Oxford: Blackwell.

Sparkes, J. (1999) *Schools, Education and Social Exclusion* (Casepaper 29). London: London School of Economics.

Whitehead, M. (1997) Life and death across the millennium, in F. Drever and M. Whitehead (eds) *Health Inequalities* (Series DS No. 15). London: The Stationery Office.

Wiggins, R.D., Bartley, M., Gleave, S. *et al.* (1998) Limiting long-term illness: a question of where you live or who you are? A multi-level analysis of the 1971–1991 ONS longitudinal study, *Risk, Decision and Policy*, 3(3): 181–98.

Wilkinson, R.G. (1996) *Unhealthy Societies: The Afflictions of Inequality*. London: Routledge.

Wilkinson, R.G. (1999) Putting the pieces together: prosperity, redistribution, health, and welfare, in M. Marmot and R.G. Wilkinson (eds) *Social Determinants of Health*. Oxford: Oxford University Press.

Part 1
Ethnicity, gender and socio-economic inequality

Introduction

Part 1 casts a critical eye over the measures of social position used to guide research and policy. It looks in particular at socio-economic status, ethnicity and gender. The chapters discuss how conventional measures can obscure and misrepresent dimensions crucial to the understanding of health inequalities and describe how alternative approaches can help to illuminate and track the interconnecting pathways through which socio-economic status, ethnicity and gender influence health.

Chapter 2 addresses the limitations of conventional measures of socio-economic status by investigating the meanings of socio-economic position within and between different minority ethnic groups. It draws on qualitative data from a larger study designed to develop socio-economic indicators appropriate for multi-ethnic studies of health. The study was carried out in 1997/8 in two cities, Bristol and Leeds, and the qualitative data were collected through semi-structured interviews with adults from White, African Caribbean and South Asian communities.

Chapter 3 is also concerned with the intersections between ethnicity, socio-economic status and health. It highlights the restricted way in which ethnicity has been understood and measured in health research. It notes how ethnicity is defined in ways which obscure the structures of racism and racial disadvantage which shape the lives and socio-economic circumstances of many minority ethnic groups. It discusses how alternative measures need to be sensitive to the dynamic ways in which ethnic identities are embodied and expressed – through a sense of nationality, through community and through language. The chapter draws on quantitative data from the *Fourth National*

Survey of Ethnic Minorities (FNS), a representative survey of ethnic minority and White people living in England and Wales in 1993–4. Because none of the White sample were asked the set of questions on ethnic identity, the chapter is restricted to minority ethnic groups for which there were sufficient numbers for reliable statistical analyses (Caribbean, Pakistani and Bangladeshi, Indian and African Asian groups).

The final chapter in Part 1 examines and applies a range of measures of socio-economic status to illuminate the multiple pathways along which it affects health. The authors note how socio-economic position is associated with differences in power, prestige and forms of consumption (like exercise routines and tastes in food). It is associated, too, with differences in employment conditions and how much control an individual exercises over the pace and content of their work. Socio-economic status also captures differences in people's material living standards: in what people can afford by way of housing, diet, etc. The chapter uses existing measures of socio-economic status which tap these different dimensions to map the pathways linking socio-economic inequality to health inequalities among women. The analysis includes both measures of health and risk factors like cigarette smoking linked to heart disease. It draws on two surveys for its analysis: the Health and Lifestyle Survey (HALS) and the Health Survey for England (HSFE).

2

Ethnicity, health and the meaning of socio-economic position

**George Davey Smith, Katherine Charsley,
Helen Lambert, Sheila Paul,
Steve Fenton and Waqar Ahmad**

Introduction

Observed differences in both health status and health service use across ethnic groups have been variously attributed to cultural, socio-economic and genetic differences, as well as to the impact of individual and institutional racism. The roles of health-related selection at the point of migration and of possible artefacts in the process of data collection have also been examined (Smaje 1995). The contribution of differences in socio-economic circumstances to health differentials between ethnic groups has been an area of particular – and often polemical – concern. Research into ethnicity and health often utilizes inappropriately crude and simplistic cultural variables, sometimes neglecting issues of social deprivation entirely (Sheldon and Parker 1992; Ahmad 1996). Alternatively, some authors who are concerned with socio-economic differences have interpreted their data as showing that differentials in mortality between ethnic groups are essentially due to income or class inequalities (Navarro 1990), while other studies suggest that this explanation is at best partial (Cooper 1993).

Health research in this area has also tended to treat the construct of 'ethnicity' itself as unproblematic, taking certain ethnic categories (for example 'Indian' or 'Asian' in Britain) for granted, and presuming that the 'ethnic groups' so termed are essentially and unproblematically different from the majority ethnic population in a concrete and unchanging manner (see Chapter 3; Senior and Bhopal 1994; Ahmad 1999; Fenton and Charsley 2000). In fact, many of the factors which, taken together, compose and constitute ethnicity – language, religion, experience of racism, migration, family life, ancestry, culture and forms of identity – are constantly changing (or their definitions are changing) and cannot be used to draw an immutable 'line' around a given population. Where the possible causal pathways for ill-health are not made explicit, 'untheorized ethnicity' (Nazroo 1998) can lead to the pathologizing of minority ethnic status in itself.

Although it is, nonetheless, possible to take some operational definition of ethnically-bounded populations as reasonable working categories, analysing ethnic differentials in terms of cultural or social class differences remains subject to several difficulties (Navarro 1990; Ahmad 1996; Lambert and Sevak 1996). Studies which emphasize cultural difference as the primary explanatory factor suffer from two main problems: they may overemphasize cultural differences between groups and neglect socio-material conditions (Lambert and Sevak 1996), while the existence of socio-economic differences within minority ethnic populations may be ignored (Ahmad 1996; Bhopal *et al.* 1999). Apparent socio-economic differentials in health status within minority ethnic communities may not be of equal magnitude or even in the same direction as those among the majority ethnic population, although this could reflect artefacts within particular studies (Smaje 1995). Whatever the reasons, simple adjustment for socio-economic position within multi-ethnic samples is clearly problematic (Davey Smith in press).

Controlling for socio-economic differences when comparing ethnically defined populations is essential if we are to avoid misleading conclusions regarding the causes of apparent health variations between and within ethnic groups; but we must also be sure that the measures of socio-economic position are not themselves misleading. In the UK, conventional measures which have long been used in studying health variations among the White majority ethnic population are generally employed in studies that include ethnicity as a characteristic of the populations being investigated, or that attempt to investigate ethnic variations in health directly. For example, a recent study concluded that tuberculosis is not associated with socio-economic disadvantage among South Asians, because area-based deprivation measures which predicted tuberculosis rates among the White majority population did not do so among South Asians (Hawker *et al.* 1999). However, if conventional indices of socio-economic position are not associated in the same way with the actual material conditions of life in minority ethnic groups as they are in the majority ethnic population, then such conclusions could be misleading. Thus it is known that income levels within social classes are lower and employment patterns more unfavourable (e.g. levels of shift work) for some minority ethnic groups than the majority ethnic population (Pirani *et al.* 1992). Occupational social class categorizations, too, will have different connotations according to labour market position. This is particularly pertinent for women in some minority ethnic communities. For example, compared to the overall population, African Caribbean women have greater involvement in the labour market, while Pakistani and Bangladeshi women remain largely outside the formal labour market, although are often engaged in piecework or homeworking (Ballard 1994).

Given these important differences, the standard practice of adjusting for occupational social class provides an inadequate way of attempting to deal with material inequalities when examining the links between ethnicity, social position and health. Moreover, other measures may also vary in relation to ethnicity and hence fail to provide reliable comparative indicators when used to adjust for socio-economic position in multi-ethnic samples. For example, current income is related to wealth, or to real purchasing power, in a different manner in different ethnic groups (Pirani *et al.* 1992; Cooper 1993).

The study on which this chapter is based confronts the limitations of conventional measures of socio-economic position directly by investigating the meanings of socio-economic position within and between different ethnic groups, including the White majority population. The chapter focuses mainly on qualitative work with members of minority ethnic populations.

Studying ethnicity and socio-economic position

The findings presented here form part of a larger study. Involving comparative work in two cities, Bristol and Leeds, the study combines qualitative and quantitative techniques in an attempt to contribute to the improvement of the use of socio-economic indicators in multi-ethnic population health studies.

The qualitative phase, from which these findings come, employed ethnographic research and in-depth interviewing. Initial consultations with 'community leaders', health professionals and other 'gatekeepers' aimed both to introduce the two full-time researchers to potential contacts in the field as well as to capture their knowledge of each city and its ethnic communities – an exercise we termed 'city mapping'. This enabled the identification of potential field sites, which were then visited to assess their suitability for participant observation. A number of community group settings were chosen and the researchers made frequent visits to these sites throughout this phase of the fieldwork.

This initial fieldwork facilitated the development of a 'topic guide' comprising issues to be explored in semi-structured interviews with adults from White, African Caribbean and South Asian communities, with a target of 90 such interviews in each city. All individuals were interviewed in the language of their choice. Initially, interviewees were recruited at field sites, and by snowballing from these contacts. As the research progressed, sections of the population which proved difficult to access through these routes were identified and new strategies, such as approaching workplaces, were employed to contact potential interviewees. Part-time research assistants/interviewers recruited from the minority ethnic communities helped to broaden the scope of potential contacts, and provided invaluable assistance to the study as key informants.

In the following sections, we draw on the qualitative material to give some indications of the complexity of the links between ethnicity and socio-economic position. Membership of a minority ethnic community does not necessarily imply that individuals and their networks possess particular characteristics; it does not predict behaviour, or even guarantee the experience of discrimination. However, the influence of different dimensions of ethnicity – including migration, language, religion, experience of racism and family formation – can create circumstances in which conventional indicators of socio-economic position, such as housing tenure, occupational class and education, have different meanings, and so may not function as expected in health research. We also show how the interlinking of different elements of ethnicity produce contingent meanings, depending on complex interactions with other aspects of life. In consequence, their meaning cannot simply be 'read off' from an initial identification of the ethnic affiliation of an individual, household or community.

Migration, racism, education and employment

The number of years of education and/or educational qualifications are commonly used in health research as a marker of socio-economic position. One problem faced by some adult migrants is the loss of recognition of their qualifications and experience in the new country. As a result, educational qualifications do not provide an equivalent degree of access to employment within all ethnic groups. This means that some migrants are being classed with those who have similar educational qualifications but greater employment opportunities and thus potentially higher standards of living. A 67-year-old Kenyan Asian man related his experience on arriving in Britain in the 1970s:

> I trained to be a teacher . . . which was again in Kenya . . . our tutors were all English, and at that time the understanding was that the training they were giving us was the same equivalent to the one which was given to the teachers there. And if we ever came over to this country our education would be . . . accepted, which well [laughs] never happened . . . Well, when I came to this country I was 41 years old. I tried to get into teaching but as I said before because they did not accept my qualifications . . . In Kenya? Oh yes, oh yes. I mean, I was a deputy head of a big junior school where we had 1100 pupils.

Although many South Asian and African Caribbean migrants arrived in Britain several decades ago, similar difficulties may face more recent arrivals. A Jamaican accountant who came to Britain four years ago complained that he was unable to gain positions which reflected his skills and qualifications:

> The thing is in Jamaica the positions were higher . . . the technical knowledge was much more demanding, here I just move through . . . The thing what I found was that the conversion wasn't accurate – although they say it's English exams, and you passed those exams, you are not classified in the same category as a man who passed it in England, . . . Anyway I scored the same marks as the [other] person and they called us back for a second interview, but then you're in that interview room and I told them my [recent accountancy exam] results and said this push me a bit further if we were on equal footing before, but yet still they didn't give me the job. That scoring thing, there's something wrong there. I mean the job was a joke really in terms of my abilities. So say if they found someone better than me, that means that people in England are very qualified or somebody is telling a lie.

A South Asian man who had brought his wife to Britain from Pakistan complained that, although she was a qualified doctor and an 'AA student', she had had to complete a conversion course before applying for jobs in this country. Having completed the course, he felt that her continuing difficulties in gaining employment were attributable to racist attitudes. For these last two people, difficulties in gaining recognition for qualifications seem to have been compounded by discrimination in the job market. These experiences show how migration and racism can combine to alter the meaning of education as an indicator of socio-economic position for sections of the minority ethnic communities.

Racism may continue to prevent the conversion of educational qualifications into employment opportunities for subsequent generations who have not themselves experienced migration. A South Asian man who had studied law had been unable to gain employment in the field: 'There's so much indirect racism in the law field, and there is about seven Asians in the whole of Bristol that studied law and can't get a job'. His younger brother had also been unable to find a job and had won a case for discrimination against one of the companies who rejected his application: 'When I wrote my CV I wrote my name, and I wrote "Singh". And probably they know he's Asian'.

Again, the influence of aspects of ethnicity is multiple and complex. Both these young men perceive that their background has hindered their prospects in other ways: as the first graduates from their household, they felt they had no familiarity with the culture of professional workplaces and no access to the 'old school tie' networks which the elder brother feels exist in law practices.

Migration, paid work and standard of living

As well as influencing the level of paid work which educational credentials can obtain for people, migration has several other influences on working lives. For example, a Pakistani woman reported how she negotiated with her husband about the propriety of women working:

> I never work before. I get two kid when I come from Pakistan, and when I had four kid, and he can't go to work properly because he was ill. And I said to him, why don't you allow me to go to work, and he was so angry with me! He said no – it's a shame for me. I said no, it's not shame for you. Because in Pakistan, it is shame, but not in here. Now, in these days, now everyone is working in Pakistan too, mind . . . and I go to work myself with my friend part-time. And he shout on me, and we fight. I said, I'm not going to stop my work because it's not wrong. Is everybody going to work. Plus you can't go to work properly and it does help when you get extra money. And after little while, he was angry but he just keep quiet because he know I won't stop. I was doing a part-time job in laundry . . .

There are other aspects of employment and standard of living that mean migrants and their families may differ from the majority ethnic population. In the years following migration to the UK, not only did many members of minority ethnic groups suffer a loss of socio-economic position exacerbated by racism, but in the struggle to establish themselves and their families in Britain, many made conscious sacrifices in terms of their standard of living. In our interviews, second generation African Caribbeans talked of the long hours their parents had worked in order to be able to afford to bring their children to Britain, and to support them once they were here. A Pakistani woman in her sixties who had been a factory worker spoke of how she had invested everything in giving her children a private education, despite the fact that they were living in poor-quality housing. While these sacrifices may themselves have had impacts on health, they could also disturb the assumed association between socio-economic position and health. However, the process of settlement has to be seen within the historical trajectory of migration: in the early phase, migrants may experience a large financial burden through remittances, while also saving for housing and children's education. Expenditures as well as income may therefore differ greatly from the majority ethnic group.

Migration, culture and social support

Strong support networks have frequently been seen as typical of certain minority ethnic families and communities, in particular of South Asian communities. It has been suggested that this 'cultural' feature has a 'buffering' effect between life stresses and health (Cochrane and Stopes-Roe 1981), although the stereotype of a 'protective Asian culture' has in turn been criticized (Sashidharan and Francis 1993; Nazroo 1998). Recent work on caring in minority ethnic communities shows that carers do not receive greater family support than White carers, and that many may be receiving considerably lower levels of support (Katbamna *et al.* 1998). In our fieldwork, several people of South Asian heritage pointed to the importance of close family ties in their communities and many testified to the vital support (from helping with housework and child care to providing employment or access to interest-free loans) that these ties provided. However, we also found close kinship networks to be an invaluable source of social and financial support among many of the White working-class families in our study. Conversely, some interviews with South Asians revealed a number of counter-examples where the 'cost' of strong social networks in terms of restrictions and obligations may be very high. In some cases, respondents reported that they had moved house, area, or even city to escape the negative influence of 'the community'. Some of those interviewed attributed a decision to move into an area with few or no other South Asians to a desire to escape constant scrutiny and pressure to conform. In a few cases, individuals had been forced to move away after transgressing the boundaries of, as they saw it, approved behaviour; or had chosen to live separately from other members of their extended families as a result of experiencing physical or mental abuse within the joint household.

As well as providing a more nuanced picture of the negative as well as positive dimensions of 'social support', our material also demonstrates that the preference of many South Asian families for living in joint households results, at least partially, from socio-economic considerations rather than from some abstract cultural imperative. Several young married couples of South Asian origin were able to save towards buying their own homes while living with their parents, thus having greatly reduced living costs. Conversely, the benefits to a South Asian woman, who had been abused, of moving into a separate household were partially offset by the increased financial burden that this entailed for her and her husband.

This latter example is not intended to suggest that extended families are necessarily a source of stress. The reduction in social support which can result from the severing of ties with family and friends as a result of migration is often felt hardest by those without the financial means to make return visits, or even keep in frequent telephone contact. One Pakistani woman who had come to Britain for marriage reported spending most of her time sleeping or crying from loneliness. She considered that language problems and pressure against women working outside the home, combined with migration and a radical shift in living circumstances from extended family to nuclear household, contributed to her depression.

Housing and ethnicity

Housing tenure is a commonly used socio-economic indicator (see Chapters 8 and 12), however, it has limitations as a marker of housing quality in multi-ethnic studies. For example, South Asian owner-occupiers are more likely to live in accommodation which is older, unmodernized and over-crowded (Jones 1993) or lacking in basic amenities (Nazroo 1997). Thus, they may not have the usual socio-economic advantages of owner-occupiers. Indeed, it has been argued that high levels of owner occupation among South Asians should be understood, at least partly, as a reaction to racism in council home allocation (Smith 1989) and as a result of the mismatch between housing availability and need in housing allocation (Bowes *et al.* 1997).

In contemporary residential distribution, the influence of differing aspects of ethnicity can act as both carrot and stick, incentive and constraint. The support gained from proximity to family, community and specialized services may combine with limited financial resources and discrimination to perpetuate areas of high minority ethnic concentration in relatively deprived inner-city locations. As the African Caribbean man quoted below shows, while social support and access to such culturally important services as specialist food shops might be seen to increase well-being, such areas often present other problems which could damage health. For example, it is widely considered that inner-city areas suffer from poor quality health service and educational provision as well as more environmental hazards, like traffic danger and lack of play space:

> This area, it's got a lot of advantages, the only thing about the areas where Black people live in Bristol is that it's all dead close to the motor-way and it's all dead polluted . . . It's a great place to live in terms of people. As far as the housing is concerned, it's difficult to have a private garden, a lot of people are living in places that are too small for them-selves, there's too much traffic around here, it's not a good place to bring kids up in terms of health. So there's all those disadvantages and if you want to change all that you need to move to an area where there's no Black people. It's a catch-22 in Bristol.

Discrimination by lenders has probably contributed to the low levels of owner occupation among Black Caribbeans (Phillips and Karn 1992), while the process of housing allocation as well as the cultural value placed on home-owning may help to explain high levels of home ownership among some South Asian groups. A national survey found much Pakistani and Bangladeshi owner-occupied property to be of poor quality and lacking basic amenities (Lakey 1997), a fact supported both by local housing sur-veys in Bristol (Lambert and Razzaque 1997) and Leeds (Law *et al.* 1996), and our own research. In our study, several members of owner-occupied

Pakistani households on low incomes in the Harehills area of Leeds reported great difficulty in meeting mortgage payments and affording household repairs, and could not envisage being able to move to more appropriate properties.

Occupational class and ethnicity

Occupational class is perhaps the most commonly used marker of socio-economic position in British health research. However, minority ethnic groups are often concentrated in less favourable locations within a given occupational grade, suffering from job insecurity, stress and unsociable hours (Nazroo 1997). Even when in the same occupation as her White colleagues, this African Caribbean former midwife felt that her working conditions in one particular hospital were much worse:

> I felt very much that I was put in situations that were very dangerous and, if I complained, it was very much that I was stirring it and making trouble. So far as me writing letters to the managers to say how unsafe I felt professionally. And I felt very unsupported yet the blond-haired, blue-eyed people had as much support as they wanted. They would be promoted far quicker than the Black or ethnic minority midwives that were there. And I had never come against that kind of racism on such a huge scale because it was very subtle, they didn't come out with it, you know what I mean.

There are also some distinct patterns of minority ethnic employment. In Bristol at the time of the 1991 census, for example, while Indians and East Africans were over-represented in occupational class 1 (professional), Pakistani men were over-represented in the category of the self-employed. High levels of self-employment among South Asians present a particular challenge to occupational classifications, as the category is very broad. Several of those interviewed had been self-employed at one time, but their businesses had failed. Others, however, are evidently doing well from self-employment, as this Pakistani man running a general store with his brother makes clear when talking about his financial situation:

> If I need something, I'll go and buy it, and that's it . . . For example, if I need a car, I'll go and buy a car. If I need a sofa, go and buy a sofa. If I want something I can go and buy it. I can't say I can go and buy a plane, but not everybody wants a plane, well I don't want a plane, but I'm saying to my own requirements, whatever I need, I can go and buy.

A recent study carried out in Glasgow confirms the difficulties in measuring occupational class which are presented by the scale of the South Asian small business economy. Williams *et al.* (1998) credit business ownership with having disrupted the relationship between class and standard of living, and therefore between class and health. Not only are the self-employed difficult to categorize, but domestic use of business goods (and vice versa), combined with sharing of goods through social networks, may raise the standard of living afforded at particular levels of income.

Even if present occupational social class can be readily assigned, current measures of socio-economic position do not necessarily provide an accurate picture of lifetime social circumstances. One African Caribbean man who had spent the bulk of his working life in the building trade until the most recent UK recession, and who described himself as poor, had grown up in a wealthy family in Jamaica until his father answered the call for labour from the 'mother country' and became a bus driver in Britain. But others who participated in the research had experienced childhood deprivation and their current classification into a particular social class would mask this past experience of poverty. With reference to some of the cases described above, the South Asian woman who had worked in a factory to send the children to private school reported that her children were currently at university or in employment. She also revealed that at one stage in their childhood, the family was living in such poor conditions, their poverty compounded by a lack of information on the benefits system, that a neighbour reported their situation to the social services. For her children, their educational attainment and occupational position reported in adulthood would mask this experience of early life deprivation.

Implications

The ways in which the measurement of socio-economic position can influence understanding and assessment of its contribution to ethnic group differentials in health status has been discussed by several authors (e.g. Kaufman *et al.* 1997; Davey Smith *et al.* 1998, Davey Smith in press). The sections above have illustrated how socio-economic categories – whether based on education, employment, occupational social class or housing tenure – may have neither the same nor consistent meanings in different ethnic groups. Aggregated socio-economic indicators (for example the area-based deprivation indices commonly utilized in British studies) and individual-level indicators may capture different aspects of socio-economic position. Areas with a high level of individual socio-economic disadvantage may also be disadvantaged with respect to transport, retail outlets, leisure facilities, environmental pollution and social disorganization, in ways that influence health independently of the individual socio-economic characteristics of the people living in these areas (see Chapters 8, 9, 10 and 12). These disadvantages may be greater in areas where a high proportion of people with minority ethnic heritage live.

A growing body of research has demonstrated that lifetime social circumstances contribute to health (see Chapter 5) and that using only data regarding social circumstances in adulthood fails to take into account the full effect of such lifetime circumstances (Davey Smith *et al.* 1997). Studies utilizing only one measure of socio-economic position will leave considerable potential for residual confounding by other health-influencing aspects of social experience. As the evidence presented in this chapter suggests, the degree to which this occurs will differ between ethnic groups. At the same apparent level of, say, current occupational class, the lifetime social circumstances or area-level social characteristics will differ across and within different ethnic groups. Similarly, at the same level of education, incomes differ between ethnic groups; or at the same level of income, there may be wealth disparities.

The qualitative research excerpted above demonstrates the different ways in which socio-economic indicators have diverging connotations in different ethnic groups or in different contexts of ethnicity. A failure to appreciate these problems when studying the contribution of socio-economic position to health differences between ethnic groups produces a form of reasoning by elimination, which leads to explanations concentrating on assumed genetic or cultural differences. For example, in a recent study of ethnic group differences in stroke in London, Stewart *et al.* (1999) compared stroke rates among two groups which they defined as Black (African Caribbean, 'Black African' and 'Black other' according to the 1991 British census categories) and White (a group they don't define). The stroke rates among Blacks were around twice as high as among Whites, and statistical adjustment for occupational social class only partly accounted for this elevated stroke rate. On the basis of this, the authors suggest that ethnic differences in genetic, physiological and behavioural risk factors for stroke require further elucidation. As demonstrated above, adjustment for occupational social class will only capture some aspects of the socio-economic environment that influence stroke risk and may not provide an index of social circumstances in the same way among the groups which Stewart *et al.* refer to as Blacks and Whites. This then produces data which apparently – but spuriously – demonstrate that health differences are due to genetic or cultural/behavioural factors.

As some minority ethnic groups are among the most disadvantaged sections of British society, measures which misrepresent the standard of living of minority ethnic groups risk not only perpetrating but exacerbating disadvantage through inadequate investment of public resources. Equally, an improved understanding of the processes which underlie ethnic differences in socio-economic position and health has the potential to lead to more appropriately targeted interventions. There is therefore a pressing need to develop more sensitive indicators of socio-economic position, particularly for use in research into the causes of ethnic inequalities in health. As a result of the qualitative fieldwork from which these findings are drawn, a survey tool has been developed and is being piloted in Leeds at the time of writing. While the qualitative findings described above have allowed for the close observation of the variety of ways in which ethnicity may change the meaning of indicators of socio-economic position, the numbers of people involved are necessarily much smaller than can be accessed by quantitative survey techniques. The two methods, qualitative fieldwork and quantitative surveys, must therefore be used in combination to produce new indicators for use in the study of health and illness across ethnic groups.

Acknowledgements

This chapter draws on research funded by the ESRC (L128251007) under the Health Variations Programme. Our thanks to Kathy Powell for fieldwork direction in Leeds and Ghazala Mir, Shakeel Razak, Marcia Hylton and Faye Scott for fieldwork assistance, and our advisory committees for guidance.

References

Ahmad, W.I.U. (1996) The trouble with culture, in D. Kelleher and S. Hillier (eds) *Researching Cultural Differences in Health*. London: Routledge.

Ahmad, W.I.U. (1999) Ethic statistics: better than nothing or worse than nothing? in D. Dorling and S. Simpson (eds) *Statistics in Society: The Arithmetic of Politics*. London: Arnold.

Ballard, R. (ed.) (1994) *Desh Pardesh: The South Asian Presence in Britain*. London: Hurst & Co.

Bhopal, J., Unwin, N., White, M. *et al.* (1999) Heterogeneity of coronary heart disease risk factors in Indian, Pakistani, Bangladeshi and European origin populations: cross-sectional study. *British Medical Journal*, 319: 215–20.

Bowes, A., Dar, N. and Sim, D. (1997) Pakistanis and social rented housing: a study in Glasgow, in A. Bowes and D. Sim (eds) *Perspectives on Welfare: The Experience of Minority Ethnic Groups in Scotland*. Aldershot: Ashgate.

Cochrane, R. and Stopes-Roe, M. (1981) Social class and psychological disorder in natives and immigrants to Britain, *International Journal of Social Psychiatry*, 27: 173–82.

Cooper, R.S. (1993) Health and social status of Blacks in the US, *Annual Epidemiology*, 3: 137–44.

Davey Smith, G. (in press) Ethnicity, health and socio-economic position in Britain and the USA: learning to live with complexity, *American Journal of Public Health*.

Davey Smith, G., Hart, C., Blane, D., Gillis, C. and Hawthorne, V. (1997) Lifetime socio-economic position and mortality: prospective observational study, *British Medical Journal*, 314: 547–52.

Davey Smith, G., Neaton, J.D., Wentworth, D., Stamler, R. and Stamler, J. (1998) Mortality differences between black and white men in the USA: contribution of income and other risk factors among men screened for the MRFIT, *Lancet*, 351: 934–9.

Fenton, S. and Charsley, K. (2000) Epidemiology and sociology as incommensurate games: accounts from the study of health and ethnicity, *Health*, 4(4): 403–25.

Hawker, J.I., Bakhshi, S.S., Ali, S. and Farrington, C.P. (1999) Ecological analysis of ethnic differences in relation between tuberculosis and poverty, *British Medical Journal*, 319: 1031–4.

Jones, T. (1993) *Britain's Ethnic Minorities*. London: PSI.

Katbamna, S., Bhakta, P., Parker, G., Ahmad, W.I.U. and Baker, R. (1998) *Experiences and Needs of Carers from South Asian Communities*. Leicester: Leicester University Nuffield Community Care Studies Unit.

Kaufman, J.S., Cooper, R.S. and McGee, D.L. (1997) Socio-economic status and health in blacks and whites: the problem of residual confounding and the resiliency of race, *Epidemiology*, 8: 621–8.

Lakey, J. (1997) Neighbourhoods and housing, in T. Modood, R. Berthoud and J. Nazroo *et al.* (eds) *Ethnic Minorities in Britain: Diversity and Disadvantage*. London: PSI.

Lambert, C. and Razzaque, K. (1997) *Asian Housing Needs in Bristol*. Bristol: UWE.

Lambert, H. and Sevak, L. (1996) Perceptions of health and the sources of ill-health among Londoners of South Asian origin: is 'cultural difference' a useful concept? in D. Kelleher and S. Hillier (eds) *Researching Cultural Differences in Health*. London: Routledge.

Law, I., Davies, J., Philips, D. and Harrison, M. (1996) *Equity and Difference: racial and ethnic inequalities in housing needs and housing investment in Leeds*. Leeds: University of Leeds 'Race' and Public Policy Research Unit, School of Sociology and Social Policy.

Navarro, V. (1990). Race or class versus race and class? *Lancet*, 336: 1238–40.

Nazroo, J. (1997) *The Health of Britain's Ethnic Minorities*. London: PSI.

Nazroo, J. (1998) Genetic, cultural or socio-economic vulnerability? Explaining ethnic inequalities in health, *Sociology of Health and Illness*, 20: 710–30.

Phillips, D. and Karn, V. (1992) Race and housing and a property owning democracy, *New Community*, 18: 355–69.

Pirani, M., Yolles, M. and Bassa, E. (1992) Ethnic pay differentials, *New Community*, 19: 31–42.

Sashidharan, S. and Francis, E. (1993) Epidemiology, ethnicity and schizophrenia, in W.I.U. Ahmad (ed.) *'Race' and Health in Contemporary Britain*. Buckingham: Open University Press.

Senior, M. and Bhopal, R. (1994) Ethnicity as a variable in epidemiological research, *British Medical Journal*, 309: 327–30.

Sheldon, T. and Parker, H. (1992) Race and ethnicity in health research, *Journal of Public Health Medicine*, 14: 104–10.

Smaje, C. (1995) *Health, Race and Ethnicity*. London: King's Fund Institute.

Smith, S.J. (1989) *The Politics of Race and Residence*. Cambridge: Polity.

Stewart, J.A., Dundas, R., Howard, R.A., Rudd, A.G. and Woolfe C.D.A. (1999) Ethnic differences in incidence of stroke: prospective study with stroke register. *British Medical Journal*, 318: 967–71.

Williams, R., Wright, W. and Hunt, K. (1998) Social class and health: the puzzling counter-example of British South Asians, *Social Science and Medicine*, 47: 1277–88.

| # Identity and structure: rethinking ethnic inequalities in health

Saffron Karlsen and James Y. Nazroo

Introduction

Since the early 1970s, ethnic differences in health have become an increasing focus of research in Britain, both in terms of general health/all-cause mortality and in terms of specific outcomes, such as heart disease (Marmot *et al.* 1984; Rudat 1994; Harding and Maxwell 1997; Nazroo 1997a, 1997b; Maxwell and Harding 1998). A summary of key findings, including a description of ethnic minority groups in Britain, can be found in Nazroo (1999). Such work, and associated discussions, have originated from a variety of competing paradigms, which have elsewhere been described as (Nazroo 1998):

- 'un-theorized' ethnicity – an apparently empirically driven approach that assumes that 'ethnic/race' variables represent true (and fixed) genetic or cultural differences between groups, which lead to differences in health across groups;
- ethnicity as structure, leading to an exploration of the inter-relationship between ethnicity, class and health; and
- ethnicity as identity, which is concerned with how cultural traditions and ethnic affiliation derived from situational and evolving identities might be related to health.

While there may be aspects of each approach which can shape our understanding of ethnic inequalities in health, only through an exploration of ethnicity as identity can we recognize the dynamic and multi-dimensional nature of ethnicity and so truly explore the inter-relationship between aspects of ethnicity minority status, structural factors and health. This chapter uses quantitative data on three broad ethnic minority groups to explore underlying dimensions of ethnicity as identity and the relationship between ethnic identity, structural factors and health.

Work on identity suggests that an individual has multiple 'identities' (related to age, gender, class, ethnicity and so on) which influence their own and others' view of who they are. The relative importance of each aspect of identity at any one time will be defined through social transactions and will affect interaction with others, which may promote group identification or alienation accordingly. Jenkins (1994) describes identity as consisting of two elements: a name (the nominal) and an experience (the virtual) – essentially, what that name means. The experience of *having* an identity will also involve the consolidation of our and others' definitions (Jenkins 1994). External characterization will significantly affect the social experience of living with that identity and the self-image of those so defined, through, for example, the experience of negative discrimination.

In terms of ethnicity, most writers draw on a notion of identity which reflects self-identification with cultural traditions that provide both meaning and boundaries between groups (see for example Barot 1996). Cultural traditions might contribute to health variations in a number of ways, including through their influence on health-related behaviours. Patterns of smoking and drinking alcohol, for example, have been shown to vary across ethnic groups (Rudat 1994; Nazroo 1997a). However, health research typically adopts an 'un-theorized' approach, where culture is mapped onto reified ethnic categories and essentialized (Ahmad 1993). Although this approach is assumed to be theoretically neutral, because genetic or cultural differences are rarely directly measured, differences are often assumed on the basis of ethnic stereotypes (Nazroo 1998).

This approach encourages the pathologizing of ethnicity, with culture itself becoming the 'cause' of health differentials. This is exacerbated by a failure to adequately explore structural dimensions of ethnicity: in particular, how racism leads to the exclusion of ethnic minority people and consequent social disadvantage (Miles 1989). Recent studies have clearly shown socio-economic gradients in mortality for different country of birth groups (Harding and Maxwell 1997). These studies have illustrated both the complexity of making adjustments for socio-economic position when drawing comparisons of morbidity experience across ethnic groups (see Chapter 2; Nazroo 1997a) and that, when more appropriate adjustments were made, there were large reductions in differences of risk of morbidity between ethnic groups (Nazroo 1998). However, these findings need to be reconciled with the theoretical work which has explored ethnicity as identity. Although socio-economic disadvantage might contribute to ethnic inequalities in health, there remains a cultural component to ethnicity that could make a major contribution to differences in health (Smaje 1996a).

When considering cultural differences in health behaviours, for example, there is a need to consider ethnicity as a hybrid identity (Hall 1992; Modood 1998): an identity that is not just given, but which is continually changed across contexts and over time. So, it is important to recognize that ethnic identity/culture is not static and that health behaviours are influenced by other factors as well, such as gender and class. Ahmad (1996: 190) sums up this position well:

> stripped of its dynamic social, economic, gender and historical context, culture becomes a rigid and constraining concept which is seen somehow to mechanistically determine peoples' behaviours and actions rather than providing a flexible resource for living, for according meaning to what one feels, experiences and acts to change. Cultural norms provide guidelines for understanding and action, guidelines which are flexible and changing, open to different interpretations across people and across time, structured by gender, class, caste and other contexts, and which are modulated by previous experiences, relationships, resources and priorities. The rigid conception of culture, which all too often is apparent in health research serves a different function, however, it provides a description of people which emphasises their 'cultural' difference and helps to obscure the similarities between broadly defined cultural groups and the diversity within a cultural group.

The demand, then, is to build on work which has explored the impact of structural factors on the health of ethnic minority people by including an assessment of the importance of ethnic identity. This is not straightforward for two reasons. First, the contextual nature of ethnic identity makes it hard, if not impossible, to operationalize in a quantitative study. Second, the relationship between culture/identity and health is unlikely to be straightforward. For example, while a strong ethnic identity may, in some circumstances, lead to improved social support (Kelleher 1996), socio-communal engagement and psychological well-being (Halpern and Nazroo 2000), in others it may also lead to negative discrimination and isolation. Here we will describe one approach to exploring the relationship between ethnic identity and health, an approach that uses quantitative techniques, but which also recognizes the multi-dimensional nature of ethnic identity.

Methods

The findings presented here are based on secondary analysis of the *Fourth National Survey of Ethnic Minorities* (FNS). The FNS was a representative survey of ethnic minority and White people living in England and Wales undertaken in 1993–4. A sample of 5196 people of Caribbean and Asian origin and 2867 White people underwent a structured face-to-face interview conducted by an ethnically-matched interviewer in the language of the respondent's choice. In addition to physical (Nazroo 1997a) and mental (Nazroo 1997b) health, the questionnaire covered a range of information on ethnicity and other aspects of the lives of ethnic minority people, including demographic and socio-economic factors (see Modood *et al.* 1997). Here we will focus on three elements of the questionnaire: ethnic identity, occupational class and self-reported health (dichotomized between those reporting very good or good health, and those reporting fair, poor or very poor health).

In terms of this analysis, the following points need noting:

- Respondents were allocated into an ethnic group on the basis of their family origins (see Modood *et al.* 1997).
- The ethnic groups included in the survey were: White; Caribbean; Indian; African Asian; Pakistani; Bangladeshi; and Chinese.
- Only half of the ethnic minority sample and none of the White sample were asked the questions on ethnic identity.
- Preliminary analysis of the FNS data showed great similarity between Pakistani and Bangladeshi people on the one hand, and Indian and African Asian people on the other (Nazroo 1997a). To overcome the problem of small numbers, these groups were combined.
- The sample for this analysis was: 591 Caribbean people, 903 Pakistani or Bangladeshi people, and 1013 Indian or African Asian people. The Chinese sample was too small to include.

The analysis of ethnic identity concentrated on questionnaire items relating to descriptions of ancestry and ethnic affiliation, lifestyle, experience of racism and social and community involvement. The full details of these questions will be shown later. To determine underlying dimensions of ethnicity that might contribute to a sense of identity, a factor analysis (Kim and Mueller 1979) of these variables was conducted. This technique is used to identify correlations among sets of inter-related variables which are represented as factors grouping variables together – in this case as underlying dimensions of ethnic identity. We first conducted this for each ethnic group separately, then for all of the ethnic minority groups combined. The principal components method of factor extraction was used. This produces factors in sequence according to the amount of the total sample variance they account for. The total variance explained by each factor is called the 'eigenvalue'. This analysis reports only factors with an eigenvalue of 1 or over (factors with a variance of less than 1 are no better than a single variable, since each variable has a variance of 1) (Kim and Mueller 1979). This process also allocated individual respondents a factor score for each of the factors identified, which represents a summary of their scores on the individual variables that make up the factor.

To explore the relationship between ethnic identity and socio-demographic characteristics, a linear regression analysis was performed separately for each identity factor and for each of the three ethnic groups. The socio-demographic indicators included were: age; gender; age of migration; religious affiliation (Indian or African Asian people only); importance of religion; registrar general's occupational class; housing tenure; economic activity; equivalent class of highest British or overseas qualification; and residential area (a measure of urbanization).

Finally, to examine the relationship between ethnic identity, class and health, a logistic regression analysis was conducted with self-reported fair or poor health as the outcome variable and the different dimensions of ethnic identity, occupational class, age and gender as the independent variables.

Results

Factor analysis of the identity questions for all ethnic minority groups combined grouped the questions into five dimensions of identity (see Nazroo and Karlsen 2000). These dimensions have been given broad 'working titles' to aid the presentation of results.

Nationality important for self-description: the questions correlating under identity 1 were:

If you were describing yourself on the phone to a new acquaintance of your own sex from a country you have never been to:
• Would your nationality tell them something important about you?
• Would the country your family came from tell them something important about you?

If a White person who knew and liked you was describing you to another White person, would they think it important to mention:
• Your nationality?
• The country your family came from?

'Ethnicity/race' important for self-description: the questions correlating under identity 2 were:

If you were describing yourself on the phone to a new acquaintance of your own sex from a country you have never been to:
• Would your skin colour tell them something important about you?
• Would the fact that you are Asian/Black tell them something important about you?

If a White person who knew and liked you was describing you to another White person, would they think it important to mention:
• Your skin colour?
• That you are Asian/Black?

Traditional: the questions correlating under identity 3 were:

How often do you wear Asian clothes/something that is meant to show a connection with the Caribbean or Africa?
- ('Never'; 'At social events'; 'At home'; 'At work, or while shopping'; 'All the time')

Who do you speak to in a language other than English?
- ('No one'; 'Older relatives'; 'Own-age relatives'; 'Younger relatives'; 'Friends outside work'; 'Work friends')

Would you personally mind if a close relative were to marry a White person?
- ('I wouldn't mind'; 'I would mind a little'; 'I would very much mind')

Do you strongly agree, agree, neither agree nor disagree, disagree or strongly disagree with these statements?
- 'In many ways I think of myself as being British'
- 'In many ways I think of myself as being Asian/Caribbean'

Community participation: the questions correlating under identity 4 were:

Does your voluntary work bring you mainly into contact with people of your ethnic origin, mainly White people or about equally with both?
- ('Don't volunteer'; 'Mainly White'; 'Both'; 'Mainly people from my own ethnic group')

Do your activities with [organization] bring you mainly into contact with people of your ethnic origin, mainly White people or about equally with both?
- ('Am not a member of an organization'; 'Mainly White'; 'Both'; 'Mainly people from my own ethnic group')

Member of a racialized group: the questions correlating under identity 5 were:

Have you ever been a victim of a racially motivated attack (verbal or physical abuse to the person or property)?

Have you ever been treated unfairly at work or been refused a job on the basis of race, colour or your religious or cultural background?

How many of the employers in Britain do you think would refuse a job to a person because of their race, colour, religion or cultural background?
- ('None'; 'A few'; 'About half'; 'Most')

The results were very similar when the factor analysis was conducted for each ethnic group separately. This would suggest that the dimensions that constitute ethnic identity are similar across different ethnic groups.

Figure 3.1 shows the distribution of respondents across the scores for each identity factor by ethnic group. In general, there was considerable overlap between factor scores for the different ethnic groups, particularly for the two South Asian groups. However, Figure 3.1 also suggests that, despite the consistency in the dimensions of ethnic identity shown above, the nature and significance of particular dimensions vary markedly, both across ethnic groups and across individuals within ethnic groups. Differences between ethnic groups were particularly marked for identities 2, 3 and 5.

We conducted linear regression analyses to explore the individual characteristics that might account for some of the variation in scores within ethnic groups. Tables 3.1, 3.2 and 3.3 show the relationship between key socio-demographic variables and the five ethnic identity factors for each ethnic group.

While the correlations for particular socio-demographic variables varied across the different factors and across the ethnic groups, some broad conclusions can be drawn:

- Being male was associated with higher scores for factors 1 (nationality important for self-description), 2 ('ethnicity/race' important for self-description), 4 (community participation) and 5 (member of a racialized group), but with lower scores for factor 3 (traditional).
- A younger age at migration was associated with higher scores for factors 1 and 4, but lower scores for factors 3 and 5.
- Reporting religion to be important was associated with a lower score on factors 1 and 2 and a higher score on factors 4 and 5.
- Having higher qualifications was associated with lower scores for factors 2 and 3, but higher scores for factors 4 and 5.
- Living in a non-urban environment was associated with higher scores on factors 1, 2 and 4, and lower scores on factors 3 and 5.

Tables 3.4 to 3.6 show logistic regression models exploring the relationship between reporting fair or poor health, ethnic identity and occupational class for each ethnic group. Each model was constructed in three stages, first with the identity factors, then with gender and age and finally with occupational class in the model. Before the inclusion of age and gender, factors 2 and 3 appeared to be associated with self-reported health for the two South Asian groups. A high score on factor 2 (importance of 'ethnicity/race' in a self-description) was associated with statistically significant increased reports of poor health for both groups. A high factor 3 score (traditional) was associated with a 60 to 80 per cent greater likelihood of reporting poor health for both South Asian groups. For the Caribbean group, a high score on factor 1 (importance of nationality in self-description) was associated with a statistically significant reduction in reported poor health.

After including age and gender in the models, the effects of the ethnic identity factors change. Both the reduced risk for Caribbean people associated

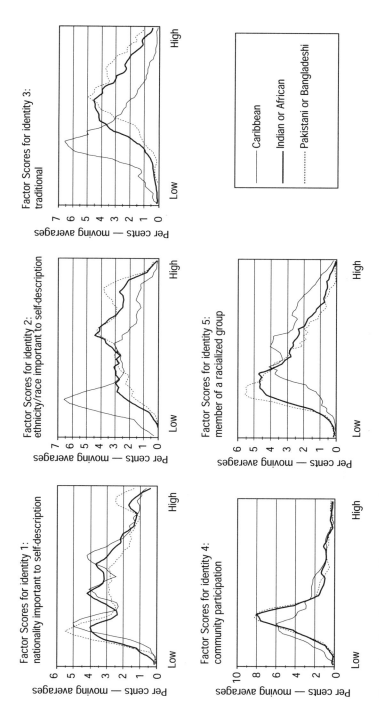

Figure 3.1 Distribution of factor scores by ethnic group

Table 3.1 Socio-demographic characteristics and dimensions of ethnic identity – Indian or African Asian group, (regression coefficients)

	Nationality	'Ethnicity/race'	Traditional	Community	Racialization
Age					
Between 16 and 29*					
Between 30 and 44	−0.10	0.17[a.s]	−0.01	0.09	0.11
Between 45 and 59	−0.20	0.15	−0.02	0.42[s]	0.12
60 or over*	0.27	0.51[s]	−0.01	0.24	−0.17
Sex					
Female*					
Male	0.03	−0.02	−0.39[s]	0.21[s]	0.30[s]
Age at migration					
16 or over*					
Between 10 and 15	0.17	−0.19[a.s]	−0.08	0.06	0.02
Under 10	0.24[s]	−0.07	−0.39[s]	0.12	0.04
Religious affiliation					
None*					
Hindu	0.05	0.14	−0.73[s]	0.12	−0.02
Sikh	−0.17	−0.01	0.97[s]	0.06	−0.10
Muslim	−0.09	−0.06	0.82[s]	0.23	−0.15
Importance of religion					
Not important*					
Fairly important	−0.19[a.s]	−0.04	0.30[s]	−0.03	0.12
Important	−0.35[s]	−0.32[s]	0.61[s]	0.12	0.04

Table 3.1 *continued*

	Nationality	'Ethnicity/race'	Traditional	Community	Racialization
Occupational class					
IV/V*					
IIIm	0.16	0.10	0.02	0.04	0.10
IIIn	0.16	0.12	−0.11	−0.07	0.09
I/II	0.11	0.11	−0.14[a.s]	0.20[a.s]	0.09
Housing tenure					
Rented*					
Owner-occupied	0.12	0.03	−0.05	−0.04	−0.04
Non-working					
Employed*					
Unemployed	0.12	0.03	−0.06	−0.12	−0.01
Sick or retired	−0.03	−0.01	0.11	−0.18	−0.08
Housewife/husband	−0.15	0.06	0.07	−0.08	0.07
Highest qualification					
No qualifications*					
CSE or O level	−0.09	−0.21[s]	−0.06	0.10	0.12
A level or degree	−0.04	−0.19[s]	−0.18[s]	0.47[s]	0.29[s]
Residential area					
Not near the city*					
Metropolitan area	0.07	−0.26[s]	0.15[s]	−0.03	0.03
Inner-city area	−0.30[s]	−0.01	0.25[s]	−0.19	0.28[s]

Notes:

* Reference category

[s] Indicates a statistically significant association ($p < 0.05$)

[a.s] Indicates an association which approaches statistical significance ($0.05 < p < 0.1$)

− Indicates negative association.

Table 3.2 Socio-demographic characteristics and dimensions of ethnic identity – Pakistani or Bangladeshi group, (regression coefficients)

	Nationality	'Ethnicity/race'	Traditional	Community	Racialization
Age					
Between 16 and 29*					
Between 30 and 44	−0.01	0.06	0.04	0.06	0.22[s]
Between 45 and 59	−0.11	0.01	0.07	−0.07	0.25
60 or over*	−0.42	0.12	0.29	0.41[a.s]	0.02
Sex					
Female*					
Male	0.36[s]	0.13	−0.25[s]	0.19	0.18
Age at migration					
16 or over*					
Between 10 and 15	−0.18	−0.08	−0.05	0.24[s]	0.05
Under 10	0.06	−0.20	−0.30[s]	0.35[s]	0.01
Importance of religion					
Not important*					
Fairly important	−0.14	−0.04	0.22	0.40[a.s]	−0.20
Important	−0.14	−0.00	0.54[s]	0.25	−0.17
Occupational class					
IV/V*					
IIIm	−0.33[s]	−0.28[s]	−0.08	0.09	0.14
IIIn	−0.27[a.s]	−0.29[s]	−0.13	0.26	0.17
I/II	−0.20	−0.28[a.s]	0.18	0.27[a.s]	0.29[s]
Housing tenure					
Rented*					
Owner-occupied	0.07	0.05	0.04	0.08	0.17[a.s]

Table 3.2 *continued*

	Nationality	'Ethnicity/race'	Traditional	Community	Racialization
Non-working					
Employed*					
Unemployed	-0.12	0.01	-0.14	-0.16	-0.15
Sick or retired	0.43	-0.13	-0.29a.s	-0.10	-0.33
Housewife/husband	0.33a.s	0.01	0.30s	-0.07	-0.28a.s
Highest qualification					
No qualifications*					
CSE or O level	-0.04	-0.12	-0.16a.s	0.11	0.07
A level or degree	-0.14	-0.06	-0.38s	0.56s	0.08
Residential area					
Not near the city*					
Metropolitan area	-0.11	0.09	-0.09	-0.26s	0.02
Inner-city area	-0.37s	-0.04	-0.04	-0.12	-0.12

Notes:

* Reference category

s Indicates a statistically significant association ($p < 0.05$)

a.s Indicates an association which approaches statistical significance ($0.05 < p < 0.1$)

– Indicates negative association.

Table 3.3 Socio-demographic characteristics and dimensions of ethnic identity – Caribbean group, (regression coefficients)

	Nationality	'Ethnicity/race'	Traditional	Community	Racialization
Age					
Between 16 and 29*					
Between 30 and 44	-0.09	-0.04	0.00	-0.15	0.07
Between 45 and 59	0.20	0.06	-0.66[s]	0.01	-0.59[s]
60 or over	0.18	0.28	-0.82[s]	-0.29	-0.73[s]
Sex					
Female*					
Male	0.18[a.s]	0.33[s]	-0.25[s]	0.34[s]	0.08
Age at migration					
16 or over*					
Between 10 and 15	0.50[a.s]	0.11	-0.25	0.01	-0.37[s]
Under 10	0.62[s]	0.40[s]	-0.89[s]	0.46[s]	-0.73[s]
Importance of religion					
Not important*					
Fairly important	0.19	0.12	0.14	-0.03	0.20[a.s]
Important	-0.10	0.09	-0.02	0.31[s]	0.20
Occupational class					
IV/V*					
IIIm	-0.06	0.08	-0.12	0.36[s]	0.04
IIIn	-0.03	-0.07	-0.11	0.33[s]	0.16
I/II	0.24[a.s]	0.29[s]	-0.05	0.26	0.03
Housing tenure					
Rented*					
Owner-occupied	0.12	0.09	-0.23[s]	-0.15	-0.17

Table 3.3 *continued*

	Nationality	'Ethnicity/race'	Traditional	Community	Racialization
Non-working					
Employed*					
Unemployed	0.22[a.s]	0.05	-0.01	-0.25	-0.17
Sick or retired	0.03	-0.04	-0.12	0.03	-0.22
Housewife/husband	0.31	0.50[s]	0.20	0.29	-0.17
Highest qualification					
No qualifications*					
CSE or O level	0.20	0.06	0.02	0.01	-0.13
A level or degree	0.16	0.24	0.11	0.38[s]	-0.09
Residential area					
Not near the city*					
Metropolitan area	-0.22[a.s]	0.01	0.23[s]	-0.15	-0.08
Inner-city area	-0.21[a.s]	-0.03	0.34[s]	0.09	0.17

Notes:

*   Reference category

[s]   Indicates a statistically significant association (p < 0.05)

[a.s]   Indicates an association which approaches statistical significance (0.05 < p < 0.1)

–   Indicates negative association.

Table 3.4 Ethnic identity and risk of fair or poor health – Indian or African Asian group (odds ratios)

	Indian or African Asian (n = 950)		
	Model 1	*Model 2*	*Model 3*
Nationality	1.02	1.09	1.09
Ethnicity	1.30[s]	1.05	1.08
Traditional	1.62[s]	1.24[s]	1.20[a.s]
Community	1.10	1.07	1.09
Racialization	1.14	1.33[s]	1.38[s]
Gender		1.58[s]	1.60[s]
Age		1.07	1.08[s]
Class			
Manual			1.63[s]
Unemployed			2.49[s]

Notes:
[s] p < 0.05
[a.s] p < 0.1

Table 3.5 Ethnic identity and risk of fair or poor health – Pakistani or Bangladeshi group (odds ratios)

	Pakistani or Bangladeshi (n = 835)		
	Model 1	*Model 2*	*Model 3*
Nationality	1.02	1.10	1.09
Ethnicity	1.25[s]	1.04	1.03
Traditional	1.76[s]	1.39[s]	1.34[a.s]
Community	0.94	1.06	1.13
Racialization	1.07	1.14	1.18
Gender		1.51[a.s]	1.57[a.s]
Age		1.09[a.s]	1.12[s]
Class			
Manual			1.45
Unemployed			2.48[s]

Notes:
[s] p < 0.05
[a.s] p < 0.1

with higher scores on factor 1 and the increased risk for South Asian people associated with higher scores on factor 2 disappear. The effect of factor 3 for the South Asian groups remains statistically significant, but the size of the association declines substantially. Entering age and gender into the models separately suggested that it was age that was accounting for the identity

Table 3.6 Ethnic identity and risk of fair or poor health – Caribbean group

	Caribbean (n = 555)		
	Model 1	Model 2	Model 3
Nationality	0.77[s]	0.95	0.94
Ethnicity	1.13	1.16	1.16
Traditional	1.05	1.08	1.06
Community	0.91	1.09	1.08
Racialization	0.90	0.94	0.94
Gender		1.81[s]	1.77[s]
Age		0.97	0.99
Class			
Manual			0.94
Unemployed			1.40

Notes:
[s] $p < 0.05$
[a.s] $p < 0.1$

effects (not shown in the tables). Interestingly, after including age in the models, the association between self-reported poor health and factor 5 (racialization) increases and becomes statistically significant for the Indian or African Asian group.

When occupational class is entered into the models, it appears to have an effect for each ethnic group. For the two South Asian groups, the class effect is significant and sizeable; for example, non-working South Asian people had a two and a half times greater chance of reporting poor health, compared with South Asian people working in non-manual occupations. There was also an effect for the Caribbean group, but this was smaller and not statistically significant. Although the inclusion of occupational class in the model did not greatly reduce the odds ratios for the identity factors, in the full model none of the identity factors made a statistically significant contribution.

Discussion

In terms of ethnic identity, the findings (see Nazroo and Karlsen 2000) support earlier work suggesting that ethnic identity has nominal and virtual components, influenced by internal and external definitions of ethnicity (Jenkins 1994). Of the dimensions derived from the factor analysis, factors 1 and 2 (based on nationality, country of origin and skin colour) appear to be related to the nominal component of ethnic identity. Of course, giving oneself a name also requires a perception of 'what it is to be that name', a perception that partly depends on the virtual component of ethnic identity, to which ethnic identity factors 3, 4 and 5 appear to be related.

Factor 3, which combined items relating to clothes, language, attitudes to mixed marriage and perception of oneself as British and Asian/Caribbean, may operate as a boundary of inclusion, providing an internal sense of identity. The elements of it that involve presentation of a public image through particular behaviours and participation in customs is similar to what Smaje (1996b) terms 'unreflective ethnicity', a phrase that suggests a form of 'innate' ethnicity. However, differences within this dimension may involve some internalization of external attitudes, reflecting the dynamic nature of what Bourdieu (1977: 97) calls 'bodily hexis', where 'political mythology is realised and embodied and turned into a permanent disposition'. Here it is important to recognize that, despite the use of the term 'traditional', a low score on this factor does not imply a 'loss' of culture or the adoption of a majority culture. Rather, these are related to reduced participation in customs seen as traditional to an ethnic group and a consequent shift in what being of that group means (see Hall's 1992 description of traditional, translated and hybrid identities for a fuller discussion of this).

Factor 4, community participation, can also be considered to reflect a boundary of inclusion. However, unlike factor 3, which could be described as 'unreflective', the perceived need to establish ethnically-identified groups would suggest both a response to exclusion by wider society and a positive celebration of ethnic group membership. It is this form of politicized identity that has led ethnicity as identity to be construed as a 'new social movement' (Nazroo 1998).

Factor 5, reflecting perceptions and experience of racism, is the most obvious indicator of external influences on ethnic identity. It could be argued that those who score highly on this factor will have recognized their ethnic status as one that has been racialized by the ethnic majority.

In terms of the exploration of patterns of ethnic identity, the key finding is the similarity of the factors across the three ethnic groups (Nazroo and Karlsen 2000). This suggests that the basic components of ethnic identity among different ethnic minority groups in Britain are broadly similar.

In terms of the relationship between ethnic identity and health, initial models that did not include age or occupational class suggested that, for the South Asian groups, higher scores on the more nominal and 'unreflective' elements of ethnic identity (factors 2 and 3) were related to increased risk of reporting fair or poor health. It could be hypothesized that, for 'unreflective ethnicity' at least, this was related to culturally determined health behaviours (such as diet, exercise and smoking). However, when age was included, these effects were substantially reduced and in the full models, which also included occupational class, they were no longer statistically significant. It seems that the initial effect was spurious – simply a consequence of the correlation between age and both identity and health. Tables 3.1 to 3.3 in fact suggest that the correlations might be slightly more complex, with the relationship perhaps being, on the one hand, between age and health, and on the other between age, age on migration and identity. Important here is to acknowledge that an apparent relationship between traditional elements of ethnic identity and health, that might be seen in a practice setting for example, may simply be confounded by age.

One reason why ethnicity as identity might not predict health is because its effect is dependent on context. In particular, a 'strong' ethnic identity may be protective of health for those living in an area with large numbers of people from a similar background, but it may produce detrimental health effects for those living elsewhere (Halpern and Nazroo 2000; Neeleman and Wessely 1999). However, an examination of these issues using these data has suggested that such contextual effects are not present.

Overall, the evidence from these data presented here and elsewhere (Karlsen and Nazroo 2000; Nazroo and Karlsen 2000) suggest that ethnicity as identity, in terms of self-description, self-presentation and behaviour, membership of ethnic minority organizations and perceptions and experiences of racism, is important to the experiences of ethnic minority people. However, we have also shown that ethnicity as identity does not appear to influence health. In the models that included all of the various ethnic identity factors, gender, age and occupational class, it appeared that those variables related to ethnicity as identity had little effect on risk of fair or poor health, while occupational class had significant and large effects for most groups and an identity as a member of a racialized group had an effect for the Indian or African Asian group. Ethnicity as structure (both in terms of racialization and class experience), rather than ethnicity as identity, is strongly associated with health for ethnic minority people living in Britain.

Acknowledgements

This chapter draws on research funded by the ESRC (L128251019) under the Health Variations Programme. The chapter is based on the Fourth National Survey of Ethnic Minorities, and thanks are due to the funders of the survey (in particular, the Department of Health, Advisory Groups, colleagues at the Policy Studies Institute and the National Centre for Social Research, the interviewers, and, most importantly, the thousands of people who responded to the survey).

References

Ahmad, W.I.U. (1993) Making black people sick: 'race', ideology and health research, in W.I.U. Ahmad (ed.) *'Race' and Health in Contemporary Britain*. Buckingham: Open University Press.

Ahmad, W.I.U. (1996) The trouble with culture, in D. Kelleher and S. Hillier (eds) *Researching Cultural Differences in Health*. London: Routledge.

Barot, R. (ed.) (1996) *The Racism Problematic: Contemporary Sociological Debates on Race and Ethnicity*. Lewiston: The Edwin Mellen Press.

Bourdieu, P. (1977) *Outline of a Theory of Practice*. Cambridge: Cambridge University Press.

Hall, S. (1992) The question of cultural identity, in S. Hall, D. Held and T. McGrew (eds) *Modernity and its Futures*. Cambridge: Polity.

Halpern, D. and Nazroo, J. (2000) The ethnic density effect: results from a national community survey of England and Wales, *International Journal of Social Psychiatry*, 46(1): 34–46.

Harding, S. and Maxwell, R. (1997) Differences in the mortality of migrants, in F. Drever and M. Whitehead (eds) *Health Inequalities* (Series DS No. 15). London: The Stationery Office.

Jenkins, R. (1994) Rethinking ethnicity: identity, categorization and power, *Ethnic and Racial Studies*, 17(2): 197–223.

Karlsen, S. and Nazroo, J.Y. (2000) 'Agency and structure: the contribution of ethnic identity to the health of ethnic minority people', unpublished manuscript. London: Department of Epidemiology and Public Health, UCL.

Kelleher, D. (1996) A defence of the use of the terms 'ethnicity' and 'culture', in D. Kelleher and S. Hillier (eds) *Researching Cultural Differences in Health*. London: Routledge.

Kim, J.O. and Mueller, C.W. (1979) *Factor Analysis: Statistical Methods and Practical Issues*. London: Sage.

Marmot, M.G., Adelstein, A.M., Bulusu, L. and OPCS (1984) *Immigrant Mortality in England and Wales 1970–78: Causes of Death by Country of Birth*. London: HMSO.

Maxwell, R. and Harding, S. (1998) Mortality of migrants from outside England and Wales by marital status, *Population Trends*, 91: 15–22.

Miles, R. (1989) *Racism*. London: Routledge.

Modood, T. (1998) Anti-essentialism, multiculturalism and the 'recognition' of religious groups, *Journal of Political Philosophy*, 6(4): 378–99.

Modood, T., Berthoud, R. and Lakey, J. *et al.* (1997) *Ethnic Minorities in Britain: Diversity and Disadvantage*. London: Policy Studies Institute.

Nazroo, J.Y. (1997a) *The Health of Britain's Ethnic Minorities: Findings from a National Survey*. London: Policy Studies Institute.

Nazroo, J.Y. (1997b) *Ethnicity and Mental Health: Findings from a National Community Survey*. London: Policy Studies Institute.

Nazroo, J.Y. (1998) Genetic, cultural or socio-economic vulnerability? Explaining ethnic inequalities in health, *Sociology of Health and Illness*, 20(5): 710–30.

Nazroo, J.Y. (1999) Ethnic inequalities in health, in D. Gordon, M. Shaw, D. Dorling and G. Davey Smith (eds) *Inequalities in Health: The Evidence*. Bristol: The Policy Press.

Nazroo, J. and Karlsen, S. (2000) 'Patterns of ethnic identity: diversity and commonality', unpublished manuscript. Department of Epidemiology and Public Health, University College London.

Neelman, J. and Wessely, S. (1999) Ethnic minority suicide: a small area geographical study in south London, *Psychological Medicine*, 29: 429–36.

Rudat, K. (1994) *Black and Minority Ethnic Groups in England: Health and Lifestyles*. London: Health Education Authority.

Smaje, C. (1996a) The ethnic patterning of health: new directions for theory and research, *Sociology of Health and Illness*, 18(2): 139–71.

Smaje, C. (1996b) Not just a social construct: theorising racial ontology. Paper presented to the British Sociological Association Annual Conference, Reading, 1–4 April.

4 | Dimensions of inequality and
         the health of women

Mel Bartley, Amanda Sacker, David Firth
and Ray Fitzpatrick

Introduction

Rapid change is taking place in women's lives. Increasing numbers of
women are entering the high-status, but also high-stress jobs in scientific,
technical and professional labour markets (Gregg and Machin 1993; Davies
and Joshi 1998). At the same time, there have been far slower changes in
attitudes towards relationships between men and women, or towards
women's 'proper' social roles. Social and economic inequality has widened,
with particularly acute effects on women caring for children (see Chapter 1).
The task of monitoring the effects of such changes on women's health is a
major challenge.

The study described in this chapter was aimed at taking forward our
understanding of social variations in women's health. It did this, first, by
taking into account changing patterns of labour market activity and domestic arrangements. Second, we regarded inequality as multi-faceted by using
separate measures of social class based on employment relations, general
social advantage based on patterns of social distance and social interaction,
and material living standards. The aim is to improve our ability to answer
the questions that must be asked if social and economic policies intended to
reduce health inequality are to be successful.

Dimensions of inequality

It is now widely accepted that the psychosocial effects of relative social and
material disadvantage play a role in the genesis of health inequalities

(McIsaac and Wilkinson 1997). The data used in the relevant studies have been of two types. Rich data have been collected by intensive studies of a cohort of men and women in the UK civil service (Marmot and Shipley 1996). In this and other studies (Davey Smith *et al.* 1994), those with the highest level of social or economic advantage enjoy better health than not just those with the lowest, but all other intermediate levels as well. These findings indicate that health inequality may not be only a matter of poverty.

Other studies of a very different kind have reported on relationships between income distribution in whole countries (Wilkinson 1992) or in smaller regions in Britain (Ben Shlomo *et al.* 1996) and the USA (Kennedy *et al.* 1996; Wolfson *et al.* 1999) and the levels of life expectancy found in these areas. Because it appears to be income distribution and not average income per capita which affects life expectancy, these studies strengthen the case for the importance of psychosocial as well as purely material effects.

There has been rather less discussion of the relationship between these two types of study, or of the issues they raise for understanding health inequality. In studies of individual men and women, it seems that the higher the income of any individual, the better their health. But in the studies of regions with different income distributions, health does not improve with every increase in the mean income per capita: above a certain level of average income, it is not the amount of income but the way it is distributed that seems to matter. And why should the distribution of income be relevant for health? Research has focused on psychosocial explanations: the effects of perceiving oneself to be worse off than other people in terms of social status or prestige (see Chapter 11). Where income is very unequal, it is argued, more people will feel 'relative deprivation' and powerlessness, resulting in both stress and risk-taking forms of behaviour.

The concepts of power and prestige may be regarded as linking the studies of health inequality between social and economic groups to the studies that compare whole countries or areas. In countries where income is more equally distributed, even those with lower incomes may have more control over their lives, and be less likely to be forced to take subservient work, or to feel that they are going to be 'looked down on' by others. A vivid example of this is the way in which, as income inequality widened in Britain, both the demand for and the supply of workers willing to become household servants such as cleaners and nannies also increased (Gregson and Lowe 1994). It seems that under circumstances of greater equality, there is also a higher degree of trust between people and a greater tendency for people to mix socially and undertake common activities (Kawachi and Kennedy 1997).

If differences in income, power and prestige are to be regarded as important causes of health inequality, we have to think of ways in which their effects could come about. This is why researchers are interested in the notion of 'lifestyle'. Poverty has an obvious relationship to living standards. However, if *relative* income is related to health due to the associated differences in power and prestige, we need to ask what are the additional processes producing this relationship? One hypothesis is that to perceive oneself as 'inferior' or subservient activates biological responses which, over the long term, increase vulnerability to heart disease and other serious illness (Brunner 1997). Another pathway which we consider here is concerned with the effects of prestige on health-related behaviour.

People with similar amounts of income may come to adopt similar patterns of beliefs, values and leisure activities as a way of acquiring or maintaining acceptance within a status group. Those with more disposable income may use it to engage in 'conspicuous consumption', which advertises their privilege (Veblen 1924). Social groups, including people with lower income, may also adopt symbolically significant activities or forms of consumption, in some cases perhaps enabling them to display their rejection of the lifestyle of those who are better off. Similar points may be made in relation to inequalities in power. Those with more power may adopt a certain lifestyle which symbolizes this, while those with less may signal their dissent or resistance by an alternative choice of, for example, music, clothes and leisure activities.

The use of forms of consumption and leisure activity to express social status has been discussed by Pierre Bourdieu, and our approach to culture and lifestyle as determinants of health is influenced by his work. Although Bourdieu's applied sociology has focused on the spheres of education and leisure rather than health, the relevance of his work for medical sociology has been pointed out (Williams 1995). In describing the ways in which musical taste expresses wider social inequality, he comments (in a discussion of the French equivalent of *Desert Island Discs*): 'There is nothing which is so effective as musical taste in enabling people to display their "class", nothing which can be used so infallibly to locate someone in the social structure' (Bourdieu 1984c: 55). He goes on to say:

> It is only perhaps taste in food which is more tightly linked to bodily experience than musical taste . . . Our self esteem suffers more from the criticism of our tastes than our opinions. In fact, our tastes express and betray us far more than our political views for example . . . Taste [*le gout*] is inseparable from disgust [*le degout*]: aversion to different life-styles is one of the most powerful barriers between the social classes.
> (Bourdieu 1984c: 56–7)

Bourdieu speaks of:

> The inclination of the privileged classes towards a 'stylized' way of life [in which] the body is treated as an end in itself which . . . inclines them towards a cult of health-consciousness and the appearance of the body: the body as a thing displayed to others . . . [t]his concern for the

cultivation of the body results in a high value being placed on moder-
ate drinking, and careful diet in the middle classes . . .

(Bourdieu 1984b: 193)

It is possible to apply these examples to understanding the importance of
financial and non-financial factors in enabling people to adopt 'healthy
behaviour'. Income *per se* is important for access to certain types of cultural
pursuit. However, it costs no more to listen to classical music than other
forms on the radio or in recorded form, and costs nothing to follow a diet
and exercise regime at home, suggesting that income alone will not explain
social differences in leisure preferences. These practices seem to be undertaken in part as a way of expressing or seeking membership of certain social
groups and social distance or differentiation from others (Bourdieu 1984a).
It is this which may enable us to understand better the link between inequalities of prestige and inequalities in health.

Income, prestige and power are by no means always equal: certain occupations carry notoriously uneven amounts of each. One group, which has
long been used as an example of this, is the clergy. Although ministers of
religion are not well paid, their lifestyles include elements such as an emphasis on intellectual culture, art and music and values such as 'deferral of
gratification' which are thought to be characteristic of the wealthy and of
those successful in business. Because of the high status placed on their occupations, clergy are able to mix with those far wealthier than themselves
without feeling 'inferior' by reason of low income. Life expectancy in members of the clergy is high in the UK, comparable to that of employers and
managers of large businesses who have far higher incomes (Office of Population Censuses and Surveys 1986).

Prestige and the associated cultural differences are by no means the only
significant dimensions of social inequality for health, however. There has
been a recent accumulation of studies showing evidence that conditions and
relationships at work (Marmot and Shipley 1996; Marmot *et al.* 1997) are
part of the aetiological pathway for psychological ill-health (Stansfeld *et al.*
1998), and, perhaps partly as a result of this, for ischaemic heart disease
(Bosma *et al.* 1997). The degree of power which other people have over the
conduct of an individual's working day – 'work control' – has been shown
to be central in this relationship. The effect of control at work does not
seem, in these studies, to be produced by different lifestyles, in terms of diet,
leisure exercise or smoking. Rather, the effect may be produced by a bio-
psychosocial process in which stress caused by low control and monotony
at work induces changes both in mood and in blood chemistry (Brunner
1997).

The third dimension of inequality we need to consider is what might be
termed the 'direct' effect of material living standards. Those on low incomes
live in poorer housing conditions, in more polluted areas with fewer

facilities, can afford less of many of the more palatable forms of healthy food, and are often employed in the most heavy and hazardous industries (Blane *et al.* 1998). However such material conditions are interpreted (given a social meaning) by the individual or group, and whatever the availability of 'counter cultures' and networks of solidarity which support self-esteem and may buffer against stress, they remain health hazards.

We can therefore see that health differences between social groups may be the result of a combination of distinct dimensions of inequality. If this is the case, we will not succeed in explaining or reducing health variations by seeking one single measure of social position, or by allowing measures of one dimension to be used as proxies for all of the others (Krieger *et al.* 1997). Income obviously buys better housing, food and other material necessities. But beyond these, which are undoubtedly important, we may also need to consider the effects of prestige on both the individual's feelings of security and self-esteem, and on the adoption of healthy lifestyles. In addition, we have strong evidence that the conditions under which people work, both in terms of work hazards and in terms of work stresses, affect their health.

In research terms, the fact that occupational groups have varying combinations of income, power and prestige makes it possible to try and single out the effect of each dimension on health. We can then contribute to policy debates by answering questions such as: 'Would it do any good to give everyone the same amount of income if we still had a situation in which some people have a lot of power over others, or if some are held in very different levels of esteem in the community?'

Measuring inequality

Researchers into health inequality in the UK are able to use two different measures of social position to indicate these different aspects of social inequality. These are the Erikson-Goldthorpe class schema (Erikson and Goldthorpe 1992) and the Cambridge scale (Stewart *et al.* 1980; Prandy 1990a).

Erikson, Goldthorpe and colleagues developed their schema as part of a comparative study of social mobility patterns in industrial societies. It is based on dimensions of the work setting such as being an employer or employee, performing manual or non-manual work and the type of relationships between employees and employers. A 'service' relationship involves higher levels of autonomy and job security, with the possibility of advancement through a clear career structure. The professional and managerial occupations in E-G classes 1 and 2 are often referred to as the 'service classes'. In contrast, a 'labour' contract is one where supervision is tighter, and motivation to work is gained through the exchange of wages for set amounts of work. Levels of job security are lower, and there is no career structure. This is the type of work relationship likely to be found in more routine jobs.

In their study of the relationship between social class and political and social attitudes, Marshall *et al.* (1988) found that women in the two 'service' groups (E-G classes 1 and 2[1]) were far more likely than those in more routine types of occupation (classes 6 and 7) to report that their job was 'more than just a way of earning a living' (85 per cent in class 1 versus 53 per cent in class 7). Women in the 'service class' were more likely to report that their job involved 'using or developing their skills' (35 per cent versus 15 per cent of working class women) or 'allowed use of initiative' (26 per cent versus 9 per cent) (Marshall *et al.* 1988: 209–11).

The Cambridge scale is intended to be a measure of more general social status outside as well as inside the workplace. It is described by its originators as a measure of 'general social and material advantage and lifestyle' as indicated by the clustering of occupations into friendship groups. Blackburn and Prandy (1997: 502) describe it as reflecting 'actual, individual behaviour in the form of choice of people with whom to interact socially on an equal basis'. These interaction choices will reflect the ways in which individuals 'will be socialised into the attitudes and behaviour appropriate to their position within their society, receive the appropriate form of education and training, move into typical early jobs, marry someone from a similar background, experience a typical career . . . and so on' (p. 502).

The scale was originally derived by asking questions about the occupations of the best friends and marriage partners of respondents, on the grounds that 'marriage and friendship choices represent instances of equality in advantage' which 'since it [the scale] uses a relational approach . . . is, in a sense, a measure of lifestyles' thus integrating concepts of both 'class' and 'status' (Stewart *et al.* 1980: 30; Marsh and Blackburn 1992: 187–9). Those pairs of occupations whose members seldom cited each other as friends were regarded as separated by a greater 'social distance', and those frequently cited as less distant from each other. Having ascertained the relative distances between all pairs of occupations, multi-dimensional scaling was used to extract the principal dimensions of the space so defined. This exercise yielded a single major dimension, supporting the concept of a 'single hierarchy of social interaction and social advantage' (Prandy 1990a, 1990b: 2). The score on this factor is the Cambridge score. The same occupation may be considered as involving a different level of general social advantage if the incumbent is male or female. For example, the Cambridge score is lower for male workers than female workers on an assembly line (male score 21.8, female score 26.6), and higher for male chefs than for female chefs (28.8 for men, 25.4 for women).

Table 4.1 Distribution of demographic characteristics (percentages) for women aged 20–59 in the Health Survey for England (HSFE) and the Health and Lifestyle Survey (HALS)

	Categories	1984 (HALS)	1993 (HSFE)
Number of women		2743	4936
Age	20–24 years	11	10
	25–34 years	28	30
	35–44 years	29	28
	45–54 years	23	24
	55–59 years	9	8
Self-assessed health	Good	77	84
	Less than good	23	16
Marital status	Married/cohabiting	80	75
	Single	10	14
	Widowed/divorced/separated	10	11
Children in household	No	48	53
	Yes	52	47
Employment status	Full-time	37	43
	Part-time	28	32
	Keeping house	35	25
Partner's employment status	Working	70	64
	Non-working	10	11
	No partner	20	25
E-G class (own occupation)	Service class	17	30
	Routine non-manual	42	36
	Self-employed	6	5
	Skilled workers	6	7
	Non-skilled workers	29	22

Source: Bartley *et al.* (1999a).

Work, lifestyle and health

We have used these two measures of social position to investigate health inequality in women, how this was affected by different social role combinations, and how these patterns changed between the mid-1980s and the mid-1990s. Table 4.1 shows the changes in women's social circumstances between 1984 and 1993.

Fewer women were married or cohabiting in 1993 and fewer had children in the household. Many more were working full-time, and almost twice as many were working in the 'service class' or more complex jobs.

Table 4.2 shows that, despite these changes, there were social inequalities

Table 4.2 Odds ratios for poor self-assessed health* by Cambridge score quintiles and Erikson-Goldthorpe (E-G) classes for women aged 20–59 in the Health Survey for England (HSFE) and the Health and Lifestyle Survey (HALS)

		HALS	HSFE
Cambridge quintiles	1	1.00 (0.79–1.26)	1.00 (0.82–1.23)
	2	1.21 (0.97–1.50)	0.94 (0.76–1.17)
	3	1.30 (1.05–1.61)	1.47 (1.23–1.77)
	4	2.06 (1.70–2.49)	1.63 (1.38–1.93)
	5	2.17 (1.79–2.64)	2.34 (2.00–2.75)
E-G class	Service	1.00 (0.78–1.29)	1.00 (0.84–1.19)
	Routine non-manual	1.21 (1.04–1.40)	1.29 (1.12–1.48)
	Self-employed	1.62 (1.11–2.36)	1.34 (0.94–1.90)
	Skilled workers	1.51 (1.07–2.13)	1.56 (1.17–2.09)
	Non-skilled workers	2.03 (1.72–2.38)	2.34 (2.01–2.71)

Note:
*Adjusted for age, marital status, working status, partner's working status, children, children by working status interaction and marital status by working status interaction.
Source: Bartley *et al.* 1999a.

in health at both times. These could be seen whether we measured inequality according to the employment-related measure (the E-G classes) or the measure of general advantage (the Cambridge scale). Because the Cambridge scale is continuous, it has been divided into five evenly sized groups to make this comparison. In Table 4.2, the degree of health inequality is shown after taking account of the fact that women in the different social positions may be more or less likely to be married, have children, have paid employment or various combinations of these social roles. Health inequality in women does not, therefore, result from different combinations of social roles.

Do the different dimensions of social inequality we have discussed affect health in different ways? In Table 4.3, we can see whether material living standards (cars and tenure), work relations (E-G classes) and general social advantage (Cambridge score) relate in different ways to a set of risk factors known to influence the risk of heart disease in women (significant odds ratios are printed in bold).

We are also asking, in Table 4.3, whether different aspects of inequality have independent relationships to risk factors. In other words, might material living standards be related to smoking, for example, regardless of employment conditions and general social advantage? In the table, the higher of their own or their partner's Cambridge scores has been allocated to married and cohabiting women. This is because we consider that attitudes and behaviours will be linked to the highest level of 'general advantage' within a household.

The effects of each measure of social position in Table 4.3 may be thought

Table 4.3 Social variation* (odds ratios) in risk factors for heart disease in women by Erikson-Goldthorpe (E-G) schema, Cambridge scale and deprivation indicators

	Behavioural factors					Work factors		Physiological factors			
	Poor diet	Smoker	Non-light drinker	No sport	Low social support	Low control	Low variety	High blood pressure (BP)	Obese	Central obesity	Breathless
Cambridge scale											
Lowest:highest score	**6.89**	**6.82**	**3.94**	**2.20**	1.82	2.03	**3.22**	0.79	**4.31**	**3.78**	1.35
p (df = 1)	0.001	<.0001	0.03	0.007	0.21	0.05	0.0003	0.66	0.0004	0.005	0.40
E-G schema											
Higher professional	1.00	1.00	1.00	1.00	1.00	1.00	1.00	1.00	1.00	1.00	1.00
Lower professional	1.66	0.94	0.96	1.05	0.77	2.74	1.57	1.10	1.01	0.78	1.48
Routine non-manual	2.70	1.00	1.31	1.13	1.08	13.33	8.46	1.19	0.86	0.72	1.84
Self-employed	2.84	1.03	1.71	1.08	0.79	1.09	5.43	0.87	1.04	1.10	1.76
Skilled manual	2.36	1.20	2.43	1.17	0.99	10.49	5.41	1.60	0.85	1.14	1.56
Non-skilled manual	2.74	1.12	1.54	1.47	1.10	19.30	15.43	1.45	1.04	1.24	1.99
p (df = 5)	0.06	0.83	0.40	0.25	0.36	<.0001	<.0001	0.53	0.71	0.03	0.04
Deprivation indicators											
No car	1.09	**1.64**	1.26	1.19	**1.49**	0.83	1.10	1.12	**1.40**	**1.32**	**1.39**
Rented accommodation	**1.86**	**1.75**	0.80	1.16	**1.61**	0.96	1.04	1.01	**1.63**	**1.54**	**1.55**
p (df = 2)	0.0002	<.0001	0.58	0.06	<.0001	0.33	0.70	0.89	<.0001	0.002	<.0001

Note:
* Odds ratios are given for each of the three indicators of social position after adjusting for the other two indicators.
Source: Bartley *et al.* 1999b.

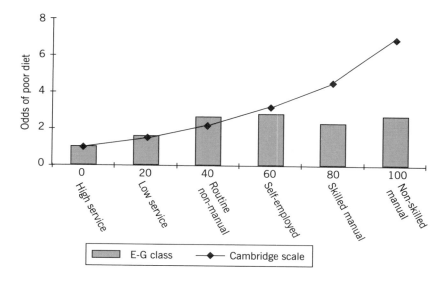

Figure 4.1 Odds of a poor diet by Erikson-Goldthorpe (E-G) class and Cambridge score for women in the Health Survey for England (HSFE)

of as those which would operate if everyone had 'average' levels of the other two measures. For example, the effect of the general advantage score on smoking assumes an 'average' type of employment and mean levels of living standards. We can see that the Cambridge scale (which we regard as a measure of prestige) does have a significant relationship to smoking regardless of the other two dimensions of inequality. By contrast the effect of E-G class based on employment relations on smoking is no longer very large when it is averaged out over all the different levels of general advantage and living standards. We might therefore say that if we really want to reduce inequality in smoking, the evidence here indicates both that material living standards need to be increased and that prestige levels should be equalized. Whereas if we are more concerned to improve social support, an improvement in living standards might suffice on its own.

Figures 4.1–4.4 show some of these relationships in graphical form. Figure 4.1 shows that at the 'average' of general social advantage and material living standards, being in a 'service class' (E-G 1 or 2) occupation makes it less likely that a woman has an unhealthy diet, but there are few differences between women in other types of employment situations.

The Cambridge score, in contrast, shows a steady gradient in relation to diet, as it does for sport participation (see Figure 4.2).

E-G class is the better discriminator of work control, however. As Figure

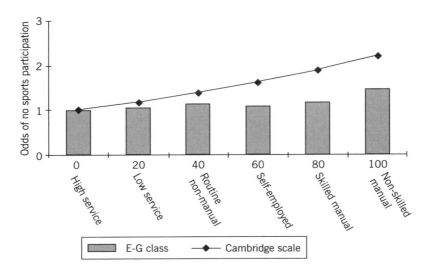

Figure 4.2 Odds of no participation in sport by Erikson-Goldthorpe (E-G) class and Cambridge score for women in the Health Survey for England (HSFE)

4.3 indicates, women in the service classes and the self-employed have more control at work than those in routine non-manual occupations while those in skilled manual jobs also have more than those in less skilled manual jobs.

Figure 4.4 shows that whereas there was a small amount of social variation in smoking when E-G class was used as the measure of inequality, there were considerably greater differences when social position was measured according to the Cambridge score.

Pathways from social inequality to health inequality

So far, we have discussed the idea that different aspects of social inequality may have different roles to play in creating health inequality in women, and have shown that there are different patterns of risk factors relating to these different dimensions. It should not be forgotten that, in reality, all three forms of inequality often go together. In fact, the originators of the Cambridge scale emphasize the importance of material advantage as well as 'social advantage' (which we are thinking of here as involving the amount of prestige accorded to people in different occupations). However, we can see from Table 4.3 that, even within groups with the same social advantage (Cambridge) score, the indicators of materially disadvantaged living standards have an independent

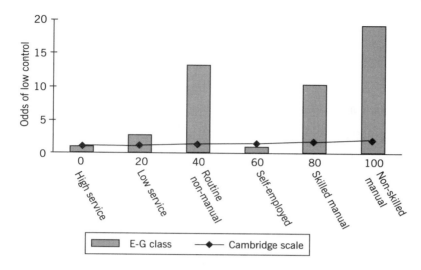

Figure 4.3 Odds of low control by Erikson-Goldthorpe (E-G) class and Cambridge score for women in the Health Survey for England (HSFE)

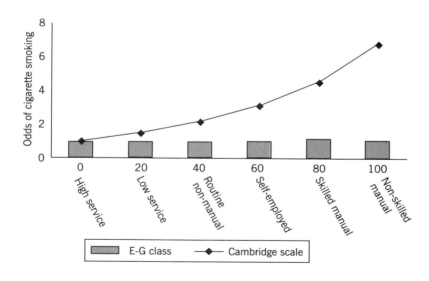

Figure 4.4 Odds of smoking by Erikson-Goldthorpe (E-G) class and Cambridge score for women in the Health Survey for England (HSFE)

relationship to diet, smoking, social support, obesity and breathlessness. Not having a car and living in a rented home is therefore telling us something more about health risk than just knowing what sort of people a woman mixes with on the basis of social equality (see also Chapter 8). Shared culture and lifestyle are not the whole answer.

The next step is to try and put these elements together, to see how far social variations in behavioural and psychosocial risk factors can go toward explaining social variations in illness and life expectancy. Are different levels of risk behaviour and psychosocial risks such as work control and social support indeed part of the reason why social inequality is reflected in health? And can we even begin to see how important each of these might be relative to the others? Such information would be valuable in policy debate and policy design.

Path models can be helpful for these purposes because they allow us to go some way towards separating out the different elements in a complex combination of causes and effects. For example, we have seen that both general social advantage and living standards are related to smoking, and we know from a lot of other research that smoking is strongly related to poor health and shortened life expectancy. But does smoking play an equally important role in the relationship between all dimensions of social inequality and poor health? Likewise for other dimensions of inequality and other risk factors such as work-related inequality and work control.

In our path models, all three measures of social position were shown to affect health both independently and via the risk factors. The results indicate that material deprivation had the greatest effect on health in terms of the total amount of variability accounted for, followed by general social advantage (the Cambridge scale) and then social class based on employment relations (E-G class). The total effect of the material deprivation measure on ill-health was over three times greater than that of the Cambridge scale and over five times that of E-G class.

In Figure 4.5, which shows the relationship between social class and women's health, positive relationships are shown by a '+' and negative ones by a '−'. The solid lines represent relationships that we expected from the theoretical framework described here, and the broken lines represent relationships which were not expected. Risk factors explained only part of the relationship between social position and health. There were also direct pathways from all three measures of social position to ill-health, showing that the effect of social position on health was only partially mediated by recognized risk factors for poor health. The strongest of the independent effects was that of low material living standards. This variable therefore had both the greatest effect due to its relationship to risk factors such as smoking and diet, and the largest additional effect which could not be explained in terms of risk factors.

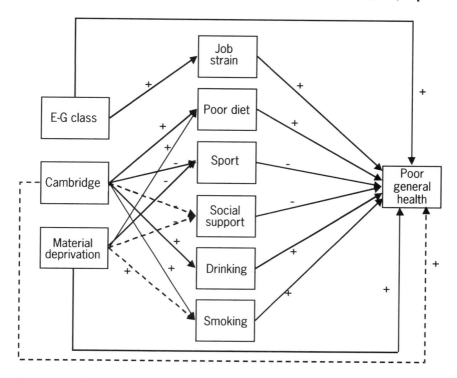

Figure 4.5 The relationship between social class and women's health: a path model
Source: Sacker *et al*. in press.

Conclusion

Understanding what determines a person's health is known to be an enormously complex problem, combining genetic inheritance with the risk of exposure to infections and other hazards and the wide variations in the degree of 'resistance' which different people seem to have. The complexity of social inequality has, however, tended not to be as fully acknowledged. It is therefore not surprising that understanding social inequality in health in a way which can contribute to reducing it is proving to be a difficult task. In this study, we have tried to show that people may experience different forms of inequality in different combinations, and that acknowledging this may be particularly important for understanding health inequality in women.

Our findings indicate that for women, different forms of inequality are related to risk factors for ill-health in different ways. Levels of social advantage as expressed in patterns of social interaction (Cambridge scores) do seem to have a strong effect on lifestyle and the health habits which are known to increase the risk of major diseases such as heart disease and cancer in women as well as men. Social class based on employment relations (E-G class) is not related to most behavioural risk factors independently of social advantage, only to job strain. Low material living standards, in contrast, are not related to job strain, but do seem to lead to less healthy behaviours even after social advantage is taken into account.

The advantage of the approach illustrated in this chapter is to suggest a way of integrating social theories of stratification (inequality) with psychological and biological theories about the causation of disease. The goal is to understand how experiences in the community, family and workplace relate to health both directly and through the influences which these experiences have on attitudes and behaviour. Social and health policy can then be directed more accurately at achievable targets.

Note

1 This study used a slightly different version from that used by Erikson and Goldthorpe (1992) in their study of international variations in social mobility, but the conceptual basis is the same.

Acknowledgements

This chapter draws on research funded by the ESRC (L128251001) under the Health Variations Programme. Data from the Health and Lifestyle Survey and the Health Survey for England were supplied by the ESRC Data Archive. Those who carried out the original collection and analysis of data bear no responsibility for its further analysis and interpretation. The Health Survey for England is Crown copyright.

References

Bartley, M., Sacker, A., Firth, D. and Fitzpatrick, R. (1999a) Social position, social roles and women's health in England, *Social Science and Medicine*, 48: 99–115.
Bartley, M., Sacker, A., Firth, D. and Fitzpatrick, R. (1999b) Understanding social variation in risk factors in women and men, *Social Science and Medicine*, 49: 831–45.
Ben Shlomo, Y., White, I.R. and Marmot, M. (1996) Does the variation in the socio-economic characteristics of an area affect mortality? *British Medical Journal*, 312: 1013–14.
Blackburn, R.M. and Prandy, K. (1997) The reproduction of social inequality, *Sociology*, 31: 491–509.
Blane, D., Bartley, M. and Smith, G.D. (1998) Disease aetiology and materialist

explanations of socioeconomic mortality differentials: a research note, *European Journal of Public Health*, 8: 259–60.

Bosma, H., Marmot, M.G. and Hemingway, H. *et al.* (1997) Low job control and risk of coronary heart disease in Whitehall II (prospective cohort) study, *British Medical Journal*, 314: 555–65.

Bourdieu, P. (1984a) *Distinction*. London: Routledge.

Bourdieu, P. (1984b) Comment peut-on etre sportif? in P. Bourdieu (ed.) *Questions de Sociologie*. Paris: Editions de Minuit.

Bourdieu, P. (1984c) L'origine et l'evolution des especes de melomanes, in P. Bourdieu (ed.) *Questions de Sociologie*. Paris: Editions de Minuit.

Brunner, E. (1997) Socioeconomic determinants of health: stress and the biology of inequality, *British Medical Journal*, 314: 1472–6.

Davey Smith, G., Blane, D. and Bartley, M. (1994) Explanations for socio-economic differentials in mortality: evidence from Britain and elsewhere, *European Journal of Public Health*, 4: 131–44.

Davies, H. and Joshi, H. (1998) Gender and income inequality in the UK 1968–1990: the feminization of earning or of poverty? *Journal of the Royal Statistical Society Series A General*, 161: 33–61.

Erikson, R. and Goldthorpe, J.H. (1992) *The Constant Flux*. Oxford: Clarendon.

Gregg, P. and Machin, S. (1993) *Is the Glass Ceiling Cracking?* London: UCL.

Gregson, N. and Lowe, M. (1994) *Servicing the Middle Classes: Class, Gender and Domestic Labour in Contemporary Britain*. London: Routledge.

Kawachi, I. and Kennedy, B.P. (1997) Socioeconomic determinants of health 2: Health and social cohesion: why care about income inequality? *British Medical Journal*, 314: 1037–40.

Kennedy, B.P., Kawachi, I. and Prothrowstith, D. (1996) Income-distribution and mortality: cross-sectional ecological study of the Robin-Hood index in the United States, *British Medical Journal*, 312: 1004–7.

Krieger, N., Williams, D.R. and Moss, N.E. (1997) Measuring social class in US public health research: concepts, methodologies, and guidelines, *Annual Review of Public Health*, 18: 341–78.

McIsaac, S.J. and Wilkinson, R.G. (1997) Income distribution and cause-specific mortality, *European Journal of Public Health*, 7: 45–53.

Marmot, M.G. and Shipley, M.J. (1996) Do socioeconomic differences in mortality persist after retirement? 25 year follow-up of civil-servants from the first Whitehall study, *British Medical Journal*, 313: 1177–80.

Marmot, M.G., Bosma, H., Hemingway, H., Brunner, E. and Stansfeld, S. (1997) Contribution of job control and other risk factors to social variations in coronary heart disease incidence, *Lancet*, 350: 235–9.

Marsh, C. and Blackburn, R.M. (1992) Class differences in access to higher education in Britain, in R. Burrows and C. Marsh (eds) *Consumption and Class: Divisions and Change*. London: Macmillan.

Marshall, G., Newby, H., Rose, D. and Vogler, C. (1988) *Social Class in Modern Britain*. London: Hutchinson.

Office of Population Censuses and Surveys (1986) *Occupational Mortality: Decennial Supplement 1979–80, 1982–83*. London: HMSO.

Prandy, K. (1990a) The revised Cambridge scale of occupations, *Sociology*, 24: 629–55.

Prandy, K. (1990b) *Sociological Research Group Working Paper 18*. Cambridge: Social and Political Sciences, Cambridge University.

Sacker, A., Bartley, M., Firth, D. and Fitzpatrick, R. (in press) Dimensions of social inequality in the health of women. *Social Science and Medicine*.

Stansfeld, S.A., Head, J. and Marmot, M.G. (1998) Explaining social class differences in depression and well-being, *Social Psychiatry and Psychiatric Epidemiology*, 33: 1–9.

Stewart, A., Prandy, K. and Blackburn, R.M. (1980) *Social Stratification and Occupations*. London: Macmillan.

Veblen, T. (1924) *The Theory of the Leisure Class: An Economic Study of Institutions*. London: Allen & Unwin.

Wilkinson, R.G. (1992) National mortality-rates: the impact of inequality, *American Journal of Public Health*, 82: 1082–4.

Williams, S.J. (1995) Theorizing class, health and life-styles: can Bourdieu help us? *Sociology of Health and Illness*, 17: 577–604.

Wolfson, M., Kaplan, G., Lynch, J., Ross, N. and Backlund, E. (1999) Relative income inequality and mortality: empirical demonstration, *British Medical Journal*, 319: 953–7.

Part 2
The influence of lifecourse and biography

Introduction

The concepts of lifecourse and biography occupy an increasingly important place in public health research and policy. They do so because they build an appreciation of time, and of individual lifetimes in particular, into explanations of health inequalities. The concepts draw attention to how social inequality influences the paths we track through childhood, across adulthood and into old age; paths which shape our access to health-promoting resources and our exposure to health-damaging risks. Lifecourse and biography thus give us an insight into the processes by which socio-economic disadvantage takes its toll on health over the lifetime of individuals. The concepts help us to get closer to understanding how disadvantage in infancy, adolescence and adulthood all have their part to play in the socio-economic gradient in adult health.

This appreciation of time and culminative impact is particularly important in affluent societies where chronic diseases, like heart disease and cancer, are the major killers. These diseases have long and complex aetiologies, where there are time-lags of years or even decades between exposure to the causes and evidence of the effects. Attending to time is important, too, because of the focus it gives to individual lives and experiences; to how we negotiate the legacy of our past and the imprint it leaves on our present. And an appreciation of lifecourse and biography is also needed to inform the development of policy. If chronic exposure to poverty in early life has life-long effects on health, then policies which tackle childhood poverty are an essential part of an effective public health strategy. If individuals draw on understandings of their family history when making decisions about their health, then health promotion programmes need to be delivered in ways which are sensitive to biographical knowledge.

The chapters in Part 2 highlight these aspects of lifecourse and biography. Chapter 5 explores the lifecourse influences on health in early old age. It is based on a study of children carried out between 1937 and 1939 in England and Scotland. The researchers traced and followed up these children in 1997–8, when they were aged 63 to 78 years. Retrospective information, using a specially designed lifegrid, was collected for a range of health-damaging exposures, including environmental hazards, inadequate nutrition and cigarette smoking. The authors describe how these exposures were patterned by social class, accumulated over the lifecourse and were related to health in early old age.

Chapter 6 focuses on how financial circumstances in childhood and adulthood affect health in adult life. Because no one survey has the information required for such an analysis, the authors used two datasets. They draw on the National Child Development Study (NCDS), which has followed up children born in 1958, and on the British Household Panel Survey (BHPS), which has collected information on a representative sample of households every year since 1991. In teasing out the influence of income, the authors take account of the complex interplay between income, education and health in childhood and the ways in which these different factors combine with current income to influence adult health. The authors then go on to draw out the implications of their analysis for policy. They highlight the importance of policies which both alleviate poverty and which tackle the factors producing and perpetuating poverty across the lifecourse, including lack of educational and employment opportunities. The authors offer an assessment of the government's anti-poverty strategy, including the New Deal, the minimum wage and the Working Family Tax Credit.

Chapters 5 and 6 draw on quantitative data to trace how past exposures and present circumstances affect current health. Chapter 7 approaches the question in a different way. It reports on a qualitative study concerned with whether and how people see themselves as at risk of ill-health because of their family history. The study focused on coronary heart disease (CHD), which in the UK is a major contributor to the socio-economic gradient in mortality. It is also one that around one in five people think 'runs in their family'. The chapter explores the understandings which lie behind this perception and how these understandings influence the decisions that people make about adopting more health-promoting behaviours.

The participants in the study were drawn from a large-scale survey conducted in the West of Scotland in 1996. This survey yielded information on middle-aged adults and on their parents, including information on whether or not the middle-aged respondents perceived themselves to have a family history of heart problems. Respondents invited to join the qualitative study, carried out in 1997/8, included both those who did and those who did not perceive that they had a family history. They were selected to ensure roughly equal numbers of men and women from contrasting social class backgrounds. Mapping the uncertainties which underlie people's perceptions of their inherited susceptibility, the chapter concludes by discussing the opportunities that health professionals have to draw on and work with individuals' understandings of risk and behavioural change.

5 | Lifecourse influences on health in early old age

**Lee Berney, David Blane,
George Davey Smith and Paula Holland**

Introduction

Our understanding of health inequalities is most advanced in relation to childhood and the years of adult working life. Yet it is among the post-retirement population that we see the highest levels of morbidity, mortality and health service utilization. Health at older ages has been relatively neglected by inequalities research. The study reported here redresses some of this imbalance.

The study draws on the increasing body of research which suggests that health in adult life is the outcome of experiences and exposures across the lifecourse (see Chapter 1). The 'lifecourse perspective' holds that inequalities in the structure of society shape life chances so that advantages and dis-advantages cluster cross-sectionally and accumulate longitudinally (DoH 1995; Davey Smith *et al.* 1997; Kuh and Ben Shlomo 1997; Power and Matthews 1997). As a consequence of this, observed social class differences in health in early old age can be seen as the biological correlates of socially structured, differential exposure to health hazards.

Numerous studies have shown that childhood circumstances have long-term sequelae for both adult health and socio-economic circumstances (e.g. Montgomery *et al.* 1996; Strachan 1997). And just as childhood conditions can be seen to influence adult health, living and working conditions in adult life can be seen to influence health after retirement. Among the post-retirement population, most of the prevalent chronic illnesses have developed slowly over several decades. While cross-sectional studies can explain some of the variations in the observed distribution of these illnesses, a method of examining the whole lifespan is needed to investigate the ways in which pre-retirement living and working conditions affect health after retirement.

Probably the most powerful research method for this purpose is the birth cohort study, a longitudinal study which tracks its subjects from birth through life. The earliest birth cohort study members in Britain were born in 1946 and are currently in their early fifties. At this age, most of the common illnesses of old age are not yet manifest. There remains, therefore, a need to extend the reach of cohort studies to include older age groups from whom retrospective lifecourse data can be collected.

Between 1937 and 1939, the Rowett Research Institute, headed by Sir John Boyd Orr, conducted a nationwide survey of diet and health. Families from 16 centres in Scotland and England took part in a detailed inquiry into their diet and health (Gunnell *et al.* 1996). This survey, one of the most valuable sources of information on diet and health in pre-war Britain, was recently 'rediscovered' by the Department of Social Medicine at Bristol University. Much of the original data has now been computerized and surviving members of the survey have been traced and flagged for death registration by the Office for National Statistics. In terms of investigating precursors of health in early old age, the Boyd Orr subjects provided an ideal opportunity to collect retrospective data which could be supplemented by the archive data on childhood diet, health and living conditions.

In 1997–8, we carried out a follow-up study of the Boyd Orr cohort. This chapter describes findings from the study which shed light on the lifecourse influences on health in early old age. Following an overview of the research design, the central three sections highlight how disadvantage accumulates across the lifecourse and how earlier exposure to disadvantage is related to current health. The sections look in turn at how childhood disadvantage is linked to subsequent disadvantage in adult life, at how disadvantage after retirement is associated with earlier disadvantage and how past and current disadvantage are related to health in early old age. The chapter concludes by drawing out some policy messages about the importance of interventions targeted at all stages of the lifecourse.

Research design and methods

Study sample

A stratified random sample of traced surviving members of the Boyd Orr cohort was taken. Our sample comprised children who were medically examined and aged between 5–14 years at the time of the original survey. Our sample was stratified on the basis of per capita childhood household food expenditure (the amount of money spent by each family on food per child per week) which was calculated by the original survey and which was available for all sample members. These data were used as a measure of childhood socio-economic circumstances in preference to using father's social class which, in a number of cases, was not recorded by the original survey. Equal numbers of subjects were chosen within each food expenditure category. From an original classification of six groups, three strata representing highest, medium and lowest food expenditure were created. Power calculations showed that 100 interviews from each of these strata would be required to detect any statistically significant differences between groups. Letters inviting subjects to give an interview were sent via local health authorities and general practitioners (Blane *et al.* 1999).

Methods

Each subject, with only three exceptions, was interviewed in their own home. The interview was conducted using a modified lifegrid (see Table 5.1) (Blane 1996; Berney and Blane 1997). Lifegrid interviews use a series of timelines to collect landmark events from different areas of a subject's life and as aids to recall when collecting additional retrospective lifecourse information. Prior to the interview, major public events such as wars and coronations were noted on the 'External' line. This provided 'benchmark' dates with which to cross-reference the dates of life events which the subject reported during the interview.

The interviews began with the completion of the 'Personal' timeline. Subjects provided a range of information on their parents and siblings, such as

Table 5.1 Section of a completed lifegrid for a woman born in 1935

	External	*Personal*	*Residential*	*Occupational*
1935			High St. Fulham	
		Sister born		
	World War II		Evacuation	
1945	War Ends		West Rd. Bolton	
				Bank clerk
	Coronation			
		Marries	May St. Dover	Housewife
1955		John born		
		Alice born		
1965		Husband promoted	Acacia Rd. Dover	

dates of birth (and death, if applicable), occupations, dates of leaving school and so on. The years of the subjects' marriage(s) and birth of children were also noted. The 'Residential' timeline noted the years when subjects changed address. The 'Occupational' timeline noted years when the subjects changed job. Having completed this part of the interview, the subjects were then asked to talk in more detail about their residences, specifically about the hazard exposures in which we were interested. Having covered all residences, the interview then went on to examine the subjects' occupations, again probing for information on hazard exposure.

Hazard exposures and health measures

Hazard exposure scores, based on years of exposure, were calculated for seven types of hazard. These were air pollution; residential damp; occupational fumes and dusts; physically arduous labour; lack of job autonomy; inadequate nutrition in childhood and adulthood; and cigarette smoking.[1] The hazards were selected on the basis that their exposure patterns may be related to the social structure (Blane *et al.* 1997; Blane *et al.* 1998). The one possible exception to this is cigarette smoking which, while undoubtedly socially structured, can be described as largely behavioural. The individual hazards also offer a biologically plausible link between exposure and morbidity/mortality. Air pollution, damp, fumes and dusts and cigarette smoking are all contributory factors for respiratory disease (Calman 1995). Lack of job autonomy has been associated with an increased risk of coronary heart disease (CHD) (Siegrist *et al.* 1990; Bosma *et al.* 1997).

To calculate the total hazard load to which each individual was exposed, the individual values for each hazard were aggregated to create a combined lifetime hazard exposure score. This provided a measure of the combined 'insults' with which the body's regenerative mechanism had to cope. It was also the case that the numbers for each individual exposure were often too small to make statistical inferences.

Once all the residential and occupational data had been collected, a range of additional information on the current socio-economic position of each subject was obtained. Subjects were asked about their housing tenure, car ownership, receipt of works or private pensions and receipt of state benefits. The interviews ended with questions on the subject's current health, freedom from serious disease, limiting long-standing illness and prescribed medication. The subject's height, weight, leg length, blood pressure and lung function were then measured.

Assigning social class

Occupational social class was assigned according to the registrar general's 1991 classification of occupations and its associated coding rules. Male subjects were assigned a class based on their last significant period of employment, with 'significant' being defined as any period greater than two years part-time. Two systems of coding were used for female subjects. The first was the conventional scheme by which married women are allocated to a social class on the basis of their husband's occupation and single women are allocated on their own occupation. The second classified women who had been in paid employment during the final ten years before the statutory retirement age, being classified on the basis of their own last significant period of employment, whether they were, or had been, married or not. Women who had not worked in this period were classified according to their husband's occupation.

Individual classes were aggregated for the analyses so that classes I, II and IIINM became the 'non-manual' category and classes IIIM, IV and V became the 'manual' category.

Childhood circumstances

Childhood height and the presence of signs of chronic disease were chosen as measures of childhood health status. Each subject's childhood stature was converted to a *z-score*: the number of standard deviations above or below the expected values for an individual's age and sex that their measurement lay. As no reference standard for the stature of pre-war children is available, internally-derived reference values were calculated (Gunnell *et al.* 1998). Subjects were then ranked into thirds according to height z-score. A symptom score was constructed to indicate the number of chronic diseases present at the childhood clinical examination. Only those signs of chronic disease which were measured in all the survey sites were included in the symptom score, namely angular stomatitis (a deficiency disease indicating a lack of riboflavin in the diet), bronchitis, knock knees and otitis media. Subjects were then classed as either 'symptom free' as children (that is, displaying none of these conditions at clinical examination) or 'symptomatic' (that is, displaying one or more of these conditions).

Childhood social class was assigned according to father's main occupation during the subject's childhood, on the basis of information given at lifegrid interview. Father's social class was coded to the registrar general's 1991 classification, rather than that in use at the time of the original survey, to allow for aggregation of classes into manual and non-manual categories.

Representativeness of the sample

In total, 294 subjects (155 women and 139 men) aged between 63 and 78 years old were interviewed. The overall response rate for the study was 43 per cent. Given that the original Boyd Orr survey was not a random sample of the British population and that families were selected from the poorer areas of the survey centres, the question of representativeness arises when placing our results in the context of the general population.

The social class distribution of the interviewees' fathers is broadly equivalent to that of the social class distribution of young adult males at the 1931 census: 66 per cent were in social classes I-III compared to 64 per cent of the male population aged 20–44 years. The interviewees, in terms of their socio-demographic characteristics in early old age, broadly resemble those aged 65–74 years in the British population at the 1991 census. The proportion in the sample who were male was 47 per cent, compared to 45 per cent in the general population. The proportion in the sample in the non-manual social classes was 50 per cent, compared to 49 per cent in the general population. In terms of current health profile, such as mean systolic blood pressure and forced vital capacity (FVC), our subjects were broadly similar to their age-group peers in the 1995 Health Survey for England (HSFE). Any bias in the results is likely to be conservative as the most disadvantaged subjects were disproportionately affected by loss to follow-up through death. Additionally, non-responders were more disadvantaged as children than the interviewees (Blane *et al.* 1999).

Childhood conditions and subsequent hazard exposure

It is well established that conditions in utero and low birth weight have long-term impacts on health in childhood and later life (Barker 1992; Power *et al.* 1996). Chronic illness and slow growth in childhood can both be described as forms of early disadvantage. They have been linked both to poor health (Strachan 1997) and to socio-economic disadvantage (Wadsworth 1986) in later life. The present study found that males and females with short stature (slow growth) in childhood accumulated greater hazard exposure than their taller peers (see Figure 5.1). There is a graded association between childhood height and mean lifetime exposure to the combined hazards: as childhood height decreases, lifetime exposure increases. There were significant linear trends for both men (p = 0.002) and women (p = 0.001) after adjusting for age at examination and age at interview (Holland *et al.* 2000).

The association between childhood symptom status and lifetime hazard exposure was less clear. Males who showed signs of chronic disease at the clinical examination carried out in the original survey accumulated greater hazard exposure than their symptom-free peers, but not significantly so. The relationship for females was reversed, with those who were symptom-free accumulating greater hazard exposure, but again this was not statistically significant. The reasons for this become clearer when we examine the association between childhood symptoms of chronic illness, lifetime hazard exposure and father's social class.

As Figure 5.2 shows, the pattern of hazard exposure for manual men is,

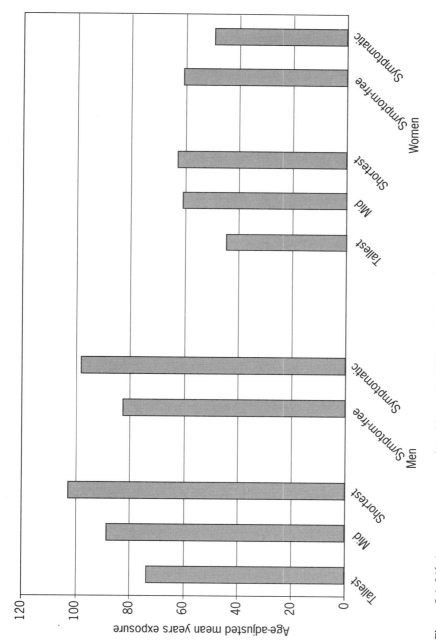

Figure 5.1 Lifetime exposure to combined hazards: childhood height and symptoms by gender

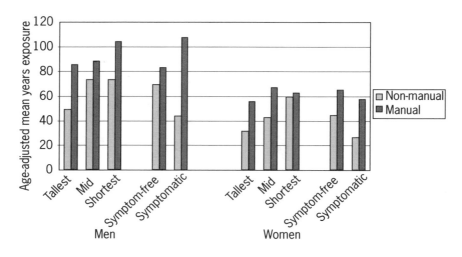

Figure 5.2 Lifetime exposure to combined hazards: childhood height and symptoms by father's social class

as we might expect, with the shortest and the symptomatic showing higher levels of exposure than the tallest and the symptom-free. The tallest children from both manual and non-manual backgrounds subsequently accumulated less exposure than their shorter peers, and there were statistically significant linear trends for men from manual backgrounds (p = 0.044) and women from non-manual backgrounds (p = 0.035). However, the pattern with respect to symptoms is more complex: among non-manual men and among non-manual and manual women, symptomatic subjects accumulated less lifetime exposure than their symptom-free peers.

One possible explanation for this is that the presence of these symptoms in childhood, more so than short stature, is likely to be recognized as a sign of physical frailty. It may well be the case that, where possible, parents set such children on a 'protective' life trajectory, thus avoiding further rapid hazard accumulation (by, for example, entering non-manual occupations). A greater accumulation of hazard exposure may be experienced by those who are not afforded such protection. Those least likely to receive such protection, for whom alternatives to paid (or, at the very least, less hazardous) employment were most restricted, were men from manual-class homes.

Health inequalities in adulthood may partly reflect a lifetime's differential accumulation of exposure to health-damaging and health-promoting environments. These results show childhood disadvantage is associated with the accumulation of further disadvantage in terms of exposure to health-damaging hazards throughout the lifecourse. This supports other evidence that individuals experiencing disadvantage as children are more likely to accumulate further disadvantages (Wadsworth 1991). The social patterning of hazard exposure is further illustrated when we look at the current socio-economic status of our subjects.

Current socio-economic status and previous lifetime hazard exposure

Measuring socio-economic status after retirement raises a number of important methodological issues. For example, how valid is it to use an occupationally-based schema when it may have been many years since the subject was employed? Similarly, there exists the widely recognized problem of assigning married women to a social class on the basis of their husband's occupation. In order to address some of these issues, the present study used a range of additional socio-economic measures. Having obtained full occupational histories for each subject, we were also able to assign women to a class based on their own last main occupation rather than their husband's (Berney *et al.* 2000).

Looking at Figure 5.3, one can see a clear trend of increasing hazard score. The main anomaly to the trend is the lower levels of hazard exposure for men in social class IIINM than in social class II. The most likely explanation for this is the social mobility of men who had spent the bulk of their working lives in the relatively high hazard exposure social class IIIM. Many of these men established their own businesses later in life and moved into social class II. In contrast to such men, it would be expected that subjects who remained in social class IIINM for the bulk of their working life would amass less hazard exposure.

When the individual classes were recoded into manual and non-manual categories, highly significant differences for both men and women ($p < 0.001$) were found between the two groups. Of the hazards examined, cigarette smoking is probably the most widely recognized and is the one most likely to be considered behavioural rather than material. The above analyses were repeated but with cigarette smoking excluded from the combined lifetime exposure score. This reduced the absolute levels of the combined hazard score but the distribution of lifetime exposure scores across classes did not change and remained statistically significant.

For women, social class differences in exposure to the combined residential hazards (air pollution, damp, inadequate nutrition) were found to be better indexed according to the social class of the head of household, while social class differences in exposure to the combined occupational hazards (fumes and dusts, lack of job autonomy, physically arduous labour) were found to be better indexed according to the social class of the women's own last main occupation. Thus, the choice of classification system used to assign social class will depend on the particular area of women's lives in which one is interested.

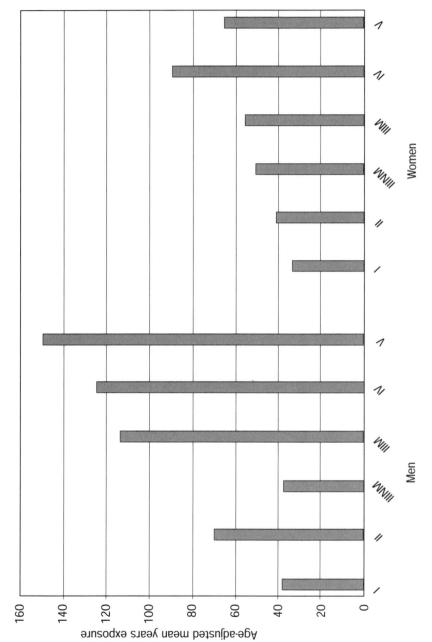

Figure 5.3 Lifetime exposure to combined hazards by subject's own current social class

In addition to information on occupation, data on a range of additional socio-economic indicators were also collected. These were housing tenure, car ownership, possession of a works or private pension, and receipt of state benefits.

Figure 5.4 shows the differences in levels of age-adjusted exposure scores which were found using the different indicators of socio-economic status position. On each measure, those who are disadvantaged after retirement have previously accumulated longer lengths of exposure to the hazards than those who are advantaged after retirement.

Linear regression modelling was used to ascertain which of the available socio-economic indicators had the strongest relationship with previous lifetime hazard exposure. For both men and women, social class of last main occupation was most strongly associated with previous lifetime hazard exposure and the largest differences in exposure score were found between the manual and non-manual groups of this indicator. Of the non-occupational indicators, housing tenure status had the strongest association for men. For women, benefit status was most strongly associated with previous hazard exposure.

Comparing the effect of social class and additional measures of socio-economic position on health in later life, Arber and Ginn (1993) found that social class was a more important determinant of disability among older people than current material resources. However, they also found that material resources had an additional effect on subjective health and sense of well-being. In the next section, we assess the relationships between socio-economic measures and objective health measures as well as self-reported health.

Social class and health outcomes in later life

When we examined health outcomes in later life, we found that the social class differences in the various measures of self-reported health (limiting long-standing illness, freedom from serious disease, regular prescribed medication) were mostly confined to men. None of the self-reported measures were related to socio-economic position during childhood. Some associations were found between the length of some individual hazard exposures during adulthood and self-reported health in early old age. The number of years exposed to low levels of job autonomy, for example, was related to both long-standing illness (p = 0.029) and lack of freedom from serious disease (p = 0.004).

Looking at each of the individual physiological measures taken at the end of the interview, it was found that lung function in women was related to factors across the whole lifecourse. Current social class, combined lifetime hazard exposure (independent of cigarette smoking status), years of

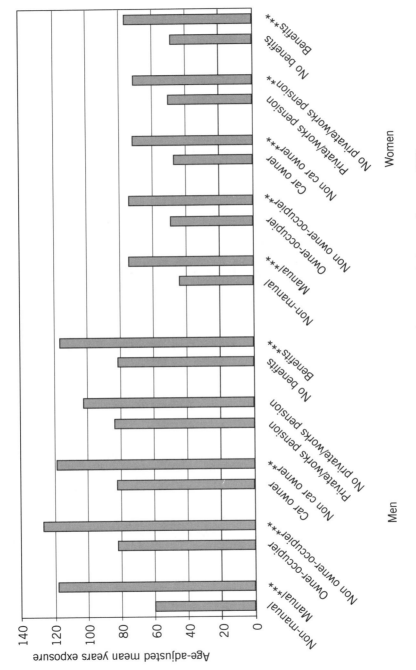

Figure 5.4 Lifetime exposure to combined hazards by measures of current socio-economic status (SES)
Note: Difference between groups: **p = < 0.01; ***p = < 0.001.

cigarette smoking and childhood socio-economic position all were related to measured lung function. Among men, lung function in early old age was found to be related to current social class and to combined lifetime hazard exposure (independent of cigarette smoking status).

Figure 5.5 shows the social class differences in lung function for both men and women. Both manual-class men and manual-class women had significantly lower levels of forced expiratory volume in one second (FEV1) than their non-manual counterparts. Similar, but slightly less significant, social class differences can be seen for levels of forced vital capacity (FVC).

Blood pressure in early old age was found to be unrelated to current social class. While non-manual men and women did have lower systolic blood pressure than their manual counterparts, the difference was not significant. However, it was found, at the individual level, that diastolic blood pressure was related to a combination of (i) shorter than average height during childhood and (ii) having a more obese than average body mass index in early old age (p = 0.002). Diastolic blood pressure was not related to either of these factors on their own; the lifecourse effect appeared only when the childhood and adult factors were placed in a sequential or conditional relationship.

Associations were also found between adult leg length, adult height and inadequate nutrition in childhood. Adult leg length, which is a sensitive indicator of growth during childhood, was associated both for men (p = 0.002)

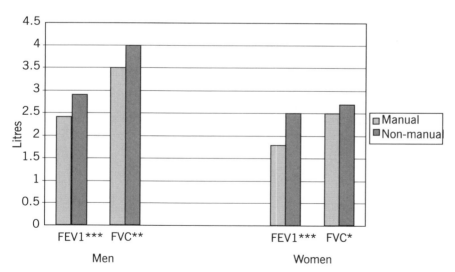

Figure 5.5 Social class differences in lung function in early old age
Note: Difference between manual and non-manual: *p = < 0.05; **p = < 0.01; ***p = < 0.001.

and women (p = 0.001) with inadequate childhood nutrition. That is to say, high inadequate nutrition scores in childhood were linked to shorter leg length in adulthood. It was also found that higher childhood inadequate nutrition scores (men p = 0.004; women p = 0.001) were associated with shorter adult height.

Conclusions

The study found evidence to support the theory that material and environmental disadvantage accumulates over the lifecourse and is linked to social class. Disadvantage after retirement from paid employment is associated with the level of disadvantage which has previously accumulated across life. Disadvantage in childhood, in terms of illness and social position, is associated with levels of disadvantage which accumulate subsequently. Such findings support conclusions from earlier studies and government committees of inquiry such as the Metter's Committee (DoH 1995) and the Independent Inquiry into Inequalities in Health (1998). Both reports state that the determinants of health inequalities are linked to the social structure and to the way that structure influences the lifestyle and quality of life of individuals. Of key importance to this process is the effect these influences exert over time.

The various dimensions of health examined by the present study related to the lifecourse in different ways. The effects of lifecourse influences are more apparent on objective than on self-reported measures of health. It may be the case that the self-reported measures are more a register of current social circumstances and psychological well-being, while objective measures register the impact of the combined lifecourse exposures on an individual's physiological state. It appears that there are at least three models of the ways in which the lifecourse influences health in early old age. In some cases, such as lung function, the influences may accumulate across the whole lifecourse, involving factors in childhood, adulthood and early old age. Alternatively, the later life relationship may have been determined largely, as in the case of adult height, at a much earlier stage of life. Finally, as in the case of blood pressure, the relationship may be conditional, with factors from different stages in the lifecourse having to occur sequentially before the later life effect is produced.

The study examined hazards which were socially and biologically plausible: socially, in that the exposure patterns were determined by the social structure; and biologically in the sense that the selected hazards were widely documented as having negative impacts on health. Differential exposure to these hazards may go some way to explaining observed social class differences in morbidity and mortality.

The last two major government investigations into health inequalities in the UK, the Black Report (DHSS 1980) and the Acheson Report (Independent Inquiry into Inequalities in Health 1998), both identified policies to improve the circumstances of children as an essential prerequisite for the reduction of health inequalities. It is undoubtedly the case that deprivation and ill-health in childhood negatively impact on adult health. We found that disadvantage and ill-health in childhood predicted disadvantage and ill-health in adulthood.

However, in addition to this, our study suggests that no stage of the lifecourse is particularly privileged. Those of our subjects who were currently in the most disadvantaged circumstances in retirement were more likely to be in poor health and more likely to have had the highest levels of hazard exposure. Such a combination of events does not occur randomly: it is socially structured. Interventions which improve living and working conditions, such as reducing exposure to the hazards we have looked at, will help no matter what stage of the lifecourse they target. In the same way as disadvantage has a knock-on effect in terms of future ill-health and further disadvantage, assistance, be it in terms of better housing, improved working conditions, cleaner air or better nutrition, will have knock-on benefits.

The Acheson Report (Independent Inquiry into Inequalities in Health 1998) emphasized that intersectorality is the key to tackling health inequalities. At home, at school, in the workplace, there are hazards to health that can be identified and acted upon. Inequalities in health in early old age may be greatly reduced by an approach that seeks to address these lifecourse influences.

Note

1 Air pollution measures were based on the level of urbanization in the area of residence and proximity to industry or main roads. Residential damp was based on subjects' recall of the presence of black mould or other signs of damp. Occupational fumes and dust scores were based upon the type and level of exposure that a subject described as being commonplace in each of their particular jobs. Physically arduous labour scores were based upon a subject's description of any occupation which involved heavy lifting, heavy sweating and where back injuries were commonplace. The job autonomy score was based upon three questions which ascertained the level of authority, variety and autonomy the subject had in each job. The three questions asked were: was the subject involved in the decision-making process; did the subject perceive the work to be repetitive; and could breaks be taken when the subject chose? Inadequate nutrition in childhood and adulthood was an indirect measure based on the number of dependent household members and the number and social class of incomes available to support them. Years of cigarette smoking were directly reported by each subject.

Acknowledgements

This chapter draws on research funded by the ESRC (L128251003) under the Health Variations Programme. The study has received assistance from Professor Stephen Frankel, Dr David Gunnell and Sara Bright of Bristol University, Dr Scott Montgomery of Royal Free and University College Medical School, the Office for National Statistics, Walter Duncan and Philip James of the Rowett Research Institute. Most thanks are due to the study's subjects for kindly agreeing to give an interview.

References

Arber, S. and Ginn, J. (1993) Gender and inequalities in health in later life, *Social Science and Medicine*, 36: 33–46.

Barker, D.J.P. (1992) *Fetal and Infant Origins of Adult Disease*. London: British Medical Journal Publishing Group.

Berney, L.R. and Blane, D.B. (1997) Collecting retrospective data: accuracy of recall after 50 years judged against historical records, *Social Science & Medicine*, 45: 1519–25.

Berney, L.R., Blane, D. and Davey Smith, G. *et al.* (2000) Socioeconomic measures in early old age as indicators of previous lifetime exposure to environmental hazards to health, *Sociology of Health and Illness*, 22: 415–30.

Blane, D. (1996) Collecting retrospective data: development of a reliable method and a pilot study of its use, *Social Science and Medicine*, 42: 751–7.

Blane, D., Bartley, M. and Davey Smith, G. (1997) Disease aetiology and materialist explanations of socio-economic mortality differentials, *European Journal of Public Health*, 7: 385–91.

Blane, D.B., Montgomery, S.M. and Berney, L.R. (1998) Social class differences in exposure to environmental health hazards, *Sociology of Health and Illness*, 20: 532–6.

Blane, D., Berney, L., Davey Smith, G., Gunnell, D.J. and Holland, P. (1999) Reconstructing the lifecourse: health during early old age in a follow-up study based on the Boyd Orr cohort, *Public Health*, 113: 117–24.

Bosma, H., Marmot, M. and Hemingway, H. *et al.* (1997) Low job control and risk of coronary heart disease, in Whitehall II (prospective cohort) study, *British Medical Journal*, 314: 558–65.

Calman, K. (1995) On the state of the public health, *Health Trends*, 27: 71–5.

Davey Smith, G., Hart, C., Blane, D., Gillis, C. and Hawthorne, V. (1997) Lifetime socio-economic position and mortality: prospective observational study, *British Medical Journal*, 314: 547–52.

DHSS (Department of Health and Social Security) (1980) *Inequalities in Health: Report of a Working Group* (the Black Report). London: HMSO.

DoH (Department of Health) (1995) *Variations in health: What Can the Department of Health and the NHS do?* (The Metter's Committee). London: DoH.

Gunnell, D.J., Frankel, S., Nanchahal, K., Braddon, F. and Davey Smith, G. (1996) Life-course exposure and later disease: a follow-up study based on a survey of family diet and health in pre-war Britain (1937–1939), *Public Health*, 110: 85–94.

Gunnell, D.J., Davey Smith, G. and Frankel, S. *et al.* (1998) Childhood leg-length and adult mortality: follow-up of the Carnegie (Boyd Orr) survey of diet and health in pre-war Britain, *Journal of Epidemiology and Community Health*, 52: 142–52.

Holland, P., Berney, L.R. and Blane, D.B. *et al.* (2000) Life course accumulation of disadvantage: childhood health and hazard exposure during adulthood, *Social Science and Medicine*, 50: 1285–95.

Independent Inquiry into Inequalities in Health (1998) *Independent Inquiry into Inequalities in Health Report* (The Acheson Report). London: The Stationery Office.

Kuh, D. and Ben Shlomo, Y. (eds) (1997) *A Lifecourse Approach to Chronic Disease Epidemiology*. Oxford: Oxford University Press.

Montgomery, S.M., Bartley, M.J., Cook, D.G. and Wadsworth, M.E.J. (1996) Health and social precursors of unemployment of young men in Great Britain, *Journal of Epidemiology and Community Health*, 50: 415–22.

Power, C. and Matthews, S. (1997) Origins of health inequalities in a national population sample, *Lancet*, 350: 1584–9.

Power, C., Bartley, M., Davey Smith, G. and Blane, D. (1996) Transmission of social and biological risk across the lifecourse, in D. Blane, E. Brunner and R. Wilkinson (eds) *Health and Social Organization*. London: Routledge.

Siegrist, J., Peter, R., Junge, A., Cremer, P. and Seidel, D. (1990) Low status control, high effort at work and ischemic heart disease: prospective evidence from blue-collar men, *Social Science and Medicine*, 31: 1127–34.

Strachan, D.P. (1997) Respiratory and allergic diseases, in D. Kuh and Y. Ben Shlomo (eds) *A Lifecourse Approach to Chronic Disease Epidemiology*. Oxford: Oxford University Press.

Wadsworth, M.E.J. (1986) Serious illness in childhood and its association with later-life achievement, in R.G. Wilkinson (ed.) *Class and Health: Research and Longitudinal Data*. London: Tavistock.

Wadsworth, M.E.J. (1991) *The Imprint of Time: Childhood, History, and Adult Life*. Oxford: Clarendon Press.

6 Income and health over the lifecourse: evidence and policy implications

Michaela Benzeval, Andrew Dilnot, Ken Judge and Jayne Taylor

Introduction

It is widely recognized that poverty is associated with poor health even in rich societies. Evidence to support this assertion is often based on cross-sectional studies using different measures of socio-economic status (SES) and health. Yet in order to develop effective policies to tackle health inequalities, we need to be much clearer about the relationship between specific dimensions of socio-economic circumstances and health. Moreover, the literature on the determinants of both SES and health make it increasingly clear that it is crucial to consider a range of factors in both childhood and adulthood. The purpose of this chapter is to contribute to understanding of the causes of health inequalities by examining the role of income levels – one of the most important determinants – for health across the lifecourse.

More specifically, this chapter has two aims. First, to investigate the importance of levels of income in childhood and adulthood for adult health, and second, to assess the contribution that current government policies might make to reducing health inequalities in the light of this evidence. Before doing this, we outline the conceptual framework that guides the analysis.

Conceptual framework

Numerous studies have found a relationship between income and health in adulthood. Evidence suggests that this association is stronger if income is measured over time, and is reduced, but remains significant, if the possibility of health selection is taken into account (Benzeval and Judge in press). In addition, a range of studies have demonstrated the significance of childhood factors for adult health (see Chapter 5; Kuh *et al.* 1997). For example, Lundberg (1993) found that economic hardship in childhood resulted in significantly raised ill-health in adulthood. In this chapter, we wish to explore the role of income in childhood and adulthood for adult health. This means we must consider both the direct and indirect effect of childhood factors on adult health. In particular, we are concerned with two potential mechanisms between childhood and adult health that we define as 'income potential' and 'health capital'.

- *Income potential* is the accumulation of abilities, skills and educational experiences in childhood that are important determinants of adult employability and income capacity. Education is seen as the key mediator in this association (Kuh *et al.* 1997), being strongly influenced by family circumstances in childhood and a central determinant of an individual's income in adulthood.
- *Health capital* is the accumulation of health resources, both physical and psychosocial, 'inherited and acquired during the early stages of life which determine current health and future health potential' (Kuh *et al.* 1997: 173).

Figure 6.1 illustrates the relationships between three key stages of life: childhood, transition to adulthood and adulthood itself; and the role of income at each of these life stages. The starting point is that an individual has certain characteristics that are fixed – such as genetic makeup, age and sex – which may affect their health and SES throughout their life.

In childhood, we are particularly interested in the effect of the financial resources available to households on the development of health and educational capital. However, the parents' own resources, in terms of their health and education, are also important factors in supporting their children's development. Family composition and relationships and, in particular, whether parents remain together throughout childhood have been shown to be significant for child development. Finally, resources in the broader community, such as the neighbourhood characteristics and the quality of schools, will also influence child outcomes.

The dimensions of an individual's transition to adulthood have been described above. In this study we focus on an individual's health capital and educational outcomes as key determinants of their adult health and living standards. However, having controlled for these factors, an individual's recent circumstances are also likely to affect their health. In this chapter, we pay particular attention to the additional effect of income levels in adulthood for health. However, we also control for an individual's social roles

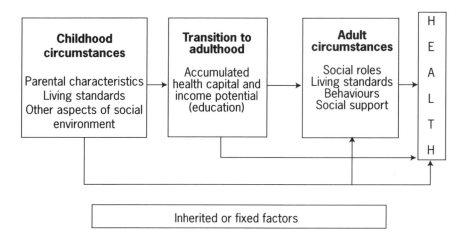

Figure 6.1 Income and health: a lifecourse perspective

because these are likely to be significant determinants of income as well as health. In addition, we recognize that a range of other adult circumstances – as illustrated in Figure 6.1 – are also significant, but there is insufficient room to explore them here.

Using this framework, we now present an analysis of income and health over the lifecourse using two longitudinal British datasets.

Empirical analysis

The purpose of the empirical part of this chapter is to examine the role of income within the framework outlined above. In particular, we ask three questions:

1 What role do financial circumstances in childhood play in shaping educational outcomes and the acquisition of health capital?
2 What contribution do education and health capital make to adult health?
3 What role does recent experience of income play in determining adult health after having taken account of accumulated health capital and educational outcomes?

There is no single British dataset that covers the breadth of information or length of lifecourse necessary to address these issues. We have therefore had to adopt a modified approach that reflects the characteristics of the datasets that can be used. The National Child Development Study (NCDS) is employed to investigate the role of financial circumstances in childhood as a determinant of health capital and educational outcomes. The British Household Panel Survey (BHPS) is employed to explore the associations between recent income and health in adulthood, having controlled for the accumulated risks in the individual's lifecourse up to the point in time when the BHPS started to collect data from respondents (1991).

Datasets

The NCDS contains information on a cohort of people born during one week in March 1958. Information is available about family circumstances at birth and when the respondents were aged 7, 11, 16, 23 and 33. For the purpose of this chapter, individuals are included in the analysis if they have valid information in all relevant waves, which gives a sample size of 8500 for predicting education and health at age 23. Full details of the survey can be found in Ferri (1993). Box 6.1 shows the variables employed in this analysis.

The BHPS is an annual household panel study which began in 1991. The analysis presented here is based on six years of the survey, and individuals are included if they have complete income and health information in all waves. The analysis is limited to people of working age but excludes those who were in full-time education during the period of the survey or those who reported themselves to be unable to work due to ill-health. For more information on the survey, see Taylor (1998).

Unfortunately, the BHPS does not systematically collect information on respondents at the start of their twenties as they make the transition from adolescence to adulthood. Instead, therefore, we focus on the accumulated risk profiles of individuals at the point at which they enter the survey in 1991. Box 6.2 shows the specific variables employed for this purpose to reflect individuals' income potential and health capital, as well as the other measures included in the study.

Methods

Multivariate analysis is employed to explore the association between income and health in detail while controlling for other factors. In the analysis of both the NCDS and the BHPS, we have chosen outcome measures that take the value 0 or 1 (according to whether or not individuals have any educational qualifications or experience ill-health). The statistical method employed is logistic regression. This estimates the odds ratios for reporting poor health (or having no educational qualifications) associated with the explanatory factors included in the models. Odds ratios show how much more likely someone with a specific characteristic is to report poor health (or have no educational qualifications) compared with someone without the characteristic. Tables 6.1 and 6.4 below show the odds ratios for the financial variables

---

Box 6.1 NCDS variables

Fixed factors

- Illness reported in first week of life (marker for inherited propensity for ill-health)
- Ethnicity
- Sex

Childhood circumstances

Financial resources
- Reported experience of financial difficulties in each childhood wave (marker for low income experience)

Parents' resources
- Parents' education
- Parents' chronic illness
- Parents' interest in child's education

Family support
- Family composition, including experience of lone parenthood

External resources
- Type of school attended
- Neighbourhood characteristics

Transition to adulthood/accumulated risk profile

- Income potential – whether or not respondent has obtained any qualifications by the age of 23
- Health capital – whether or not respondent reports a limiting long-standing illness at age 23

Adult health outcomes

- Health – age 33 self-assessed health as fair or poor vs. excellent or good

---

of interest, controlling for the other factors in the models. The statistical significance ($p < 0.1$) of sets of variables can be assessed by comparing the change in scaled deviance associated with their inclusion in the models with the X^2 distribution. The tables show the change in scaled deviance together with its p-value, which indicates the probability that the association between each set of variables and health is due to chance. Hence, the smaller the p-value the more significant the set of variables. Tables 6.2 and 6.3 below show the change in scaled deviance and p-values associated with adding

---

Box 6.2 BHPS variables

Fixed factors

- Age
- Sex
- Ethnicity

Childhood circumstances

- Father's social class when respondent was aged 14
- Whether the respondent was ever in a lone-parent family before the age of 16

Accumulated risk profile (wave 1 of survey)

- Income potential – whether or not respondent has any educational qualifications in wave 1
- Health capital – whether or not respondent reported a limiting illness in wave 1

Adult circumstances (accumulated across waves 1–6)

- Living standards – quintiles of equivalent weekly family income averaged over six years
- Social roles – employment, marital and parental status across six years

Adult health outcomes (wave 6 of the survey)

- Subjective assessment of health as fair or poor vs. excellent or good in wave 6

---

different sets of variables to models containing all of the other factors in order to assess their relative significance.

Results

What role do financial circumstances in childhood play in shaping educational outcomes and the acquisition of health capital?

This question is addressed with the NCDS dataset. Separate models are developed for both educational qualifications and limiting long-standing illness at age 23. Because of poor quality income data in the NCDS, as described elsewhere (Meghir and Taylor 1999), a measure of financial circumstances based on parental reporting of financial problems during childhood is employed here.

First, base models are constructed that include fixed factors – sex, ethnicity and illness at birth – and the number of times that the individual's family experienced financial difficulties during their childhood. Second, other resources in childhood – parental characteristics, family composition and changes, and neighbourhood resources – are added to these models.

Table 6.1 shows how the number of times someone experiences financial difficulties in childhood is associated with an increased risk of both low educational attainment and poor health at age 23. It shows that people who experienced financial difficulties in childhood are at greater risk of poor health as they move into adulthood. Persistent poverty appears to be particularly harmful. Children of families that experienced financial difficulties on all of the three occasions which they were recorded are nearly nine times more likely to have no educational qualifications (column 1) and over 3.5 times more likely to have a limiting illness (column 3), than those whose childhood was free of financial problems. However, as column 2 shows, the odds ratios for financial difficulties are reduced, but remain statistically significant, when other childhood circumstances are added to the education model. This suggests that financial circumstances are only one, albeit

Table 6.1 The effect of childhood financial difficulties on educational attainment and health capital at age 23

	Odds ratios for financial difficulties in childhood			
	No qualifications age 23		*Poor health age 23*	
Number of times financial difficulties were experienced in childhood	*Fixed factors and childhood financial difficulties* *(1)*	*Plus other childhood circumstances* *(2)*	*Fixed factors and childhood financial difficulties* *(3)*	*Plus other childhood circumstances* *(4)*
Once	3.08	1.71	1.45	1.37
Twice	6.39	2.41	1.08^{ns}	1.01^{ns}
Three times	8.97	2.46	3.64	3.15
Change in scaled deviance for financial difficulties (X^2)	436.15	59.64	17.49	10.33
p-value	<.0001	<.0001	0.0016	0.0353
Change in scaled deviance for overall model (χ^2)	437.05	1283.21	23.15	80.94
p-value	<.0001	0.0001	0.0032	0.0028

important, dimension of a range of childhood factors that affect child development. A similar, but much less extreme, pattern is observed for the health model (column 4). The group of variables producing this effect include parents' education and family composition, both of which are known to be strong determinants of family income. However, these are also likely to have an independent effect on children's educational outcomes. For example, well-educated parents may 'develop social and personal skills in their offspring (such as motivation and self-direction, manners of speech and peer identification)' (Kuh *et al.* 1997: 172). Parental marital breakdown has also been shown to have a strong detrimental effect on child development (Duncan and Brooks-Gunn 1997).

What contribution do education and health capital make to adult health?

This question can be addressed with both the NCDS and the BHPS. Final subjective assessments of health as fair or poor (at age 33 or in wave 6 respectively) are employed as the dependent variables. Tables 6.2 and 6.3 show the change in scaled deviance and p-values associated with adding different sets of variables from across the lifecourse to the models.

Table 6.2, based on the NCDS, shows that education and health capital and broader childhood circumstances are highly significantly associated with adult health. Having controlled for these sets of factors, financial circumstances in childhood remain significantly associated with adult health. Table 6.3, based on the BHPS, shows that each set of variables from across the lifecourse that we have highlighted is significantly associated with health. Health capital and education appear to be the most significant factors for adult health, followed by living standards and social roles, particularly employment status. Nevertheless, having controlled for these factors, childhood social circumstances are still significantly associated with adult health.

Table 6.2 The role of health capital and education in determining adult health at age 33 (NCDS)

Factors	Change in scaled deviance χ^2	p-value
Financial difficulties in childhood	8.34	0.0798
Other childhood factors	161.48	<.0001
Health capital and education	108.51	<.0001

Table 6.3 The role of health capital and education in determining adult health, wave 6 (BHPS)

Factors	Change in scaled deviance X^2	p-value
Living standards	15.7	0.0034
Social roles	26.4	0.0152
Health capital and education	92.2	<.0001
Childhood circumstances	11.1	0.0494

What role does recent experience of income play in determining adult health after having taken account of accumulated health capital and educational outcomes?

This question is addressed by investigating the association between health and recent financial circumstances, after controlling for relevant historical information available within the BHPS. The models predicting subjective health assessments are developed in four stages. First, dummy variables for each quintile (fifth of the distribution) of average income over six years are added to the base model containing the fixed factors. Second, the variables summarizing individuals' social roles over the six years are included. Third, the measures of accumulated risk – educational outcomes and health capital – are added to the models. Finally, the two measures of childhood circumstances – parents' social class and living in a lone-parent family – are included.

Table 6.4 shows the odds ratios for the income quintiles and the change in scaled deviance associated with them at each of these stages. With only fixed factors and income in the model, individuals in the lowest income quintile are twice as likely, and those in the second poorest quintile 1.4 times as likely, to report poor or fair health, when compared to those in the top income quintile. The other two income quintiles do not have significantly different risks of ill-health to the top 20 per cent, suggesting that there may be a non-linear relationship between income and health. Although the odds ratio for the lowest income quintile is reduced by adding the other sets of variables, this pattern remains broadly consistent. It is important to note, however, that the measures of social roles – especially employment – education and health capital are highly significant and substantially improve the overall statistical significance of the models (as is evident by the large increase in the change in scaled deviance of the overall model). Nevertheless, recent experience of low income in adulthood appears to be an independent determinant of poor health even after adjusting for a range of lifecourse factors.

Table 6.4 The effect of lifecourse on the association between recent income and health (BHPS)

6-year average income quintiles	Income and fixed factors	Plus social roles	Plus health capital and education	Plus childhood circumstances
5 poorest	2.09	2.11	1.96	1.86
4	1.40	1.47	1.42	1.37
3	1.10ns	1.14ns	1.15ns	1.12ns
2	0.99ns	0.98ns	1.05ns	1.04ns
1 richest	1.00	1.00	1.00	1.00
Change in scaled deviance for income (X^2)	42.4	29.9	18.2	15.7
p-value	<.0001	<.0001	0.0011	0.0034
Change in scaled deviance for overall model (χ^2)	76.9	100.4	191.5	202.8
p-value	0.0000	0.0000	0.0011	0.0034

Note: ns = not significant.

Summary

The results presented above illustrate the complexity of the determinants of health across the lifecourse. We want to highlight five key findings:

1 Financial circumstances in childhood are important determinants of educational attainment and health capital.
2 Other childhood circumstances, in particular parental education and family disruption, are also significant determinants of both education and health.
3 Educational attainment and health capital are strong predictors of adult health outcomes.
4 However, having controlled for accumulated health capital and educational attainment, recent financial circumstances and social roles – especially employment – are also significantly associated with health outcomes.
5 Finally, having controlled for all of these factors, childhood circumstances still have a small but significant effect on adult health.

The next section examines the implications of these findings for policy and discusses the extent to which New Labour's social exclusion strategy addresses them.

Policy analysis

The analysis has shown the enduring importance of childhood poverty for health capital and educational attainment, and the additional health damaging consequences of low income in adulthood. The results suggest that practical policies to reduce poverty, especially for families with children, should be an essential ingredient in any concerted effort to tackle health inequalities. However, as the above analysis shows, the statistical importance of the poverty variables is reduced when other factors, particularly education, employment and parents' circumstances, are introduced into the models. It is important to be aware that these factors are also significant causes of poverty itself (Jenkins 1999). Taken together, this suggests that other policy developments are also required: to promote educational opportunities, to provide support for parents, to reduce the harmful consequences of marital breakdown and to promote employment opportunities.

New Labour's policies to improve living standards suggest that a sophisticated understanding of lifecourse influences has been taken into account and that new initiatives are 'intend[ed] to tackle the *causes* of poverty and social exclusion not just alleviate the *symptoms*' (DoH 1999: 5; DSS 1999). The strategy focuses on: tackling worklessness, making work pay, improving skills through education and training, and providing financial security for those who cannot work (social security benefits). Action in each of these areas is briefly assessed below.

Tackling worklessness

The central theme of the government's welfare reform is 'work for those who can; security for those who cannot' (DSS 1998: iii). The government has introduced a range of policies to reduce barriers to employment – for example, the National Childcare Strategy and Employment Action Zones. However, their single biggest investment – £5.2 billion – is on a range of New Deal initiatives to promote employment for a number of different groups. The main focus has been on young people who have been unemployed for six months and people over 25 who have been unemployed for two years. The schemes are different for each population group, but basically involve three distinct components:

1 A single gateway for benefit claims and job advice with intensive personalized support to find work.
2 A requirement to take up one of a range of options including a subsidized job, training or full-time education, a job in the voluntary sector or as part of the Environmental Task Force.
3 Some groups, but not all, who refuse to take one of these options are faced with benefit sanctions.

The key determinant of the success of initiatives such as the New Deal is whether providing people with short-term employment opportunities (through subsidizing jobs or developing special employment schemes) increases their long-run effectiveness at work and hence employability (Bell *et al.* 1999). Using a cohort of similar people in the Labour Force Survey (LFS) prior to the introduction of the New Deal, Bell *et al.* (1999) simulated the effects of the initiative for young people.

For young people who are unemployed for 6–12 months, 41 per cent find employment in the following six months without the New Deal, although 64 per cent of those are unemployed again within another six months. Many of those who find jobs during the gateway period, therefore, would have found employment anyway, representing a large deadweight cost for the New Deal scheme. At the same time, these statistics show that experiencing six months employment will not necessarily promote long-term employability.

The young people eligible to join the New Deal are disproportionately male and low skilled. The £60 wage subsidy currently offered under the New Deal is therefore likely to represent a substantial proportion of their wage (it represents approximately 50 per cent of the current value of the national minimum wage). Simulation using the LFS suggests that, for such people, having a job will have very little effect on their competence after six months and even after a year it will only be increased by an average of 15 per cent. Hence Bell *et al.* conclude that 'the productivity effects are relatively modest compared to the size of the subsidy deemed necessary to get the group into jobs. Thus it is likely that the effects of the policy will be far more modest than its proponents have hoped for' (1999: 37).

Making work pay

There are three main elements to the government's efforts to 'make work pay'. First, in April 1999, the government introduced the first ever national minimum wage in Britain. The rate was set rather modestly at £3.00 per hour for people aged 18 to 21 and £3.60 for others. The aim is to reduce in-work poverty and float people off dependency on social security (Cash 1998). Second, the government has increased in-work income for low-paid workers by making the Working Family Tax Credit (WFTC) more generous than its predecessor, Family Credit. From October 1999, the child element of WFTC was increased, the threshold at which benefits start to be withdrawn as wages rise was raised and the rate at which benefits are then withdrawn was lowered. In addition, the associated Childcare Tax Credit has been made much more generous (McCrae and Taylor 1998). Finally, the government has introduced a new 10p income tax rate and reformed the National Insurance system by raising the threshold and removing the 'entry fee' to reduce the burden on those in low-paid jobs.

The extent to which these policy changes encourage individuals back into the labour market or reduce low income among workers is open to question. Gregg *et al.* (1999) have used the LFS to simulate the effect of these policies on income and unemployment levels. Their analysis suggests that all the policies will increase average in-work income, with the national minimum wage having the biggest effect on women's income and the WFTC and the reforms to the National Insurance system being the most important for men. It is impossible to predict the effect that the national minimum wage will have on the availability of jobs and hence the level of unemployment. However, all the other changes are expected to reduce unemployment. The changes in the National Insurance system are expected to have the biggest effect on unemployment levels. The WFTC appears to be the best value for money, while the 10p income tax rate is the most expensive (although it is important to remember that creating new jobs is not the only policy goal). The combined effect of these policy changes is expected to reduce the overall level of unemployment by 300,000 or 4 per cent. As Gregg *et al.* conclude, 'this decrease is unlikely to be large enough to completely transform the labour market, [but] the finding is good news for those (including the present government) who see "welfare to work" as a means of reducing unemployment' (1999: 141).

Education and training

Focusing on the longer term, the government has made education their 'number one priority because without skills and knowledge children will not succeed in life' (Blair 1999). For pre-school children, the government has introduced Sure Start in 60 disadvantaged areas across the country, which provides additional resources (£452 million over three years) to promote early education, health and family support services. In addition, Education Action Zones have been established in 25 deprived areas to provide added impetus to efforts to enhance learning opportunities for disadvantaged children.

More generally in education, *Excellence in Schools* (DEE 1997) sets out a commitment:

- to boost literary and numeracy rates by the age of 11;
- to reduce truancy and school exclusions;
- to raise attainment levels in general;
- to increase the proportion of children from lower income households staying on in education.

To achieve these aims, an extra £19 billion has been committed to education over three years. However, the specific policy changes that are required to meet these goals are less clear. A raft of strategies have been introduced, for example, the Social Exclusion Unit's report on truancy and pilot schemes for an Education Maintenance Allowance to encourage children from low-income families to stay on at school. Whether these initiatives add up to a coherent strategy to promote educational opportunities in Britain is debatable. Moreover, their success in achieving the government's objectives remains to be seen.

Social security benefits

The government has focused its benefit reforms on helping families on low incomes. For example, in successive Budgets, on top of the in-work tax and benefit changes described above, the government has increased the rate of universal child benefit and the child element of income-related benefits, as well as introducing a tapered Child Tax Credit. Figure 6.2 shows that altogether these changes have redistributed income towards people in the lowest income deciles and to families with children.

Bringing all of these measures together, the government estimates that they will have lifted 700,000 children out of poverty by 2002 and that it will take 20 years to eradicate child poverty altogether (Blair 1999). In a detailed assessment of these policy changes, Piachaud (1999) confirms that the government should achieve their target for the end of the first term, but that they are unlikely to meet their longer term goals without further substantial increases in benefit levels.

Overall assessment

The government's response to the Independent Inquiry into Inequalities in Health (1998) sets out what it describes as 'the most comprehensive programme of work to tackle health inequalities ever undertaken in this country' (DoH 1999: 4). However, the bulk of their response simply lists their pre-existing policies to reduce poverty and promote social inclusion. This is not in itself a problem since most commentators (Independent Inquiry into Inequalities in Health 1998) and the government have acknowledged that 'tackling inequalities generally is the best means of tackling health inequalities in particular' (Secretary of State for Health 1998: 12). However, reducing health inequalities as a policy goal has not obviously had any specific influence on the priorities the government has adopted within its overall anti-poverty strategy. Moreover, the additional policies that have been designed to target health inequalities (e.g. Health Action Zones, Health Improvement Programmes and the reform of the NHS resource allocation system) are unlikely to have more than a marginal impact on the health divide, certainly in the short to medium term.

The main thrust of the government's anti-poverty strategy has two distinct elements. First, it emphasizes the central role of formal work as the best route out of poverty. Second, it prioritizes families with children. Our

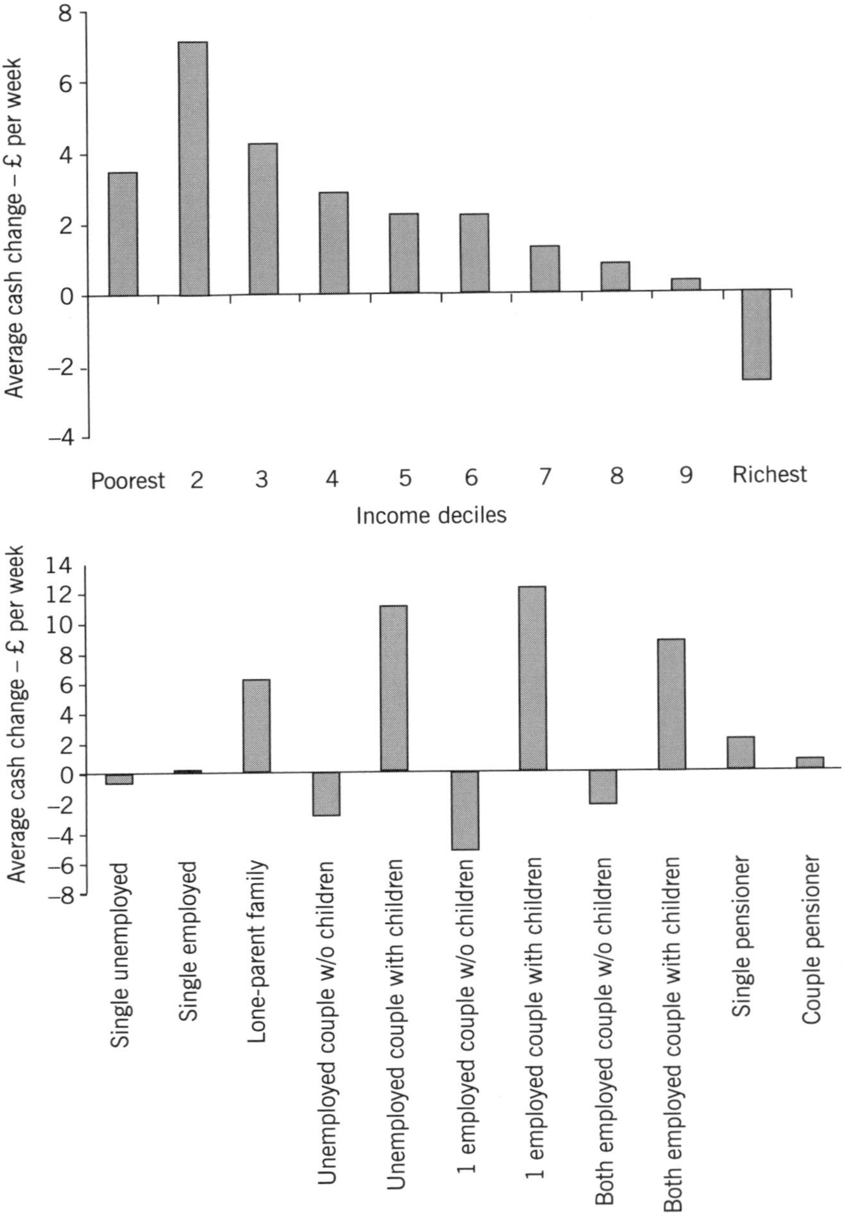

Figure 6.2 Redistribution effects of New Labour's budgets
Source: IFS tax and benefit simulation model based on 1996–7 Family Expenditure Survey.

analysis suggests that both of these are important parts of any strategy to reduce health inequalities. However, as the brief review above indicates, although the government has promoted policies to meet these objectives, they have only had marginal effects to date and are unlikely to make a major impact on the levels of poverty or unemployment in Britain in the future. Moreover, some key groups are excluded from the government's anti-poverty strategy. Although the New Deal does not exclusively focus on families with children, most of the tax and benefit reforms to date have favoured this group. Overall, therefore, single people and couples without children have all experienced reductions in their real living standards (see Figure 6.2). This is likely to adversely affect their health.

Conclusion

Financial circumstances in childhood are an important determinant of an individual's educational attainment and health capital as they enter adulthood. These, in turn, have a significant effect on people's living standards and health in adulthood, and low incomes then also have a detrimental effect on health. The government has introduced a range of policies to improve living standards by creating opportunities for employment and education as well as reforming the benefit system. It is too early to assess how successful these policies will be in reducing poverty or health inequalities. However, evidence suggests that they may only have a marginal effect on the groups that have been targeted. Furthermore, they may run the risk of further excluding other significant groups in the population who are also at increased risk of ill-health. On the other hand, it must reasonably be expected that reducing the health divide will take at least a generation. We welcome the fact that health inequalities are being treated as a serious issue and that some attempt is being made to address their causes. The challenge for the future will be to find ways of sustaining and reinforcing these efforts over the longer term.

Acknowledgements

This chapter draws on research funded by the ESRC (L128251013) under the Health Variations Programme. We are grateful to all of the researchers who have made it possible for us to use the BHPS. The data were originally collected by the ESRC Research Centre in Micro-Social Change at the University of Essex, and made available through the ESRC Data Archive. Particular thanks goes to Sarah Jarvis and Stephen Jenkins, who calculated the net family income variables and deposited them at the Archive. We are also grateful to the ESRC Data Archive for providing the NCDS data used in this project.

References

Bell, B., Blundell, R. and Van Reenen, J. (1999) *Getting the Unemployed Back to Work: The Role of Targeted Wage Subsidies*, Working Paper Series No. W99/12. London: IFS.

Benzeval, M. and Judge, K. (in press) Income and health: the time dimension, *Social Science and Medicine*.

Blair, T. (1999) Beveridge lecture, Toynbee Hall, London, 18 March.

Cash, T. (1998) Lessons from the international experience of statutory minimum wages, *Labour Market Trends*, 106(9): 463–7.

DEE (Department of Education and Employment) (1997) *Excellence in Schools*, Cm 3681. London: The Stationery Office.

DoH (Department of Health) (1999) *Reducing Health Inequalities: An Action Report*. London: Department of Health.

DSS (Department of Social Security) (1998) *New Ambitions for our Country – A New Contract for Welfare: A Consultation Paper*, Cm 3805. London: The Stationery Office.

DSS (Department of Social Security) (1999) *Opportunity for All: Tackling Poverty and Social Exclusion*, Cm 4445. London: The Stationery Office.

Duncan, G. and Brooks-Gunn, J. (eds) (1997) *Consequences of Growing Up Poor*. New York: Russell Sage Foundation.

Ferri, E. (1993) *Life at 33: The Fifth Follow-up of the National Child Development Study*. London: National Children's Bureau and City University.

Gregg, P., Johnson, P. and Reed, H. (1999) *Entering Work and the British Tax and Benefit System*. London: IFS.

Independent Inquiry into Inequalities in Health (1998) *Independent Inquiry into Inequalities in Health Report* (The Acheson Report). London: The Stationery Office.

Jenkins, S. (1999) *Modelling household income dynamics*, Working Paper 99–1. Colchester: ESRC Research Centre on Micro-social Change, University of Essex.

Kuh, D., Power, C., Blane, D. and Bartley, M. (1997) Social pathways between childhood and adult health, in D. Kuh and Y. Ben-Shlomo (eds) *A Life-course Approach to Chronic Disease Epidemiology*. Oxford: Oxford Medical Publications.

Lundberg, O. (1993) The impact of childhood conditions on illness and mortality in adulthood, *Social Science and Medicine*, 36: 1047–52.

MaCrae, J. and Taylor, J. (1998) How will the new Working Families Tax Credit work? *Poverty*, 100: 7–9.

Meghir, C. and Taylor, J. (1999) Parental investments and adult health outcomes. *Proceedings of the Eighth European Workshop on Econometrics and Health Economics*, University of Catania, Italy, 8–11 September.

Piachaud, D. (1999) Progress on poverty, *New Economy*, 6(3): 154–60.

Secretary of State for Health (1998) *Our Healthier Nation – A Contract for Health: A Consultation Paper*, Cm 3852. London: The Stationery Office.

Taylor, M. (ed.) (1998) *British Household Panel Study User Manual: Introduction, Technical Reports and Appendices*. Colchester: ESRC Research Centre on Micro-social Change, University of Essex.

7 | Barriers rooted in biography: how interpretations of family patterns of heart disease and early life experiences may undermine behavioural change in mid-life

Kate Hunt, Carol Emslie and Graham Watt

Introduction

Coronary heart disease (CHD) is a major cause of morbidity and premature mortality in older industrialized countries and is strongly patterned by social class and gender. Inequalities in CHD thus make a major contribution to overall inequalities in health and life expectancy. Health-related behaviours, which continue to be strongly patterned by social class, are risk factors for CHD at both the population and individual level and have been a focus of public health policy (see Chapters 1 and 4). However, attempts to modify behavioural risk factors at a population level have met with mixed success (Ebrahim and Davey Smith 1999) and the individualistic focus of much health promotion in the 1980s and 1990s has been widely criticized (see for example Davison *et al.* 1991; Bunton *et al.* 1995 for more detail). Current government policy recognizes these criticisms and acknowledges that 'our cultural attitudes and lifestyles have a vital bearing on our health' (SODH 1998: 1; see also DoH 1999).

Notions of heredity and perceived family histories of illness are one important aspect of the cultural context in which decisions about behaviours are made (Davison *et al.* 1992). Research has shown that, among the general population, around 20 per cent of people think that heart disease runs in their family (Hunt *et al.* 2000), more than for any other illness.

Research on people's understandings of heart disease suggests that 'having' a family history may be a barrier to the adoption of less detrimental health behaviours (Davison *et al.* 1989). Davison *et al.* suggested that, for those who made some kind of assessment of their inherited risk of heart disease, there were four orientations or 'logical possibilities' to 'lifestyle' choices that they might adopt. Those who thought they had inherited a high risk of getting heart trouble might either think 'I will be especially careful about smoking, weight, food and exercise' or 'I may as well not bother to follow advice about smoking, weight, food and exercise'. Conversely those who thought they had inherited a low risk might think either 'I will build on that by being careful about smoking, weight, food and exercise' or 'I don't have to take any notice about advice about smoking, weight, food and exercise' (Davison *et al.* 1989: 339). Analyses of quantitative data following on from this research (Hunt *et al.* 2000) have shown that people who reported that they had a family history of heart disease were more likely to see themselves as a 'candidate for heart disease', to ascribe greater importance to 'family illnesses and weaknesses' in the aetiology of heart disease and to ascribe a 'very' important effect to health-related lifestyles. However, the odds of being a current smoker were only decreased for people with a perceived family history when account was also taken of whether people saw themselves as a candidate for heart disease and the extent of their endorsement of current coronary health promotion messages.

As about a quarter of all deaths in the UK are attributed to CHD (Charlton *et al.* 1997), many people have direct experience of the impact of the disease in their own family or their wider social networks. However, there has been little research on how people come to define themselves as 'having' or 'not having' a family history and few studies have related such perceptions to other relevant attitudes or behaviours (Ponder *et al.* 1996). Furthermore, although the epidemiology of CHD suggests that experiences of heart disease within families should vary between people from different class backgrounds, class (and gender, see Emslie *et al.* in press) have been largely ignored in studies of beliefs about heart disease and inheriting heart trouble.

In this chapter, we report on a qualitative study which reinforces earlier research showing that people commonly link notions of family history to behaviour. However, we also draw out some of the complexities of meaning underlying the notion of 'having' heart disease in the family. In particular, we demonstrate that categorizations of familial risk may be neither straightforward nor static, and highlight the difficulties that many people have in disentangling notions of 'family history' from the history of their family.

The sample and methods

Interview respondents were selected from a cross-sectional survey, the Family Study of Cardiorespiratory Disease (FASTCARD), which was conducted in the Paisley-Renfrew area of the West of Scotland in 1996. The 2338 FASTCARD participants were themselves the adult offspring (aged 30–59) of couples who had taken part in an earlier epidemiological study, the Midspan study between 1972–6 (Hawthorne *et al.* 1995). We thus had information about the health and social position of potential respondents (in 1996) *and* their parents (in 1972–6) to inform our sampling strategy. We restricted our qualitative interviews to people aged 40–49 years at the time of the 1996 survey since research has shown that this is a time when people often become increasingly aware of their own morbidity and potential mortality.

In anticipation of this qualitative research, two questions were included in the 1996 survey to enable us to identify people who apparently perceived, or did not perceive, that they had a family history of heart problems. Respondents were asked: 'Some people think that particular illnesses or weaknesses run in their family, others don't. Do you think that there are any conditions, weaknesses or illnesses which run in your family?' Those who said yes were asked to indicate which conditions 'ran' in their family; answers making reference to heart problems were taken to indicate a perceived family history of heart disease (pFH). Nineteen per cent of women and 13 per cent of men indicated that they had a pFH of heart disease (Watt *et al.* in press). In our qualitative interviews, people with a pFH of heart disease were contrasted with people who indicated that *no* illnesses or weaknesses 'ran' in their family (no pFH). Throughout the remainder of this chapter, we use this notation to indicate which of these two groups respondents were from. One of the aims of our research was to compare accounts of heart disease in family members across these groups and our qualitative data demonstrate some of the complexities which underlie respondents' responses to such survey questions (see below).

We randomly selected names from eight pre-identified groups of interest since we wished to interview roughly equal numbers of men and women from contrasting class backgrounds: non-mobile working class and middle class groups – that is, people who had manual jobs whose father had also had a manual job – and people with non-manual jobs whose father had also had a non-manual job, with and without a pFH (as identified in the 1996 survey). Saturation point, where no new themes seemed to be emerging, occurred after 61 interviews. Thus, as Table 7.1 shows, seven or eight people were interviewed within each of the eight groups.

A topic guide was used to ensure that certain areas were covered while allowing respondents flexibility to introduce or pursue topics. The interview began with general questions about the respondent's health, their beliefs about the causes of ill-health generally and heart disease specifically. This enabled respondents to mention heredity spontaneously. Respondents were again asked whether any illnesses or weaknesses 'ran in their family'. A health family tree was also constructed (Ponder *et al.*

Table 7.1 The sample by gender, social class and perceived family history (achieved n/potential n[1])

	Class background (n aged 41–51)	pFH of CHD	No pFH of any illness
Men	Non-mobile working class (n = 145)	8/18	7/103
	Non-mobile middle class (n = 72)	7/14	8/37
Women	Non-mobile working class (n = 103)	8/13	7/57
	Non-mobile middle class (n = 95)	8/53	8/41

Note:
1 n = number of survey respondents fulfilling criteria.

1996) by asking respondents about the age and health, or cause of death, of family members. This allowed the interviewer to refer back to specific family members when exploring understandings about mechanisms of inheritance. In order to focus on possible links with health-related behaviours, respondents were asked whether their attitudes to health had changed over their lifetime and whether particular events had changed their views or behaviours. We also presented respondents with a scenario based on research by Davison *et al.* (1989) to explore links between perceptions of familial risk and health-related behaviours (see below and Emslie *et al.* submitted for more detail).

Transcripts, each checked against the tapes, and field notes were studied and discussed repeatedly to identify common themes and explore the underlying reasoning of respondents. The NUD.IST software package was used to facilitate analysis.

Repeated readings and discussions of the first 14 interviews by two researchers (CE and KH) to identify major themes informed a coding frame based on these themes. NUD.IST was used to extract sections of transcripts for more detailed re-examination, enabling us to compare the accounts of the different subgroups (for example, comparing accounts of heart disease in the family between men and women from different class backgrounds). The analysis followed the principles of grounded theory (Strauss 1987).

Defining 'family history' – a simple dichotomy?

The 'taking' of a family history is a common feature of many medical consultations and is often treated unproblematically. Although there is some debate among epidemiologists about defining a 'positive' family history of heart disease (Hunt *et al.* 1986; Silberberg *et al.* 1998), clinical definitions are usually based on the occurrence of heart problems in first degree relatives.

However, decisions about behavioural change will be mediated through an individual's *own* perceptions of risk (Love *et al.* 1985). It is therefore crucial to explore how people weigh up whether or not they have heightened familial risk of heart problems and to be aware of ways in which their interpretation of their familial risk may differ from externally imposed definitions.

Our research design allowed us to examine and compare the accounts of family health of equal numbers of people who had indicated in a prior survey that heart disease did or did not 'run' in their family.

The accounts of family health which both groups of respondents gave in our qualitative interviews revealed a spectrum of (un)certainty underlying these two apparently distinct groups. Some were convinced that they were (or were not) at heightened familial risk, while others were undecided and continued to weigh up the significance of continuing events in their families (see Emslie *et al.* submitted). The accounts also demonstrate variability in the amount of family health information available to people. Not only did family size vary enormously, but people often said that they knew less (or nothing) about one side of the family.

Other studies have demonstrated an association between reporting higher numbers of relatives with heart disease and reporting a pFH (Hunt *et al.* 2000; Watt *et al.* in press), but our interviews suggest that the process of defining oneself as having a family history depends on more than the simple identification and totalling of cardiac events in one's family. Some cardiac events are discounted (for example, cardiac deaths of elderly relatives were often attributed to old age by our respondents), while others are accorded more weight. Age of death was almost always mentioned and respondents' accounts suggested that this could take on even greater significance if there was some discernible pattern of events (for example, if more than one family member had died at a particular age). Often this was judged within a complex of other factors.

Some respondents did not think that heart disease ran in their family despite having several relatives with heart problems. Some interpreted this as being due to chance, citing examples of 'anomalous deaths' (either fit, healthy, young people who had 'dropped dead' of heart problems or others who flaunted coronary prevention advice but lived to a 'ripe old age') (see Davison *et al.* 1991). Other strategies for downplaying familial risk of heart problems included stressing differences rather than similarities between themselves and family members with heart disease (Emslie *et al.* submitted).

Working-class respondents who had indicated in the survey that they had a pFH of heart problems tended to be more equivocal about this in the in-depth interviews than middle-class respondents. Working-class men in particular expressed ambivalence about whether heart disease ran in their family (see Emslie *et al.* submitted for more detail). This ambivalence is interesting given the class patterning of CHD and the common perception of it as a male disease. It ran counter to our prior expectation that the greater burden of premature mortality among people from less affluent back-grounds might make them *more* likely to think they had a family history. These men may not be convinced that heart problems 'run' in *their* family, in particular, in the context of greater numbers of premature deaths in their wider social networks.

One crucial finding was that respondents commonly made a distinction between inherited risk within their family *as a whole* and for themselves *per-sonally*. Thus, some thought that heart disease ran in their family but did not *personally* feel at increased risk of heart disease because they thought that they did not 'take after' affected family members in crucial ways. Con-versely, some respondents who did not perceive themselves as having a family history of heart problems had relatives affected by heart disease. Analysis of quantitative data from the FASTCARD population as a whole shows that 23 per cent of men and 21 per cent of women who did *not* per-ceive themselves as having a family weakness due to heart disease had at least one parent who had died of CHD (Watt *et al.* in press).

One practical consequence of these observations is that a 'family history' may mean different things to patients and to health professionals. This leaves potential for misunderstanding and miscommunication if patients and doctors assume that they are operating with shared understandings of 'family' risk.

Perceptions of family risk in discourses around health behavioural change

In our interviews, almost all respondents spontaneously mentioned heredity when speaking about the aetiology of heart disease, irrespective of whether they thought that heart disease 'ran' in their own family. The imputed mechanisms of inheritance were often complex, intertwining biological and social processes, and more often than not, family history was seen as just one of many factors. For example, Morag said:

> I think heart problems can be hereditary to a degree, like your genes, coming from your mum and dad like things like that, but I do think overweight people . . . would be a higher risk. My husband smokes Capstan full strength cigarettes and I keep saying, I don't know how you don't have a heart attack with all these cigarettes . . . you smoked all these years and you should get something, you know, 'cause he's 51. In saying that, my husband was at the doctor's and they said, 'oh you're as healthy as anything', so it's your luck . . . So, I don't know, but, er, no I canna say that I would turn and go [you're a] definite heart attack, oh you're a definite heart attack person, you're not . . . I think

it can be hereditary, probably it definitely is hereditary, a lot of it, you also have the kind of stress factor or the smoking factor and you're overweight, I think they all add to it.

(Morag working-class pFH)

Morag's quote is typical in linking notions of candidacy (Davison *et al.* 1991; Emslie *et al.* in press) to family and in demonstrating knowledge of the behavioural risk factors for heart disease. But, although the evidence on behavioural risk factors was accepted at a general level, most, like Morag, knew that there was no certainty in predicting whether a particular individual would succumb to CHD. Like earlier research (see Davison *et al.* 1991), our respondents' accounts suggest that what epidemiologists have called the 'prevention paradox' (Rose 1985) continues to undermine people's confidence in the effect of making behavioural changes. Responses such as 'you can do all these things right, you can not smoke, you can not get overweight and you can keep yourself fit, and then drop dead running the marathon' (Roger middle-class pFH) were typical.

In trying to explore the links between family history and behaviour, we presented all respondents with what we have referred to as the 'family history conundrum' (that is the dilemma about behavioural decisions for 'someone' with a strong family history of heart disease as outlined by Davison *et al.* 1989). We were particularly interested in comparing the responses of men and women, with and without a family history, and from different class backgrounds. Most men (particularly middle-class men) with a pFH said that it would not be 'worth' someone with a strong family history trying to adopt less coronary-prone behaviours. Men without a pFH appeared reluctant to judge people in this situation, but generally said that they thought they should 'be more careful', and none said it was 'not worth' making changes (see Hunt *et al.* 1999 for more detail). Unlike the men, women's responses were not obviously patterned by class and pFH. Just three women said that there would be 'no point' doing anything and about half said that they thought they would try to make some changes. The remaining half described themselves as being 'somewhere in the middle', and said that, while they felt they 'should' make changes, they did not think there were enough convincing reasons to make them actually modify their behaviour. One woman said: 'I think it's the same as in most aspects of human nature, that you start out with these intentions but not necessarily carry it through' (Kate working-class pFH).

However, elsewhere in the interviews it was clear that many people were continually wrestling with decisions about modifying their behaviour, particularly expressing concerns about their weight and slowing the process of bodily depreciation with age and increasing morbidity. Many explicitly linked worries about whether to modify their behaviours to concerns about their family history (Hunt *et al.* 1999). Chloe, for instance, said: 'Well heart disease does frighten me 'cos my mother took a heart attack and died when she was 53 . . . because I'm getting near that age and my brother's a bit the same, he, he's overweight and he's going to diet classes, I'm trying to stop smoking' (Chloe working-class pFH).

Respondents' accounts also suggested that other factors had encouraged them to adopt more healthy behaviours (see Table 7.2). These included distinct health events or 'warnings', getting older and the increasing reality of mortality, financial factors, having children, information when it was seen to be credible and consistent, and enjoyment and enhanced well-being.

However, their accounts also suggested a number of barriers to change (see Table 7.3). Many respondents expressed uncertainty that making changes to their behaviour would materially affect their own risk. This lack of certainty stemmed from a perception that much of the evidence was changing or contradictory as well as from awareness of lack of prediction of individual events. Many respondents (and middle-class men in particular) appealed for 'some kind of logical reasoning' to bolster lifestyle changes (Hunt *et al.* 1999). One powerful image which recurred was that CHD was seen as a 'good way to go'.

Some barriers appeared to be rooted in people's sense of their biography, particularly their family environment as a child. Thus, some

Table 7.2 Factors encouraging less coronary-prone behaviours

Factors	*Comments or examples*
Bodily markers of decline, ageing or deterioration in health	Being overweight, losing fitness, having high blood pressure or raised cholesterol reading, awareness of reaching an age where risk of mortality is increasing
Health events or 'warnings'	Chest or arm pain, death or serious disease in a close family member or friend
Having children	Desire to 'be around' for and 'fit enough to enjoy' children as they grew up
Credible and consistent information	
Finance	Desire not to 'waste' money on things that they knew to be health-damaging anyway
Enjoyment	Immediate or cumulative benefits of change; giving up something which they 'didn't miss' anyway

Table 7.3 Barriers to adopting less coronary-prone behaviours

Barriers	Comments or examples
Lack of certainty about benefits	Awareness of lack of 'guarantees', conflicting information, and 'counter-examples'
Legacies which were perceived to be unchangeable or very difficult to change	Family history, effects of past exposures (including both 'conditioning' and existing 'damage' which could not be undone)
Costs	Loss of enjoyment, can't accommodate within working life, lack of time and so on
Image of heart disease as a 'good way to go'	Focus of narratives on 'quick' deaths and little discussion of cardiac morbidity
Time constraints	Limitation imposed by long hours in paid work, shift work or commuting; family or caring responsibilities
General lack of motivation	

people identified a number of 'legacies' from their past which they felt could not be 'undone'. Their family history (in the sense of the pattern of illness and deaths in their family), their past exposure to tobacco smoke and particularly their past diet were the most commonly mentioned. Some working-class respondents made explicit links between diet and wealth or class. For example, Katherine said that people without money 'havenae any option but to eat fish and chips, or constant chips' and Jane said:

I think your class certainly defines your diet, I would say. I mean it's easier if you're middle class and you can shop at whatever, say, you can buy everything at a Marks and Spencer, right, it's a lot easier, you can get your lettuce and your carrots and whatever. But money comes into everything, so money does affect your health as well.

(Jane working-class pFH)

Both women went on to imply that this had both material and cultural roots, linking diet (and heart disease) to money, upbringing and education:

I think if you've got the money and are taught how to shop. And I don't think we were ever taught how to shop . . . I think how people have been brought up in their family is how they are today . . . it may be how I was brought up would have caused me to have heart [problems], because of maybe how, well, I make the same meals as my mum would make.

(Katherine working-class pFH)

And Jane said:

> Being working class, you were kind of uneducated, I mean there were four of us, we were never hungry or anything like that, we got, what I'd say would be the basics. You never knew about real food, it was basic stuff, potatoes and mince and stuff like that, but you were very uneducated about food . . . [my parents'] priorities were, quite rightly, just paying the rent and getting you fed, getting you to school.
>
> (Jane working-class pFH)

One working-class woman, who described herself as coming from a family that was 'no rich, but comfortable, working-class comfortable', described her mother's attempts to provide a healthy diet in a time of scarcity:

> I was born in '48 . . . I was a kind of war baby . . . so I love all farm things, I love all cheese, and I love eggs and I love milk, and, all those fat things, and when I was young, my mother was dead pleased to be able to get you all them, and as the years have went by now, they're telling you everything's bad for you . . . my mum always made good home-made meals, I mean you came in at 4 o'clock from school, the six of us used to always get our hot chocolate or our bovril or our Haliborange and my mother made a point of giving you all these things, you know, you used to queue up . . . I think it gave us, stayed us in good stead.
>
> (Tina working-class pFH)

Tina's account suggests that she perceives her childhood diet to have a mixed legacy, some elements standing her 'in good stead' and others (having a high fat diet) reflecting changes in public health wisdom over her lifetime and thus sowing the seeds for some scepticism about dietary advice. She also said of 'all those fat things' 'that's all the things I love', implying that her early diet had also affected her tastes many decades later.

Others made comments which suggested, too, that a legacy of their early diet was to 'condition' their tastes, and limit the changes they could make now, sometimes using quite deterministic language. For example, Douglas said: 'I wasn't brought up with vegetables so I still can't eat carrots and I can't eat lettuce. Eh the only things I can actually take are turnips and peas. So that was just from an early age we didn't get vegetables. It was chips instead of vegetables' (Douglas middle-class pFH).

Earlier in the interview, Douglas had expressed a conviction that heart disease 'definitely' ran in his family, graphically describing the inscription of the age of death of three successive generations of men on their tombstones.

However, his later account of the food that he ate (and liked) earlier in his life demonstrates the complexities of how early life experiences and 'family history' can become intertwined:

> I can remember my mother's mother making me fried bread and I loved it. A big white lump of fat into the frying pan and a piece of bread and so that's the way we were brought up. Maybe that's why we've had so many heart problems in the family. So I think heart problems are definitely more diet than genetic. I put *my* problems down to the fact to eh 40 years of bad food. Certainly not because my father and mother had problems.
>
> (Douglas middle-class pFH)

Family history or histories of families: conclusion and policy implications

Like earlier work, our research demonstrates that the perception of inherited risk of disease is an important factor in people's decisions about health-related behaviours and lifestyles. However, it also demonstrates that perceiving oneself to have high or low family risk of what is widely recognized as a disease with multi-factorial aetiology is not linked to behaviour in a simple or predictable way. Indeed, much of the discourse around perceived familial risk and decisions about health-related behaviours is characterized by ambivalence, an ambivalence which seldom comes from lack of thought or knowledge, but is rooted in an accumulation of uncertainties.

First, there are the uncertainties which people perceive in the scientific evidence (and professional evidence and advice on diet was treated with most scepticism). Second are the exceptions to the epidemiological or aetiological guidelines which people observe, the 'counter-examples' to the rules, which continue to fuel scepticism about health promotion advice (Davison *et al.* 1991). Third is the very complexity and, for some people the ambiguity and uncertainty, in establishing whether they really are at increased family risk of getting heart disease. Fourth is the uncertainty about whether trajectories projected forward by past experiences can be changed.

These uncertainties are set in the context of the lifecourse, often one that is seen to be strongly shaped by past material and cultural circumstances. These middle-aged respondents have reached a time in their lives when they have increasing experience of the reality of death and illness within their families and wider social networks and a growing awareness of their increasing likelihood of experiencing ill-health themselves. Our interviews have shown that people recognize the long shadows that earlier life experiences have for their health, mirroring the increasing interest within 'expert' or 'professional' epidemiology in the accumulation of risk and disadvantage over the lifecourse (see for example Kuh and Ben-Shlomo 1997; Graham 2000). It is clear that the public take a lifecourse perspective and base their own understandings of the aetiology of disease not only around their own biographies, but also around those of their families. Within this, a number of mechanisms (upbringing and learning from the family, 'conditioning', cumulative exposures and so on) become very intertwined. While studies of health beliefs have shown changing orientations as people grow older (Backett and Davison 1995), much of this represents the ageing of families and the distillation of experiences in one's own, subsequent and preceding generations. Our research suggests that, in addition to people struggling with their sense of family history (in the sense of some genetic or constitutional factor that puts them at higher risk of the disease), there is need for the recognition that every family has a history, and that death and disease, wealth and health, figure highly in these histories. It is crucial to recognize that the family is a primary and perhaps the most intimate site for observation within lay epidemiology. This is not only because, as a rule, family deaths or occurrences of serious illness have the greatest import and consequences, but also because the family is a more intimate arena for observing risk patterns over a lifetime. Thus, counter-examples within the family carry even greater weight, persuading someone to accept or reject the plausibility of a putative aetiological pathway, or the potential for any constructive intervention to reduce risk.

It is important for health professionals seeking to engage in discussions about behavioural risk factors with clients/patients to recognize that, whether or not people find it straightforward to categorize their familial risk of heart disease, their accumulated observations of family health and lifestyles are likely to be at the root of their orientation to behavioural change. Failure to recognize these complexities gives rise to a potential (and potentially destructive) mismatch between lay and professional constructions of family risk for individuals. This may mean that valuable opportunities for supporting or promoting behavioural change are squandered.

Acknowledgements

This chapter draws on research funded by the ESRC (L128251028) under the Health Variations Programme.

References

Backett, K.C. and Davison, C. (1995) Lifecourse and lifestyle: the social and cultural location of health behaviours, *Social Science and Medicine*, 40: 629–38.
Bunton, R., Nettleton, S. and Burrows, R. (eds) (1995) *The Sociology of Health*

Promotion: Critical Analyses of Consumption, Lifestyle and Risk. London: Routledge.

Charlton, J., Murphy, M., Khaw, K., Ebrahim, S. and Davey Smith, G. (1997) Cardiovascular diseases, in J. Charlton and M. Murphy (eds) *The Health of Adult Britain 1841–1994.* London: The Stationery Office.

Davison, C., Frankel, S. and Davey Smith, G. (1989) Inheriting heart trouble: the relevance of common-sense ideas to preventive measures, *Health Education Research*, 4: 329–40.

Davison, C., Davey Smith, G. and Frankel, S. (1991) Lay epidemiology and the prevention paradox: the implications of coronary candidacy for health education, *Sociology of Health and Illness*, 13: 1–19.

Davison, C., Frankel, S. and Davey Smith, G. (1992) The limits of lifestyle: re-assessing 'fatalism' in the popular culture of illness prevention, *Social Science and Medicine*, 34: 675–85.

DoH (Department of Health) (1999) *Saving Lives: Our Healthier Nation.* London: The Stationery Office.

Ebrahim, S. and Davey Smith, G. (1999) Multiple risk factor interventions for primary prevention of coronary heart disease (Cochrane Review), *The Cochrane Library*, 2.

Emslie, C., Hunt, K. and Watt, G. (in press) Invisible women? The importance of gender in lay beliefs about heart disease. *Sociology of Health and Illness.*

Emslie, C., Hunt, K. and Watt, G. (submitted) What constitutes a 'family history' of heart disease? A qualitative study of lay reasoning.

Graham, H. (2000) Socio-economic change and inequalities in men and women's health in the UK, in E. Annandale and K. Hunt (eds) *Gender Inequalities in Health.* Buckingham: Open University Press.

Hawthorne, V.M., Watt, G.C.M. and Hart, C.L. *et al.* (1995) Cardiorespiratory disease in men and women in urban Scotland: baseline characteristics of the Renfrew/Paisley (Midspan) study population, *Scottish Medical Journal*, 40: 102–7.

Hunt, K., Davison, C., Emslie, C. and Ford, G. (2000) Are perceptions of family history of heart disease related to health-related attitudes and behaviours? *Health Education Research: Theory and Practice*, 15: 131–43.

Hunt, K., Emslie, C. and Watt, G. (1999) The chip pan's out the door. Lay perspectives on health behaviour in the context of family history of heart disease. Tackling inequalities in health, 7th Annual Health Forum, Brighton, 17–18 March.

Hunt, S., Williams, R. and Barlow, G. (1986) A comparison of positive family history definitions for defining risk of future disease, *Journal of Chronic Diseases*, 39(10): 809–21.

Kuh, D. and Ben-Shlomo, Y. (1997) *A Lifecourse Approach to Chronic Disease Epidemiology.* Oxford: Oxford Medical Publications.

Love, R.R., Evans, A.M. and Josten, D.M. (1985) The accuracy of patient reports of a family history of cancer, *Journal of Chronic Diseases*, 38: 289–93.

Ponder, M., Lee, J., Green, J. and Richards, M. (1996) Family history and perceived vulnerability to some common diseases: a study of young people and their parents, *Journal of Medical Genetics*, 22: 485–92.

Rose, G. (1985) Sick individuals and sick populations, *International Journal of Epidemiology*, 14: 32–8.

Silberberg, J., Wlordarczyk, J., Fryer, J., Robertson, R. and Hensley, M. (1998) Risk associated with various definitions of family history of coronary heart disease: the Newcastle Family History Study II, *American Journal of Epidemiology*, 147: 1133–9.

SODH (Scottish Office Department of Health) (1998) *Working Together for a Healthier Scotland: A Consultation Document.* Edinburgh: The Stationery Office.

Strauss, A. (1987) *Qualitative Analysis for Social Scientists.* Cambridge: Cambridge University Press.

Watt, G., McConnachie, A., Upton, M., Emslie, C. and Hunt, K. (in press) How accurately do adult sons and daughters report and perceive parental deaths from coronary disease? *Journal of Epidemiology and Community Health.*

Part 3
The influence of home and place

The spatial polarization of poverty and affluence in older industrial societies like the UK is focusing government attention on the need for and potential of area-based approaches to tackling health inequalities. Investing in areas is a central plank of the UK's new public health policy. A range of initiatives, spearheaded at local, regional and national level, are seeking to regenerate the physical fabric and the social relationships which hold communities together.

Underlying the area-based approach to tackling health inequalities is the assumption that areas make a separate and distinct contribution to health. Improving the physical and social infrastructure of poor areas can therefore help to reduce the socio-economic gradient. The chapters in Part 3 put this assumption to the test. In their different ways, the chapters examine whether poorer areas have poorer health profiles simply because of the poorer people who live there, or whether the poorer health profiles of poor areas are also and additionally the result of their health-damaging character.

Chapter 8 begins the complex process of testing for and teasing out the influence of place. The authors describe the differing socio-economic and health profiles of those who own and those who rent their homes. They describe, too, how their homes and neighbourhoods differ in ways which may be health-promoting (gardens, safe place areas) or health-damaging (damp homes, neighbourhoods with discarded syringes and needles), and note the important differences in the privacy, autonomy and social status that owners and renters derive from their homes. The chapter draws on a postal survey of adults living in and around Glasgow, carried out in 1997.

Chapter 9 extends the analysis of the influence of place by combining data relating to individuals with data about the areas in which they live. It uses multi-level modelling, a technique which enables the effects of individual characteristics and area characteristics to be separated and measured. The authors apply this technique to two datasets: the Office for National Statistics Longitudinal Study (ONS-LS) and the Health and Lifestyle Survey (HALS). Confirming that areas make a difference to the health of residents, the authors go on to examine possible mechanisms through which areas may be exerting their influence. The chapter focuses on one aspect of the economic environment of areas, looking at the influence of de-industrialization, and one aspect of the social environment, assessing evidence that social capital may have a role to play in explaining area differences in health.

Chapter 10 continues the focus on the quality of the physical and social environment. The authors present findings from a household survey based in four localities in North-West England. Two of the localities are relatively affluent and two are relatively poor. The researchers collected both quantitative and qualitative data from the respondents in each locality, mapping their perceptions of their health and socio-economic circumstances, their home and their neighbourhood. Weaving together these data, the authors discuss how differences in the health status of those living in the four localities are related both to differences in their individual circumstances and to differences in the places in which they live.

Chapter 11 is again concerned with the ways in which areas may have an effect on health. The authors focus on CHD, a cause of death with marked geographical variations and a sharp socio-economic gradient. They look at recovery from first heart attack (myocardial infarction). In mapping the factors which might explain the relationship between material disadvantage and physical recovery, they pay particular attention to psychosocial factors. They examine whether social comparisons – perceiving oneself to be better or worse off than others – play a part in the recovery process. The study is based on a survey of 200 patients who have recently experienced their first heart attack, interviewed around 5 weeks and 15 weeks post myocardial infarction. The patients were recruited at a large Scottish hospital, with information on the areas in which they live derived from the 1991 census.

Part 3 concludes with an analysis of the latest evidence on geographical inequalities in mortality in Britain. It examines patterns of premature mortality (under the age of 65) from the early 1950s to the late 1990s. It describes the increase in geographical inequalities since the late 1960s and the particularly rapid increase since the early 1980s. The authors go on to examine the part played by selective migration: a process in which better-off and healthier people leave areas of high mortality and move into areas of low mortality while poorer and less healthy people become concentrated in areas of high mortality. The authors describe how changes in the housing market, and the position of those excluded from it, may be contributing to the spatial polarization of mortality. The authors conclude by noting that strategies which seek to reduce health inequalities should give priority to narrowing income inequalities and equalizing access to housing.

8 | Housing tenure and health inequalities: a three-dimensional perspective on people, homes and neighbourhoods

**Sally Macintyre, Rosemary Hiscock,
Ade Kearns and Anne Ellaway**

Introduction

Owner-occupiers have lower risks of death and better health than people who rent their homes. The reasons for this association have rarely been studied directly, it usually being assumed that housing tenure is associated with health because it is acting as a marker for social class or for income and wealth.

In this chapter, we seek to examine some of the correlates of housing tenure in order to help unravel the reasons for these well-known associations. Using data from a postal survey of a random sample of adults in the West of Scotland, we investigate the extent to which owner-occupiers and social renters differ in demographic, socio-economic and psychological characteristics, and how their dwellings and local neighbourhoods differ in ways which might be health-promoting or health-damaging. We argue that unpacking the correlates of housing tenure in this way will help planners design healthier communities and reduce inequalities in health.

The relationship between housing tenure and health

Data from the Office for National Statistics Longitudinal Study (ONS-LS) show that, between 1971 and 1981, age standardized mortality rates were around 25 per cent higher for social tenants than for owner-occupiers (Filakti and Fox 1995). Moreover, although death rates have declined since that time, the falls have been larger among owner-occupiers (Harding *et al.* 1997). Housing tenure is also associated with a range of health measures, including higher rates of long-term illness among social renters as reported at the 1991 census (Gould and Jones 1996) and psychosocial problems (Lewis *et al.* 1998). This association has been reported from other European countries, for example Sweden (Sundquist and Johansson 1997).

Explanations for the observed associations between housing tenure and health

In the nineteenth century, public health practitioners and theorists regarded housing conditions as a major determinant of population health and of the differences in health between social groups (Chadwick 1842). In contrast, in some of the discussion on inequalities in health in the modern era, housing tenure and housing conditions are seen as epiphenomena of social class or income. However, this rather begs the question of what it is about social class or income which directly impacts on health. If we are to move forward in understanding, and in devising policies to reduce, inequalities in health, then we need to understand the ways in which key axes of social stratification such as social class and income expose people to different social and physical risks, and how these risks influence health. Thus, if housing tenure is consistently observed to be associated with measures of health, we believe it is important to examine why this should be so, over and above its obvious role in demarcating the poor from the better-off (see also Chapter 12).

Housing tenure has not been used as an indicator of socio-economic position, or of material or social deprivation, because of any theory about how it might relate to socio-economic hierarchies or to deprivation; rather, its use has been largely pragmatic. Information on housing tenure has been collected in UK decennial censuses since 1961. The question was not originally intended as a general measure of deprivation. However, once it was observed that tenure was predictive of mortality, it increasingly began to be seen as an indicator of deprivation and to be used in some census-based classifications of small areas (Townsend *et al.* 1988; Wallace and Denham 1996). These are widely used in the UK by the public and private sectors to measure and monitor health status in localities, to allocate resources, and to target markets.

The frequent, but usually implicit, hypothesis underlying the use of housing tenure in planning and in social epidemiology is that it is simply a marker of income or social class, both of which are major determinants of health but are difficult to collect in surveys or are inappropriate for some groups. If this hypothesis were correct, then tenure would have little or no relationship with health once income or social class are taken into account. A less common but equally implicit hypothesis is that tenure is simply a marker of psychological characteristics (such as optimism, self-efficacy, deferred gratification or perceived control), which are major determinants of health. If this hypothesis were correct, then tenure would have little or no relationship with health once these characteristics are taken into account. A third hypothesis, even less often examined in the health inequalities literature, is that features of housing tenure are directly health-promoting or health-damaging. If this hypothesis was correct, then aspects of tenure (such as housing conditions or quality of residential environment) might be directly health-promoting or damaging, and, since they are associated with social class, might help to explain social class gradients in health.

Some of our previous work on housing tenure and health in the West of Scotland provides some support for the third hypothesis. We found that the different distribution between tenure categories of housing stressors (for example, overcrowding, dampness, health hazards, difficulty with heating the home) and perceptions of the local environment (for example, crime, neighbourliness, area reputation, amenities) helped to explain the association between tenure and health (Ellaway and Macintyre 1998). We also found that a range of mental and physical health measures were all significantly associated with housing tenure even after controlling for age, sex, income and self-esteem (Macintyre *et al.* 1998). We interpreted these findings as indicating that tenure may be associated with health not only because it is a marker of income or psychological traits, but because features of tenure may also directly promote or damage mental and physical health.

In the project reported here, we took a broad social perspective on the significance of housing tenure. We examined the role of housing quality and residential environment in influencing mental and physical health, and in mediating observed associations between asset-based measures of socio-economic status and health. We also explored the personal and social significance of housing tenure in people's everyday lives.

The project had two components: a postal survey of a representative sample of adults in a range of neighbourhood types, and in-depth interviews with a purposive sub-sample of these respondents. In this chapter, we report on data from the postal survey. Our aim here is to describe the ways in which owner-occupiers differ from social renters – in terms of demographic, socio-economic, psychological and health characteristics – and how owner-occupied homes, and the areas in which they are located, differ from socially-rented homes. We also aim to examine the extent of overlap between these and other commonly used measures of social position and material or social deprivation. In these ways, we can unpack the notion of housing tenure and begin to identify those dimensions of housing occupancy and residency which might be important for health outcomes.

Design and measures

In 1997, we drew a random sample of 6500 adults from the electoral roll in eight local authority areas in the Glasgow and Clyde Valley Structure Plan area in the West of Scotland. The processes of polarization and residualization have been slower to hit the social rented sector in Scotland than in England. The social rented sector in Scotland (34 per cent) is larger than in England (22 per cent), as is the proportion of owner occupation accounted for by Right to Buy sales of public housing (25 per cent of all owner-occupiers in Scotland compared to 10 per cent in England), so that the experience of social rented housing in Scotland is more extensive and enduring than in England.

The sample was stratified by a geodemographic classification of neighbourhood type (using ACORN, Scottish version) to ensure that all types of residential neighbourhoods (ranging from 'affluent consumers in large houses' to 'poorest council estates') were included in the correct proportions. The postal questionnaire achieved a response rate of 50 per cent, which is typical for this type of general population survey (Roberts and Pearson 1993), giving 2838 completed responses for analysis. In the postal survey, 63 per cent of respondents were owner-occupiers, which is slightly higher than the Scottish figure (61 per cent).

The postal questionnaire included standard demographic, socio-economic, psychological and health variables, and also more innovative measures about the dwelling, how it was used, the psychosocial benefits it might confer, and the area of residence. These are listed in Box 8.1.

We developed a measure of the psychosocial benefits derived from the home, based on theories of ontological security (Saunders 1990; Giddens 1991; Dupuis and Thorns 1998). A Likert-type scale ('strongly agree' to 'strongly disagree') was initially used on nine items, from which we derived three factors which we have called protection, autonomy and prestige. Protection measured the extent to which the home is a private haven, autonomy is concerned with being able to do as one wishes in the home and prestige is about living in a high status home (Hiscock *et al.* in press; Kearns *et al.* 2000). Examples of items are: 'I feel I have privacy in my home' (protection), 'I can do what I want when I want with my home' (autonomy), and 'my home makes me feel I'm doing well in life' (prestige).

Results

First, we examine the demographic and socio-economic characteristics of owners and renters. As Table 8.1 shows, owners were slightly more likely to be male, much more likely to be married or cohabiting, less likely to be living in a one-person household and were somewhat younger than renters.

Box 8.1 Measures to examine housing tenure

Demographic

- Age
- Sex
- Marital and cohabiting status

Socio-economic

- Reported monthly household income (standardized for household composition (Goodman and Webb 1994))
- Proportion of household income derived from benefits
- Occupational social class (OPCS 1992)
- Housing tenure (owner-occupiers vs. social renters)
- Household car access

Psychological

- Mastery (Pearlin *et al.* 1981)
- Self-esteem (Rosenberg 1965)
- Ontological security
- 'Faces scale' (a seven-point scale representing happiness or satisfaction) (Andrews and Withey 1976)

Health

- Long-standing illness and limiting long-standing illness (OPCS 1992)
- Self-perceived health ('excellent', 'good', 'fair' or 'poor')
- Number of symptoms in the last month
- Hospital Anxiety and Depression Scale (Zigmond and Snaith 1976)

Dwelling

- Length of residence
- Type of accommodation (house vs. flat, whether has garden, number of rooms)
- Problems (dampness, keeping warm in winter, overcrowding, noise, poor state of repair)
- Fixtures (central heating, security lighting, burglar alarm, smoke alarm)
- Amount of time spent in dwelling

Area

- ACORN code
- Area stressors (see Table 8.4)
- Location in relation to range of amenities (see Table 8.4)
- No neighbours with whom to exchange small favours
- Whether feels part of the community

Owners had significantly greater monthly household income adjusted for family size and were much less likely to receive all the household income from benefits. Owners were more than twice as likely to be in paid employment than renters and were more likely to be in non-manual occupations.

However, there was some within-tenure variation in the socio-economic indicators. For example, some owner-occupiers were in the lowest income (7 per cent) and social class (13 per cent) groups, while some social renters were in the highest income (9 per cent) and social class (15 per cent) groups, suggesting that tenure cannot be used as a precise marker of socio-economic status and material resources (Danesh *et al.* 1999; McLoone and Ellaway 1999).

Second, we examine the association between housing tenure and psychological and health characteristics. As Table 8.2 shows, owners have significantly higher levels of mastery, self-esteem and overall life satisfaction than renters. Owners also report deriving more ontological security from their homes, as measured by the total ontological security scores and by each of the subscales of protection, autonomy and prestige. They are much more likely to report their general health as being excellent or good, less likely to report long-standing or limiting long-standing illness, have lower depression and anxiety scores, and report fewer symptoms in the last month.

Third, we examine social and physical characteristics of the home by tenure. As Table 8.3 shows, most features of the home which are considered socially desirable in our society are more commonly found in owner-occupied properties. This includes the dwelling being a house rather than a

Table 8.1 Association between housing tenure and demographic socio-economic characteristics (percentage unless specified otherwise)

	Tenure		
	Owner-occupier	Renter	Significance
Demographic			
Male	43.2	38.8	*
Married/cohabiting	67.7	32.3	***
One-person household	18.2	42.1	***
Mean age	49.4	54.5	***
Socio-economic			
Mean adjusted monthly income (£)	1354.7	611.8	***
All income from benefits	6.8	46.8	***
Non-manual RG's social class	70.7	39.3	***
In paid work	60.8	24.2	***

Notes: *p < 0.05, **p < 0.01, ***p < 0.001.
RGs = Registrar General's.

Table 8.2 Association between housing tenure and psychological health characteristics (percentage unless specified otherwise: m = mean)

	Tenure		
	Owner-occupier	Renter	Significance
Psychological			
m mastery	20.3	18.7	***
m self-esteem	31.2	29.0	***
m life satisfaction score	5.4	4.8	***
m ontological security (total) #	36.1	34.2	***
m ontological security (protection)	0.1	−0.1	***
m ontological security (autonomy)	0.1	−0.1	***
m ontological security (prestige)	0.2	−0.2	***
Health			
General health excellent or good	70.7	39.7	***
Long-standing illness	38.2	59.6	***
Limiting long-standing illness	24.8	47.2	***
HADS depression score	11.1	13.1	***
HADS anxiety score	13.6	15.0	***
m symptoms last month	3.2	4.6	***

Notes: $*p < 0.05$, $**p < 0.01$, $***p < 0.001$
# Higher scores are more positive.
HADS = Hospital Anxiety and Depression Scale.

flat, having more rooms, the presence of a garden and the main accommodation being on the ground floor rather than in the basement or above the fifth floor. With the exception of smoke alarms, desirable fixtures were more commonly found in the owner-occupied properties, which were reported to have fewer problems such as damp and cold. Owner-occupiers were more likely to say that they thought the home was worth more than others in the locality and to report higher satisfaction with their home. Because average household size was larger among owner-occupiers, 'objective' levels of overcrowding (as defined by numbers of rooms per person) differed little between the two tenure groups. Renters spent significantly more of their time actually in their homes, both during the week and at weekends.

Fourth, we examine social and physical characteristics of the neighbourhood. As Table 8.4 shows, renters are more likely to report that a range of stressors (with the exception of burglaries) are a serious or minor problem in their neighbourhood. However, with the exception of safe play areas, a similar and high proportion of owners and renters report that their homes are well-placed for a list of amenities, suggesting that these variables, at least as self-reported, are unlikely to explain much of the relationship between tenure and health. There is no difference between owners and renters in

Table 8.3 Housing variables (percentage unless specified otherwise: m = mean)

	Tenure		
	Owner-occupier	Renter	Significance
House (rather than flat)	69.0	32.4	***
Garden (communal or owned)	94.0	68.1	***
Central heating	90.4	81.5	***
Security lighting	47.6	19.5	***
Burglar alarm	40.3	9.2	***
Smoke alarm	85.1	92.3	***
Problem with:			
Damp	20.8	38.3	***
Keeping warm in winter	25.2	50.9	***
Overcrowding	19.1	26.5	***
Noise	20.2	40.2	***
Poor state of repair	13.9	39.8	***
Home worth more than others in locality	22.1	6.3	***
Number of rooms	4.9	3.6	***
m rooms per person	2.3	2.2	*
Main accommodation at ground level	77.2	51.2	***
Main accommodation fifth floor or above	0.2	9.8	***
m hours per day at home, weekday	15.4	17.1	***
m hours per day at home, weekend	16.6	17.2	***
m satisfaction with home score	5.8	5.0	***

Notes: $*p < 0.05$, $**p < 0.01$, $***p < 0.001$.

reporting feeling very much part of their neighbourhoods, but renters are more likely (21 per cent compared with 12 per cent) to say they have *no* neighbours with whom they can exchange small favours. Overall, owners report higher satisfaction with their neighbourhoods than do renters.

Discussion and policy implications

Our aim in this chapter is to describe, in a more fine-grained fashion than is usually done, the demographic, socio-economic, psychological, housing, area and self-perceived health correlates of housing tenure in Britain in the 1990s. We believe it is important to document differences between owners and renters, and between owned and socially-rented homes, because in the health inequalities field these are often inferred in rather crude ways rather than studied directly.

Table 8.4 Area variables (percentage unless otherwise specified: m = mean)

	Tenure		
	Owner-occupier	*Renter*	*Significance*
Reported serious or minor problem in neighbourhood with:			
Vandalism	66.5	82.3	* * *
Litter and rubbish	64.8	76.1	* * *
Smells and fumes	24.2	43.5	* * *
Assaults or muggings	34.7	59.8	* * *
Burglaries	71.5	70.2	ns
Disturbance by children/youngsters	52.2	70.9	* * *
Speeding traffic	59.1	72.3	* * *
Discarded syringes/needles	10.1	33.4	* * *
Uneven pavements	56.3	74.7	* * *
Nuisance from dogs	50.4	62.2	* * *
Reputation of area	18.8	45.7	* * *
Poor public transport	29.2	36.2	* * *
Noise	27.8	54.6	* * *
Other people	16.3	37.3	* * *
Has no neighbours with whom can exchange small favours	11.5	20.8	* * *
Feels very much part of neighbourhood	31.1	30.1	ns
Satisfaction with neighbourhood	5.8	5.0	* * *
Home is very or fairly well placed for:			
Food stores	88.8	84.9	*
General practitioner's surgery	83.1	79.7	*
Accident and emergency department	75.5	62.6	* *
Safe play areas	64.2	50.1	* * *
Work	88.6	86.0	* *
Public transport	88.3	89.2	ns
Library	85.2	85.0	ns
Pharmacy	88.7	87.5	ns
Primary school	94.5	94.6	ns
Secondary school	83.9	83.2	ns

Notes: $^*p < 0.05$, $^{**}p < 0.01$, $^{***}p < 0.001$.

The results point towards a conceptual model along the lines shown in Figure 8.1, with five sets of factors contributing to the relationship between housing tenure and individual health. Two of the sets of factors (home and area features) are represented as being a direct consequence of housing tenure. A third set of factors, the psychological characteristics of occupants, may be indirectly dependent upon housing tenure.

We have shown that owners and renters differ markedly in demographic characteristics and in socio-economic status. Since it is known that these demographic and socio-economic characteristics are associated with health, and we have found this to be the case in this sample (data not shown), the observed relationship between tenure and a range of health measures may be due to these personal characteristics, which we are assuming mainly determine tenure rather than vice versa. Moreover, we have also shown in some detail that physical and social features of the dwelling and of the area, and psychological characteristics of residents, are distributed unequally across tenure categories in ways which might be more health-damaging for social renters than owners.

Negative views about the dwelling, the area and health may be due to negative affect, or 'plaintive set' – that is, some types of people have negative views about everything (Watson and Pennebaker 1989). However, if plaintive set were the explanation for tenure differences in perceptions of the dwelling, the area and one's health, this would still leave open the question of why plaintive set is distributed differently by tenure. Moreover, differences in perceptions between tenure categories are not uniform, suggesting that people are responding to specific features of their environment rather than expressing global views of general satisfaction or dissatisfaction. In addition, in previous work comparing socially contrasting neighbourhoods, we found greater differences when we measured access to amenities directly than when this was reported by respondents (Macintyre *et al.* 1993).

In considering the poorer health of social renters, we also have to

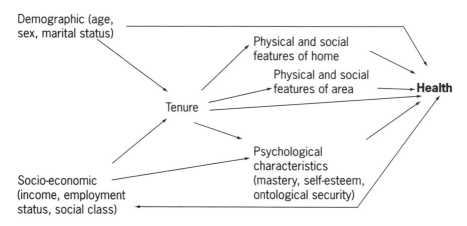

Figure 8.1 The relationship between housing tenure and individual health: a conceptual model

recognize that access to social-rented housing is restricted and that medical priority (being in poor health) is a major factor in determining access (Karn and Stafford 1990). In addition, many social-rented tenants are out of work and there has been a tendency for the long-term unemployed to move out of unemployment into long-term incapacity for both legitimate and illegitimate reasons (Beatty and Fothergill 1999), which may influence their reporting of long-standing illness.

The literature on the direct effects on health and longevity of housing and area conditions is surprisingly sparse (Scottish Office 1998). However, we would suggest that there are plausible physical and psychosocial mechanisms through which features of the home, and of the area in which it is located, might have health-promoting or health-damaging effects on physical and mental health. Housing and area influences on health seem likely to be more proximate and direct (including, for example, the effects of damp, temperature, ventilation, crowding, access to amenities and stressors in the dwelling or its environs) than the more generalized effects of income and social class. Finding that housing tenure is more strongly predictive of mortality than social class (Chandola 2000) lends support to our view that tenure is more than simply a marker for social class. Social class may be predictive of housing tenure, which may predict housing and area conditions, which have a direct effect on physical and mental health, and thus generate observed inequalities in health.

In terms of policy interventions, there are clearly features of social-rented housing which could be improved in ways which we would expect to impact positively on health and feelings of self-worth. This applies to dwelling features, fixtures and fittings, and standards of repair and maintenance. In addition, social renters live in areas with greater problems than owner-occupiers face in their localities (see Table 8.4). But in our study, social-rented neighbourhoods were reported to have equally good access to most facilities and amenities (though we have not assessed their quality, which may be an issue) and residents felt part of a neighbourhood and of a reciprocal community at least as often as did owners. Thus, as well as having features which might be damaging to health, social-rented neighbourhoods also have social characteristics which might mitigate the worst health effects of poor environments.

Recent research into disadvantaged neighbourhoods has illustrated how social cohesion is a major means of coping with material deprivation, and 'resilient reciprocity' becomes something to be proud of in the face of external stigma (Anderson and Munck 1999; Forrest and Kearns 1999). This suggests that attention should be given to reducing the incidence of neighbourhood stressors and increasing local provision of resources and opportunities for even greater social cooperation and interaction.

A major issue for housing policy is whether the attempt to create 'balanced communities' in social-rented estates, through either tenure diversification or the relaxation of housing allocation rules, can achieve social and health gains if the problems of low income and worklessness among social-rented tenants are not also tackled. What little evidence there is, suggests that tenure diversification on council housing estates does not readily deliver community outcomes (Atkinson and Kintrea 1998), though it may boost the psychosocial benefits to be derived from homes which are no longer in mono-tenure areas (and this may be an important gain). The current drive towards joined-up, holistic approaches to the improvement of disadvantaged social-rented neighbourhoods, in which poor health is identified as a key dimension of social exclusion (Social Exclusion Unit 1998; Scottish Office 1999) presents a major research challenge in evaluating the health impacts of regeneration programmes whose individual elements may have mixed and contrary effects. A greater understanding of how people live in their homes and neighbourhoods is needed to attain a three-dimensional perspective of residency as a relational resource and experience, and so move beyond the simple view that health is associated with housing tenure because housing tenure is simply a proxy for social class or income.

Acknowledgements

This chapter draws on research funded by the ESRC (L128251017) under the Health Variations Programme.

References

Anderson, H. and Munck, R. (1999) *Neighbourhood Images in Liverpool: It's All Down to the People*. York: York Publishing Services.

Andrews, F.M. and Withey, S.B. (1976) *Social Indicators of Well Being: Perceptions of Life Quality*. New York: Plenum Press.

Atkinson, R. and Kintrea, K. (1998) *Reconnecting Excluded Communities: The Neighbourhood Impacts of Owner Occupation*. Edinburgh: Scottish Homes.

Beatty, T. and Fothergill, S. (1999) *Incapacity Benefit and Unemployment*. Sheffield: Sheffield Hallam University.

Chadwick, E. (1842) *General Report on the Sanitary Conditions of the Labouring Population of Great Britain*. London: W. Clowes & Sons.

Chandola, T. (2000) Social class differences in mortality using the new UK National Statistics Socio-Economic Classification, *Social Science and Medicine*, 50(5): 641–9.

Danesh, J., Gault, S., Semmence, J., Appleby, P. and Peto, R. (1999) Postcodes as useful markers of social class: population based study on 26,000 British households, *British Medical Journal*, 318: 843–4.

Dupuis, A. and Thorns, D. (1998) Home, home ownership and the search for ontological security, *Sociological Review*, 46: 24–47.

Ellaway, A. and Macintyre, S. (1998) Does housing tenure predict health in the UK because it exposes people to different levels of housing related hazards in the home or its surroundings? *Health and Place*, 4: 141–50.

Filakti, H. and Fox, J. (1995) Differences in mortality by housing tenure and by car access, *Population Trends*, 81: 27–30.

Forrest, R. and Kearns, A. (1999) *Joined up Places? Social Cohesion and Neighbourhood Regeneration*. York: York Publishing Services.

Giddens, A. (1991) *Modernity and Self Identity: Self and Society in the Late Modern Age*. Cambridge: Polity.

Goodman, A. and Webb, S. (1994) *For Richer for Poorer: The Changing Distribution of Income in the UK 1961–1991*. London: Institute of Fiscal Studies.

Gould, M.I. and Jones, K. (1996) Analyzing perceived limiting long-term illness using UK census microdata, *Social Science & Medicine*, 42: 857–69.

Harding, S., Bethune, A., Maxwell, R. and Brown, J. (1997) Mortality trends using the longitudinal study, in F. Drever and M. Whitehead (eds) *Health Inequalities: Decennial Supplement*. London: The Stationery Office.

Hiscock, R., Kearns, A., Macintyre, S. and Ellaway, A. (in press) The significance of residence: housing tenure and area variations in ontological security derived from the home, in C. Gurney (ed.) *The Value of Place: Changing the Meaning and Experiential Aspects of Residential Areas*. London: Avebury.

Karn, V. and Stafford, B. (1990) *Housing Allocations: Report of a Survey of Local Authorities in England and Wales*. Coventry: Institute of Housing.

Kearns, A., Hiscock, R., Macintyre, S. and Ellaway, A. (2000) Beyond four walls. The psychosocial benefits of home: evidence from West Central Scotland, *Housing Studies*, 3: 387–410.

Lewis, G., Bebbington, P. and Brugha, T. *et al.* (1998) Socioeconomic status, standard of living and neurotic disorder, *Lancet*, 352: 605–9.

Macintyre, S., McIver, S. and Sooman, A. (1993) Area, class and health: should we be focusing on people or places? *Journal of Social Policy*, 22: 213–34.

Macintyre, S., Ellaway, A., Der, G., Ford, G. and Hunt, K. (1998) Are housing tenure and car access simply markers of income or self esteem? A Scottish Study, *Journal of Epidemiology and Community Health*, 52: 657–64.

McLoone, P. and Ellaway, A. (1999) Postcodes don't indicate individual's social class, *British Medical Journal*, 319: 1003–4.

OPCS (Office of Population Censuses and Surveys) (1992) *General Household Survey*. London: The Stationery Office.

Pearlin, L., Lieberman, M., Menaghan, E. and Mullan, J. (1981) The stress process, *Journal of Health and Social Behaviour*, 22: 337–56.

Roberts, H. and Pearson, J. (1993) Impact of a postcard versus a questionnaire as a first reminder in a postal lifestyle survey, *Journal of Epidemiology and Community Health*, 47: 334–5.

Rosenberg, M. (1965) *Society and the Adolescent Self Image*. Princeton, NJ: Princeton University Press.

Saunders, P. (1990) *A Nation of Home Owners*. London: Unwin Hyman.

Scottish Office (1998) *Poor Housing and Ill Health: A Summary of Research Evidence*. Edinburgh: Central Research Office.

Scottish Office (1999) *Social Inclusion – Opening the door to a better Scotland*. Edinburgh: Central Research Office.

Social Exclusion Unit (1998) *Bringing Britain Together: A National Strategy for Neighbourhood Renewal.* London: The Stationery Office.

Sundquist, J. and Johansson, S.E. (1997) Self reported poor health and low educational level predictors for mortality: a population based follow up study of 39,156 people in Sweden, *Journal of Epidemiology and Community Health*, 51: 35–40.

Townsend, P., Phillimore, P. and Beattie, A. (1988) *Health and Deprivation: Inequality and the North.* London: Routledge.

Wallace, M. and Denham, C. (1996) *The ONS Classification of Local and Health Authorities of Great Britain.* London: The Stationery Office.

Watson, D. and Pennebaker, J. (1989) Health complaints, stress and distress: exploring the central role of negative affectivity, *Psychological Review*, 96: 234–54.

Zigmond, A. and Snaith, R. (1976) The Hospital Anxiety and Depression Scale, *Acta Psychiatrica Scaninavica*, 67: 361–87.

9 | Putting health inequalities on the map: does where you live matter, and why?

**Heather Joshi, Richard D. Wiggins,
Mel Bartley, Richard Mitchell,
Simon Gleave and Kevin Lynch**

Introduction

The analysis of geographical differentials in health in Great Britain has a long tradition. In the mid-nineteenth century, William Farr established the practice of taking 'healthy districts' as a baseline from which to compare the state of industrial cities. In those times, most of the healthy districts were in more rural areas and in the South and East of England. The spatial distribution of health and illness has changed remarkably little in the past century and a half, despite the passage of the UK through the 'epidemiologic transition'. This transition, from a situation in which infectious diseases of childhood and young adulthood were the most common causes of mortality, to one in which the chronic diseases of older age predominate, might have been expected to bring about a shift in the geography of disease. But this has not proved to be the case.

The dominant paradigm, within which these persistent spatial inequalities have been understood, has been one based on individual characteristics and behaviour. One generally accepted reason for spatial health inequality derives from a spatial variation in employment structure. There is still a preponderance of manual work in the old northern industrial areas. Manual workers and their families are more likely to experience economic deprivation and are less likely to adopt the health education messages aimed at countering the new major diseases such as heart disease and cancer. For example, manual workers are still smoking when other groups are giving up; neither have they adopted wholeheartedly the recommended changes in diet and exercise (see Chapter 7).

Research on the reasons for observed area differences now distinguishes between the effects of social composition and of social context (Macintyre *et al.* 1993). Composition refers to the aggregated characteristics of individuals living in an area, while context refers to characteristics of the area which are independent of its individual inhabitants. Context could include features of the physical environment, such as climate or pollution, and features of the local economy, such as the housing stock or the structure of employment. It could also include the provision of services such as shops, transport and schools, as well as the quality of healthcare available. Finally, there are features of the social fabric which may make a place less or more 'healthy', such as the level of crime or community cohesion.

Sooman *et al.* (1993) have studied the types of shops and transport available in different areas of Glasgow, an example of clearly contextual features. However, at a certain level of density, composition may become a form of context: as one example, when in deprived areas with high rates of smoking, an individual is more likely to smoke than a similar individual in an area with lower smoking rates (Duncan *et al.* 1996).

In order to disentangle these complex influences, evidence is required both about individuals and the places they live in. We also need a statistical framework capable of analysing the relationships between them. An appropriate statistical framework is provided by a multi-level model, which allows for separate relationships between individual and area characteristics (Goldstein 1997).

A multi-level model explicitly recognizes that individuals behave in context. They act out their lives in households and within neighbourhoods, and in larger areas and broad regions. Areas provide natural groupings, or clusters of units, for our analysis, reflecting features of context or population composition. In contrast to conventional regression analysis, the multi-level framework provides an appropriate way of being able to take account explicitly of any clustering (Cheung *et al.* 1990). We are also able to examine the interplay of individual and area-level characteristics in determining individual health. By separating out the between-area and within-area contribution of area effect, it is possible to see the extent to which they actually explain any differences between areas, once the characteristics of the individuals who reside there have been taken into account. The failure of many studies to take account of the multi-level nature of the data obtained has been a prominent theme in methodological criticisms of epidemiological (Langford and Bentham 1996), educational (Goldstein 1997) and sociological (Willms and Patterson 1995) research over the last 20 years. We were able to avoid the 'ecological fallacy' by making a pioneering application of multi-level modelling to the Office for National Statistics Longitudinal Study (ONS-LS), not previously possible with individual data.

Earlier analysis of individual and ward-level data in this study (but which did not use the multi-level technique) suggested that individual characteristics are the most important source of geographical variations in mortality (Sloggett and Joshi 1994, 1998a). However, some ward and regional 'effects' remained in models of limiting long-term illness (LLTI), even after allowance for effects at both personal and community levels (Sloggett and Joshi 1998a, 1998b). In these models, the risk of LLTI was raised by about 17 per cent, moving across areas towards those with worse composite indices of deprivation in steps of one standard deviation. Shouls *et al.* (1996) also analysed limiting long-term illness in the 1991 census, using multi-level modelling on larger areas (local authorities or groups thereof). With more information at the area-level included (for example, affluence as well as deprivation), a greater geographical element was detected alongside the effects of individual inequality on health.

This chapter explores some of the evidence on area-based inequalities in health. It begins by describing the evidence before asking what role may be played in these area effects by two specific factors among the many: economic change and social cohesion. It concludes with a discussion of the relevance of the spatial aspect of health inequality for policy.

Individual disadvantage or area type?

The ONS-LS allows us to look at the health of individuals within areas with the additional dimension of time by examining social and spatial mobility. This is because the ONS-LS links information from the 1991 census of England and Wales, to information from 1971 and 1981 for up to 800,000 individuals (Hattersley and Creeser 1995). The 1991 census asked a question on limiting long-term illness. We used this information to examine whether a certain type of work life-history between 1971 and 1991 was more likely to result in LLTI in men of working age. We also examined how far geographical differences in typical work life-histories could go towards explaining the marked regional inequalities in health.

The first step was to look at differences in LLTI between all 403 of the county districts of England and Wales. County districts are administrative units averaging 120,000 population. Previous analysis of the 1991 census data had shown large differences in the prevalence of LLTI, ranging between 48 per cent of all households having at least one person with a long-term illness, in the Rhondda (Wales), to 15 per cent in Surrey Heath (southern England) (Charlton and Wallace 1994). Were these area differences any more than a matter of the collection of individuals with higher susceptibility to ill-health? This question was approached by using multi-level models, a technique not previously available on ONS-LS microdata. These showed that individual characteristics were indeed important, the more so as we looked at movement between social classes, and into and out of unemployment over successive census reports. Having been out of work in either 1971 or 1981, having been in a manual job in 1971, having moved from a higher to a lower social class, not having a degree and being a member of an ethnic minority were all risk factors for LLTI. These variables explained around half of the area differences. However, after taking account of the fact that some areas contain far more disadvantaged men than others, it still seemed to matter where a man lived.

In order to begin the task of discovering what it might be about areas which makes a difference to health risks, each of the 403 county districts was classified according to the ONS grouping of local authorities (Wallace and Denham 1996). The classification is based on a range of social and economic data collected at the time of the 1991 census, concerning what kinds of industries predominate in different areas, car and home ownership, unemployment, the type of housing and the area's demographic structure. Table 9.1 shows that the prevalence of LLTI varies sharply between categories of this area classification.

Including this information on area type in the multi-level model explained another quarter of the differences in illness between areas. Fewer inhabitants of areas described as 'growth areas' or among the most economically prosperous areas had LLTI, having already taken account of their individual characteristics and the occupational histories. Conversely, the health of men in coalfield areas, and areas dominated by ports and heavy industries, was poorer than would have been expected on the basis of their own social and

Table 9.1 The ONS area classification of county districts in England and Wales

Type of county district	*Mean prevalence (%) of limiting long-term illness in men aged 36–65 in 1991*
Coalfields	21.76
Ports and industry	20.50
Inner London	16.55
Manufacturing	16.39
'Scotland'*	16.31
Coast and countryside	13.19
Mixed economies	13.11
Resort and retirement	12.54
Mixed urban and rural	12.20
Services and education	10.68
Most prosperous	9.94
Growth	7.18
Average LLTI, all areas	13.39

Note: *'Scotland' does not refer to the country itself, but rather to areas in England and Wales deemed to be socio-economically similar to Scotland.
Source: Wallace and Denham (1996).

occupational histories alone. This leaves about one quarter of the health variations (age-standardized) between districts unaccounted for, either by measured characteristics of individuals or by their local economy: a variation possibly explained by climate, culture or other particular local conditions (Wiggins *et al.* 1998).

This type of analysis of the ONS-LS was extended to consider health variations among women as well as men, taking car ownership and housing tenure as indicators of individual circumstances (Wiggins *et al.* 1999). These analyses looked at the influence of a third, intermediate level – that of the electoral ward, of which there are 9369 in England and Wales.

For women and men, the chance of reporting LLTI was affected by the persistence over time of disadvantaged individual circumstances. Each observed occurrence of a disadvantageous state added to the chances of an adverse outcome: those who were, say, unemployed or council tenants at both previous censuses reported worse health than those who reported such states only once. There was a milder effect of repetition of residence in a deprived area, but otherwise little difference in LLTI for those who were geographically mobile or not. Migration into the South-East region did, however, appear to be beneficial. In line with findings by Macintyre and Ellaway (1998), cars and tenure appear to be useful markers of social and material advantage. For individuals, owning a car and a home in 1971 and 1981 both protected against the risk of reporting LLTI; not having either at either date raised the odds of LLTI by a factor of 1.7.

After adjusting for individual circumstances and histories, area differences persisted. A deterioration in ward poverty by one standard deviation of an index (based on census small area statistics) raised the chances of LLTI by a factor of about 1.18: much the same as in the analysis of Sloggett and Joshi (1998a), but less than the impact of individual circumstances. For men, the majority of local authority districts with a worryingly high level of unexplained rates of LLTI are largely accounted for by virtue of their classification as a former coalfield. For women, almost all of the remaining variation between county districts is explained by taking account of the composition of the wards in these areas. Multi-level analysis also revealed the existence of variation between wards in otherwise unspecified effects of place – however, investigation of these variations would require more information than is available in the census.

How far did this combination of individual and area variables explain the 'North–South divide' in illness? Once the geographical distribution of people with different kinds of employment histories, and the characteristics of areas in terms of industry, housing and degree of urbanization, are taken into account, little difference in health remained between northern and southern areas of England and Wales. This does not mean there is no role for health-related behaviour, as it still may be that individuals with certain types of work histories, living in certain types of area, smoke more, take less exercise and eat a poorer diet. This analysis tells us that area does matter, as well as individual factors, but it does not tell us all the reasons why this might be.

How might area make a difference to health?

What specific characteristics of an area might affect the health of its inhabitants? Of the various ways in which an area itself might generate poor or good health, we focus here on one aspect of the economic environment (de-industrialization) and one of the social environment (social capital). In these analyses, the source of data was the Health and Lifestyle Survey (HALS), a representative sample of the British population in 1984–5 spatially clustered in electoral wards (Cox *et al.* 1987). Poor health was defined as having more than the average number of symptoms in the past two weeks.

De-industrialization

One area characteristic with a potential health effect is de-industrialization: economic decline with associated socio-demographic change. Champion and Townsend (1990) report a net loss of 2.8 million manufacturing jobs in Britain between 1971 and 1989. Since the manufacturing and mining industries were spatially concentrated, the effects of their loss were also spatially (and therefore socially) concentrated. There are likely to be changes in the nature of everyday life for the entire population of a de-industrialized community, even for those not directly involved in the declining industries. Areas experiencing de-industrialization during the 1980s have shown a relative deterioration in health (Phillimore *et al.* 1994). We therefore investigated the relationship between local de-industrialization and levels of health reported by all residents, men and women, employed and unemployed.

The source of data on de-industrialization was the Small Area Statistics for 1981 and 1991. We categorized wards into those with high and low levels of heavy industrial employment in 1981, which experienced high or low decreases in this type of employment up to 1991. To see whether differences in the degree of community cohesion made any difference to the health impact of economic recession, we also included in the analysis people's answers to a question on how far they felt they were part of the local community.

Residents in areas that had once had a high level of heavy industry, and then lost a large number of such jobs between 1981 and 1991, were indeed more likely to report poor current health. Of residents in such areas, 14.2 per cent reported a high number of symptoms, compared with 10.5 per cent in areas with low levels of industrial employment in 1981 and with low loss of industrial employment over the next ten years. These two types of area accounted for 38 per cent and 40 per cent of the sample respectively. The remaining 22 per cent lived in areas with other combinations of the level and change of industrial employment and had intermediate levels of health. Multi-level analysis expressed the higher risk of poor health among individuals in the de-industrializing areas as an odds ratio of 1.35 relative to the areas of low industrialization and low industrial decline. This took account of whether they themselves were unemployed or employed in manual work, and applied regardless of the extent to which they felt integrated into their community. The odds of poor health for those in unskilled social class V were 1.78 (relative to social class I); while the odds for those who did not feel part of the community (relative to those who did) were 1.33.

Thus, while there was a specific effect on health of adverse change in the local economic structure, regardless of the situation of individual people, there were still bigger health differentials for individual disadvantageous situations like being in social class V. Socially integrated people who felt part of their communities were healthier, too, but this was so whatever the economic state of the area they lived in. Feeling part of their community might help protect people against the effects of de-industrialization, but de-industrialization does not explain the whole of the area differences in health (Mitchell *et al.* 2000).

Social capital

The concept of social capital has been described as 'the resources that emerge from one's social ties' (Portes and Landolt 1996: 26). Putnam, in his highly influential analysis, suggests that social capital is a community-based resource which includes 'civic engagement'. This he defines as 'people's connections with the life of their communities' (1995: 1).

We examined whether a higher level of civic engagement was positively associated with health, independently of other socio-economic characteristics of individuals and the areas in which they live. HALS records the frequency and nature of contact with family and friends, attendance at a place of worship and any voluntary or community work, in the two weeks prior to interview. Responses revealed three distinct tendencies characterized by high levels of contact with family, with friends and with fellow citizens. A civic orientation was characterized by attendance at church and by involvement in voluntary work. We tested directly the nature of the relationship between health and these orientations to family, friends and fellow citizens.

Logistic regression analysis of poor health (again measured as having above average numbers of symptoms) controlled for the individual's age and fitness and then successively introduced controls for the individual's socio-economic circumstances and those of the local population. Individual fitness (as measured by sports participation and limiting long-standing illness) was included in the model to allow for the effects of chronic ill-health, as well as the effect of current symptoms, on social contacts. Area deprivation was measured by the Breadline Britain Index (Gordon and Pantazis 1997). This estimates the number of households likely to be in poverty in an area, using the local rates at the 1991 census of non-home ownership, non-access to a car, low social class, unemployment, lone parents and LLTI, weighted in accordance with responses to the Breadline Britain survey. It is positively, but not perfectly, correlated with the de-industrialization score (0.25) and more closely related to the ward scores used in the ONS-LS, though these use different weights and do not include LLTI.

The analysis is shown in Table 9.2. The effects of any explanatory variable are shown as odds ratios: any ratio under 1 suggests that the attribute will improve the chances of good health, whereas a ratio greater than 1 suggests the opposite.

The first model (column labelled social orientation, individual fitness) showed those with a greater degree of civic engagement or family contact gave a significantly better report on their state of health than those with less, whether or not they had a chronic disease. Civic engagement was the form of social activity most strongly related to current health (odds of reporting above average symptoms of 0.65, in comparison with 0.86 and 0.88, for family and friend orientations respectively).

The second model (column labelled social orientation, individual fitness, individual socio-economics) adds a simple indicator of low or high social class, and a three-category measure of income. The effect of being in a low social class is to raise the chances of experiencing more than average symptoms (odds ratio 1.48). Those in the highest income band are only about half as likely to report poor health as those in the lowest band. The effects of class and income are independent of the other characteristics already in the model. Although the association between civic orientation and health was weakened after adjusting for socio-economic circumstances, it remains significant.

The final model (column labelled social orientation, individual fitness, individual socio-economics, area characteristics) introduces a measure of area deprivation. An increase of 10 per cent in the proportion of households estimated to be living in poverty in the area is associated with an increase of 21 per cent in the chances of a person reporting poor health. It is a significant, independent, predictor of poor health at the individual level despite the inclusion of individual socio-economic characteristics. Its inclusion slightly reduces the impact of these individual terms, but makes no difference to the association between civic orientation and health. Indirectly, this tells us that the poor areas do not have systematically less civic engagement. Civic engagement has about the same protective effect in the full model (0.72) as does 'feeling part of the community' in the de-industrialization model (0.75). The reason that civic engagement appears to protect health is not that it is more common in rich areas. Poor areas seem to have health disadvantages beyond

Table 9.2 Results of logistic regression models, predicting ill-health.[1] Odds ratios (and confidence intervals)

Model Predictor variable	Social orientation, individual fitness		Social orientation, individual fitness individual socio- economics		Social orientation, individual fitness individual socio- economics, area characteristics	
More civic oriented[2]	0.65	(0.57, 0.74)	0.72	(0.63, 0.83)	0.72	(0.63, 0.83)
More family oriented[2]	0.86	(0.77, 0.96)	0.81	(0.72, 0.91)	0.80	(0.72, 0.90)
More friend oriented[2]	0.88	(0.79, 0.99)	0.93	(0.82, 1.04)	0.93	(0.82, 1.04)
Age[3]	0.95	(0.92, 0.98)	0.90	(0.86, 0.93)	0.91	(0.87, 0.94)
Does sport/physical activity[4]	0.59	(0.52, 0.67)	0.64	(0.56, 0.72)	0.65	(0.57, 0.73)
Has LLTI[5]	5.78	(5.03, 6.64)	5.60	(4.86, 6.45)	5.59	(4.85, 6.44)
Manual class[6]			1.48	(1.30, 1.67)	1.41	(1.25, 1.60)
Low income[7]			1.45	(1.67, 1.26)	1.39	(1.58, 1.20)
High income[8]			0.68	(0.65, 0.69)	0.71	(0.68, 0.73)
Area poverty[9]					1.21	(1.13, 1.30)
−2 Log likelihood	7525		7360		7341	

N with full data for this analysis = 7020

Notes:

1 Reporting more than the mean number of symptoms in the past two weeks.
2 Odds relative to those who had a negative score.
3 Age in 10 years, modelled as a continuous variable.
4 Those who reported doing some kind of sport/physical activity in the two weeks prior to interview. Odds relative to those who did not report any such activity.
5 Those reporting limiting long-term illness. Odds relative to those who did not.
6 Those in social classes IIIM, IV or V. Odds relative to classes I, II or IIIN.
7 Those in the lowest income bracket (under £79 per week, net, per week in 1984) relative to those in the middle income bracket (£79–£173). There are 28 per cent of cases in the low income bracket, just under half all cases in the middle bracket and another 28 per cent in the top.
8 Those in the top income bracket (£174 or more per week in 1984). Odds relative to the middle bracket.
9 The Breadline Britain Index. Unit equivalent to a 10 per cent difference in the fitted proportion of households in poverty in the respondent's ward of residence in 1991.

those associated with the individual and with the community as we have measured them.

The socio-economic health divide therefore has individual, social and local components. Although a low level of civic engagement is associated with poorer health, socio-economic status is no less important at both the individual and area levels. In the presence of wealth, weaker friendship networks and lower levels of civic orientation have relatively small health penalties attached to them. Personal circumstances seem at least as strong an influence as area. The odds of poor health increase by 1.39 between the median to the poorest income group, and by 1.21 if the deprivation score is increased by ten points (which it does between the middle of the most deprived quarter of the sample and its mid-point). Combining the impact of individual and local deprivation, the model predicts that a gap in income of this magnitude accompanied by an equivalent contrast in area deprivation and a shift from non-manual to manual occupation, would more than double the odds (2.37) of poor health.

The size of the Breadline Britain area effect on current illness is very similar to the corresponding analyses of LLTI in the ONS-LS, despite the difference in outcome measures. When adjusted by the standard deviation of the Breadline Britain Index, the odds ratio is 1.16. For the ONS-LS, we have around 1.18.

Other mechanisms

The analyses reported in this chapter do not address all aspects of area differences in health, nor do they cover all the ways in which the health and circumstances of individuals may vary. Some of these dimensions have been examined by members of this team during the course of the project. Blane *et al.* (in press), for example, investigated links between poor climate, poor housing and lung function, noting that these links make a further contribution to explaining poor health in the North-West for reasons beyond smoking behaviour. Our investigations have also been extended to the data on 33-year-olds in the National Child Development Survey (NCDS). Preliminary results suggest that self-assessed health and mental state (but not, at that age, LLTI) have a social and regional pattern, but that ward level indicators of deprivation and de-industrialization do not have much independent impact.

Conclusion

Do individual or area characteristics matter? Both do. Our analyses of the ONS-LS and HALS produced a remarkably consistent set of findings about the contribution of context and composition to area differences in health. Area differences in self-reported ill-health, long-term or current, are mainly, but not simply, attributable to the socio-economic characteristics, occupational and migration histories of individual residents. But where people live also matters. Both men and women living in deprived wards have higher risks than those with similar characteristics in more affluent wards of reporting LLTI in the census and of reporting high numbers of symptoms in HALS. Men are especially at risk of ill-health if they live in former coalfields or other areas of industrial decline. The magnitude of ward effects is strikingly similar in the present and previous analysis of census data, and in the survey data on current illness in the working-age population. In all cases, too, the estimates of the impact of individual disadvantage were more important, even if they did not account for all the area variation.

As well as looking at individuals' socio-economic circumstances, we attempted to look at social relations. We have not been able to identify areas which are rich in the kinds of collective activity and public provision which adds value to the quality of life of poorer residents. But we have found evidence, in two separate exercises, for individual social inclusion having an independent impact on health. But lack of participation in the community and lack of civic engagement are not the only reasons that poor people in poor places are at a health disadvantage.

What are the implications for public health policy? Should policies be targeted at particular areas (Smith 1999)? The geographical clustering of people at high health risk makes area-based initiatives look attractively cost effective. This would apply even if local health variations were all due to local concentrations of individual disadvantage, assuming some economies of scale in delivering services at these points. This would be all the more effective if the place itself gives rise to poor health. However, if only individuals living in particular areas are to benefit, then individuals at risk who happen to live outside targeted areas will obviously miss out. In the 1981 census of England, the majority (55 per cent) of the most 'deprived' individuals (those owning neither a home nor a car at both 1971 and 1981) lived outside the most deprived wards (Sloggett and Joshi 1994). Similarly, for England and Wales in 1991, 51 per cent of 'deprived' individuals did not live in the wards containing the most deprived fifth of the population. A similar picture emerges from our analysis of HALS. The bottom income group in our HALS sample, though over-represented in the bottom fifth Breadline Britain wards, or those with high de-industrialization, were not confined to these areas. Of the low-income group, 71 per cent lived in the better-off four fifths of wards, and 53 per cent lived outside the areas of greatest industrial decline.

Equally, if individuals rather than areas are targeted, the nature of area differences will continue to deflate potential benefits to those individuals. This suggests that policymakers need targeting strategies which combine redistributive initiatives at an individual and area level. Policies could be crafted which start with individuals and provide enhancements/premiums, depending on the deprivation profiles persisting at ward and broader levels of aggregation. Such resource allocation mechanisms cannot be foolproof, particularly as much variation in health remains unaccounted for by our models. To improve allocation, we need to continue to deepen our understanding of why area differences persist.

Our finding that individual dimensions are important sources of health disadvantage implies that public health needs to be concerned with economic inequalities. Our finding that there are spatial dimensions to these disadvantages further suggests that area-based initiatives need not be futile. But they will not be a panacea, if individual inequality is neglected.

Acknowledgements

This chapter draws on research funded by the ESRC (L128251012) under the Health Variations Programme. We thank the ONS for access to the Longitudinal Study and the ESRC Data Archive for providing the HALS.

References

Blane, D., Mitchell, R. and Bartley, M. (in press) The 'Inverse Housing Law' and respiratory health, *Journal of Epidemiology and Community Health*.
Champion, A. and Townsend, A. (1990) *Contemporary Britain: A Geographical Perspective*. London: Edward Arnold.
Charlton, J. and Wallace, M. (1994) Long-term illness: results from the 1991 Census, *Population Trends*, Spring: 18–25.
Cheung, K.C., Keeves, J.P., Sellin, N. and Tsoi, S.C. (eds) (1990) The analysis of multilevel data in educational research: studies of problems and their solutions, *International Journal of Educational Research*, 14: 215–319.
Cox, B.D., Blaxter, M. and Buckle, A.L.J. *et al.* (1987) *The Health and Lifestyle Survey*. London: Health Promotion Trust.
Duncan, D., Jones, K. and Moon, G. (1996) Health related behaviour in context: a multilevel approach, *Social Science and Medicine*, 42(6): 817–30.
Goldstein, H. (1997) *Multilevel Models in Educational and Social Research*. London: Charles Griffin & Co. Ltd.
Gordon, D. and Pantazis, C. (1997) *Breadline Britain in the 1990s*. Aldershot: Ashgate.
Hattersley, L. and Creeser, R. (1995) *Longitudinal Study 1971–1991: History, Organisation and Quality of Data*. London: HMSO.
Langford, I.H. and Bentham, G. (1996) Regional variations in mortality rates in England and Wales: an analysis using multilevel modelling, *Social Science and Medicine*, 42: 897–908.
Macintyre, S. and Ellaway, A. (1998) Ecological approaches: rediscovering the role of the physical and social environment, in L. Berkman and I. Kawachi (eds) *Social Epidemiology*. Oxford: Oxford University Press.
Macintyre, S., MacIvers, S. and Sooman, A. (1993) Area, class and health: should we be focusing on places or people? *Journal of Social Policy*, 22: 213–34.
Mitchell, R., Gleave, S., Bartley, M., Wiggins, R.D. and Joshi, H. (2000) Do attitude and area influence health? *Health and Place*, 6: 67–79.
Phillimore, P., Beattie, A. and Townsend, P. (1994) Widening inequality of health in Northern England, 1981–91, *British Medical Journal*, 308(6937): 1125–8.

Portes, A. and Landolt, P. (1996) The downside of social capital, *The American Prospect*, 26: 18–21.

Putnam, R. (1995) The strange disappearance of civic America, *The American Prospect*, 24(Winter).

Shouls, A., Congdon, P. and Curtis, S. (1996) Modelling inequality in reported long term illness: combining individual and area characteristics, *Journal of Epidemiology and Community Health*, 50(3): 366–76.

Sloggett, A. and Joshi, H. (1994) Higher mortality in deprived areas: community or personal disadvantage? *British Medical Journal*, 309(6967): 1470–4.

Sloggett, A. and Joshi, H. (1998a) Deprivation indicators as predictors of life events, 1981–1992, *Journal of Epidemiology and Community Health*, 52(4): 228–33.

Sloggett, A. and Joshi, H. (1998b) Indicators of deprivation in people and places: longitudinal perspectives, *Environment and Planning A*, 30(6): 1055–76.

Smith G.R. (1999) *Area Based Initiatives: The Rationale for and Options for Area Targeting*, CASEpaper 25. London: London School of Economics.

Sooman, A., Macintyre, S. and Anderson, A. (1993) Scotland's health – a more difficult challenge for some? The price and availability of healthy foods in socially contrasting localities in the West of Scotland, *Health Bulletin*, 51(5): 276–84.

Wallace, M. and Denham, C. (1996) *The ONS Classification of Local and Health Authorities of Great Britain*. London: HMSO.

Wiggins, R.D., Bartley, M. and Gleave, S. *et al.* (1998) Limiting long-term illness: a question of where you live or who you are? A multilevel analysis of the 1971–1991 ONS Longitudinal Study, *Risk, Decision and Policy*, 3(3): 181–98.

Wiggins, R.D., Gleave, S. and Bartley, M. *et al.* (1999) Health, area and the individual: a multilevel analysis of reporting a limiting long-term illness for men and women in the ONS Longitudinal Study of England and Wales. Paper presented at Royal Statistical Society Conference on Risk, University of Warwick, July.

Willms, J.D. and Patterson, L. (1995). A multilevel model for community aggregation, *Journal of Mathematical Sociology*, 20(1): 23–40.

10 Understanding health inequalities: locating people in geographical and social spaces

**Anthony Gatrell, Carol Thomas,
Sharon Bennett, Lisa Bostock,
Jennie Popay, Gareth Williams
and Said Shahtahmasebi**

Introduction

Over the last 20 years, there has been a great deal of work that documents patterns of health inequalities in British society, as well as considerable progress in developing theoretical explanations of such inequalities. To date, much of this work has been of a quantitative nature, using either aggregate or individual data. More recently, there has been a growing recognition that many of the questions concerning the existence of health inequalities require more detailed exploration of the lives of individuals within particular localities. We argue that, via a mix of both quantitative and qualitative methods, it should be possible to develop more rounded explanations of health inequalities. Here, we explore the nature of the relationship between health status and material and social circumstances, within and between differing geographical and 'social' spaces.

We first consider what has motivated the present study. We pay particular attention to the meaning of area effects on health since, in common with the other chapters in this section, concerns with 'place' and 'locality' underpin our work. Following an overview of research methods, we present some findings, before reflecting upon these and their policy implications.

Theoretical context

There is a long tradition in the disciplines of geography, public health and epidemiology of mapping health outcomes – whether mortality or morbidity – in geographical space. Such mapping is done at a variety of scales, including quite small areas. Invariably, such maps portray geographical health inequalities. But how are these to be understood? More specifically, to what extent are observed differences due to the mix of people living in different areas, and to what extent do they reflect the social and physical environments in which such people live? Put another way, do differences between areas reflect *compositional*, as opposed to *contextual*, effects? As Chapter 9 indicates, the evidence to date is that, while health variations are indeed accounted for by individual-level (compositional) variables, area-level (contextual) influences are also significant.

Research on such area-level influences has highlighted a range of potential health determinants. These include the physical environment (air and water quality, for example), the provision of services and facilities (such as good schools and healthcare), socio-cultural features of a neighbourhood (community integration and levels of crime, for example) and neighbourhood reputation (see Chapter 9; Macintyre *et al.* 1993; Curtis and Jones 1998). For Phillimore (1993), the industrial legacies of areas also merit attention, as do variations in social divisions or polarization. Macintyre and colleagues have sought to discriminate between areas (rather large parts of Glasgow, comprising perhaps 50–60,000 people) in terms of measures of the resource base and social environment. Data are presented on counts of recreation and health facilities, transport facilities, and so on, while crime rates are also compared (see also Chapter 8). Analysis of data on both health status and health behaviours confirms that area of residence has an effect, over and above that of individual-level variables.

Good progress has therefore been made in understanding the relevance for health of the geographical spaces in which people live. But less progress has been made in understanding these areas as social spaces within which people live and express their being (Popay *et al.* 1998). What is the nature of social relationships within these areas, and how is individual health experience and behaviour shaped by the feelings that people have about the areas in which they live and those who live among them?

Some researchers have begun to address these issues looking, for example, at community engagement and perceptions of neighbourhood quality (see Chapter 8; Sooman and Macintyre 1995). In addition, there is a long tradition of community studies both in British and American sociology, examining ways of life in different neighbourhoods, although this has not, in general, looked specifically at health inequalities. An exception is the work of Cornwell (1984) whose research in Bethnal Green in East London examined how the beliefs and knowledge of individuals were shaped by local living and working environments. This has informed our own work, in the sense that it situates a socio-cultural analysis of people's beliefs and lived experiences in the context of a materialist analysis of socio-economic circumstances. We also draw on the growing body of literature that prioritizes psychosocial determinants of ill-health: the ways in which 'despairing circumstances, unsurmountable tasks, or lack of social support, can influence disease-related parameters' (Elstad 1998: 41). The self-efficacy approach that Elstad reviews, conceptualizing individuals as 'acting subjects and not only as being governed by external and structural forces' (1998: 45) therefore needs consideration, but we need to see how self-efficacy is both enabled and constrained by living within particular social spaces.

Considerable attention, too, is being given to operationalizing measures of social capital and social cohesion, prompted in part by Wilkinson's (1996) thesis (itself drawing on Putnam's 1993 work on the strength of community life in Italy). This is not the place for an extended review and critique of this growing literature, but following Bullen and Onyx (1998) we understand social capital to comprise: participation in the local community, feelings of trust and safety, social connections within the neighbourhood and among friends and family, a tolerance of diversity, and a valuing of life and work connections. Cooper *et al.* (1999) have drawn on these dimensions to construct operational measures of social capital and we have devised similar measures in the work reported below.

The important contribution that can be made by qualitative research on social capital is also being recognized (Campbell 1999). There is certainly a need to examine in depth how people live their lives in particular places or neighbourhoods. We consider such places to be loci of social meaning in which macrosocial structures impact on the lives of ordinary people. As Stanley and Wise (1990: 44) put it, 'individuals do not exist except as socially located beings: thus social structures and categories can be "recovered" by analysing the accounts of particular people in particular material circumstances'. While the concept of social capital is useful in principle, we want to understand how people experience these places and how the quality of social relations, as revealed in qualitative accounts as well as quantitative surveys, influences health.

Explaining and understanding health inequalities in Lancaster and Salford: data and methods

There are two strands to our empirical work. The first is a survey of people living in four localities, while the second comprises a series of in-depth interviews with purposively-sampled individuals drawn from each of those localities. Since these interviews are still ongoing, we draw on two pilot interviews which we attempt to weave into our analysis of survey data. The aim here is to examine the extent to which such accounts shed light on the connections between social space and health outcome.

Our surveys were conducted in four urban localities, two each in the districts of Lancaster and Salford. Salford forms part of the major conurbation of Greater Manchester, while Lancaster is a large town in North-West England. In each district, we sought to identify a relatively affluent and a relatively deprived locality, drawing on detailed explorations of small-area data from the 1991 census, as well as local knowledge. Three of the localities (Worsley/Boothstown and Torrisholme, the two more affluent study areas in Salford and Lancaster respectively, and Weaste/Seedley/Langworthy, a more deprived area in Salford) comprised a number of enumeration districts (EDs) within electoral wards. The fourth study area, Skerton (a more deprived part of Lancaster), comprised a set of EDs across two electoral wards. The localities had to be based around EDs, since these were the smallest units for which census data are available; but we wished to define localities that were not simply electoral wards, since the latter are defined purely for the purposes of local government and do not define socially meaningful community boundaries.

Across the four localities, 2000 names and addresses were selected from the electoral registers; 600 in each of the more deprived areas and 400 in the relatively affluent localities. The differences in sampling fractions reflected the expectation of differing response rates across the two sets of localities. Each person was contacted by letter and subsequently at the doorstep, when they were asked to take part in a short interview concerning their own health and that of household members. Data on household type, age, gender and ethnicity were also collected. They were then asked to complete, and to return by post, a questionnaire. If the person declined to take part, a second household member was invited to participate.

The questionnaire sought detailed information on the respondent's health, their home, length of residence in the area, work status, family finances, availability of a car, levels of social support, smoking behaviour, diet and how they felt about living in their neighbourhood. Social class was defined on the basis of last reported occupation. We asked about perceived access to facilities and resources (such as food stores, schools and public transport), as well as perceived problems with the neighbourhood (such as crime levels and nuisances). From the survey data, we were able to construct a number of variables relating to social capital, as well as access to facilities and the perceived physical fabric of the locality (following Macintyre *et al.* 1993). The definitions of the social capital variables are presented in Table 10.1. They were defined partly on the basis of work by Bullen and Onyx (1998), although we did not have data on tolerance of diversity or the value of life and work used in their study.

We present here some analyses of the question on self-reported health. This asked 'would you say that for someone of your age your own health in

Table 10.1 Variables relating to social capital

Feelings of trust and safety

In this area how much of a problem are the following?
Assaults and muggings
Burglaries
Disturbance by children or youngsters
Speeding traffic
Lack of safe places for children to play
Walking around after dark

Neighbourhood connections

How much do you agree with the following statements about your neighbourhood?
I feel like I belong to this neighbourhood
I visit my neighbours in their homes
The friendships and associations I have with other people in my neighbourhood mean a lot to me
If I need advice about something I could go to someone in my neighbourhood
I believe my neighbours would help in an emergency
I borrow things and exchange favours with my neighbours
I plan to remain a resident of this neighbourhood for a number of years
I like to think of myself as similar to the people who live in this neighbourhood
I regularly stop and talk with people in my neighbourhood
Living in this neighbourhood gives me a sense of community

Connections with family and friends

In the last two weeks, not counting people you live with, have you
Seen someone in your family to chat to?
Had contact by telephone or letter with your family?
Seen a friend to chat to?
Had contact by telephone with a friend?
Do you feel you have people you can talk to when you have problems?
Apart from those who live with you, do any of your *relatives* live in the area or within easy reach?
Apart from those who live with you, do any of your *friends* live in the area or within easy reach?

Participation or willingness to engage in local social action

I would be willing to work together with others on something to improve my neighbourhood
Are you actively involved in any of the following clubs or associations?
Political party
Neighbourhood watch scheme
Tenants group
Residents association
Neighbourhood council
Volunteers

Table 10.1 continued

Participation in other community groups/organizations (including leisure, religious or educational groups)

Are you actively involved in any of the following clubs or associations?
Sports club
Sports supporters club
Social club
Hobby or interest group
Church or religious group
Other

general is: excellent, good, fair or poor?' It is conventional to examine the risk of ill-health, and logistic regression was therefore used to estimate a model with a binary response (poor/fair vs. good/excellent health). Variables were fitted in the model one at a time and a sequence of multi-variate models was then estimated, with particular variables dropping out if they were not significant at the 5 per cent level. In essence, the aim is to find a set of variables that predict whether people are more likely to report poor, as opposed to good, health.

The overall response rate to the survey was 44 per cent, though this varied by locality (35–7 per cent in the more deprived areas and 47–56 per cent in the more affluent localities). A total of 777 questionnaires were returned and analysed.

Locating people in geographical and social space

In all four study areas, approximately 60 per cent of the respondents were women. The overwhelming majority (ranging from 93 to 100 per cent) of respondents described their ethnic group as 'White'. The age structure of each locality was broadly similar in three localities (approximately 20 per cent aged under 30, 25 per cent over 60 years), though Torrisholme had an older age structure (9 per cent under 30, 40 per cent over 60 years).

As expected, there were marked differences between the two sets of localities in terms of material circumstances, as evidenced by indicators such as social class, unemployment, low income and tenure (see Table 10.2). About 30 per cent of those in Skerton and Weaste/Seedley/Langworthy had household incomes of less than £6000, compared with about 10 per cent in the more affluent localities. Likewise, 30 per cent of those in the more deprived localities were in social classes IV and V (manual occupations), compared with 8 per cent in Worsley/Boothstown and 13 per cent in Torrisholme. Turning to simple indicators of perceived quality of life, there are clear differences between the deprived and more affluent areas, in terms of perceptions of vandalism and hazards from drug abuse, although vandalism seems a particular problem in Weaste/Seedley/Langworthy and discarded needles and syringes in Skerton. Speeding traffic is a problem in both the more disadvantaged study areas but less so in the other localities. Access to leisure and public transport is more complex, with those in Worsley/Boothstown feeling relatively poorly served (though presumably better placed materially to counteract this lack of access). A 'sense of community' is lacking in a third of our respondents in the more disadvantaged areas, while only 12 per cent of respondents elsewhere agreed that there was no sense of community where they lived. We now consider the extent to which these and other variables shape health.

Describing and explaining health outcomes

Our results from the multivariate analysis indicate that both material circumstances (as represented by household income) and health behaviours (diet) are predictive of poor self-reported health (see Table 10.3). For example, taking the lowest income as a reference category, we see that those with household incomes of between £6000 and £10,000 are 18 per cent less

Table 10.2 Individual material circumstances and perceived quality of life among respondents in the four localities

	Weaste/ Seedley/ Langworthy %	Skerton %	Worsley/ Boothstown %	Torrisholme %
Material circumstances				
Social class IV and V	30	30	8	13
Unemployed	7	9	1	2
Income < £6000	27	29	8	12
Between 75% and 100% of income from benefits	36	36	19	21
Renting	27	32	8	5
Perceptions of area				
Poor leisure facilities	68	64	75	36
Poor public transport	33	28	46	20
Vandalism	60	23	9	5
Discarded needles	2	12	1	1
Speeding traffic	45	40	32	23
No sense of community	36	32	12	13
No one to chat to	11	7	7	3

Note: Numbers are percentages of respondents in each locality.

likely than the poorest group to report ill-health; this is the interpretation of the odds ratio of 0.82. However, since the confidence interval (0.50–1.35) includes 1.0 we cannot say that this reduction in the odds of poor health is statistically significant. But those on higher incomes have consistently lower

Table 10.3 Logistic regression analysis exploring correlates of poor self-reported health

Explanatory variables	Odds ratio	95% Confidence intervals	
		Lower	Upper
Income			
< 5999	1.00		
6000–9999	0.82	0.50	1.35
10,000–19,999	0.65	0.40	1.05
20,000– 39,999	0.29	0.15	0.53
> 40,000	0.21	0.07	0.65
Missing	1.13	0.60	2.13
Loneliness			
Most of the time	1.00		
Quite often	0.70	0.25	1.99
Occasionally	0.73	0.28	1.89
Seldom	0.51	0.20	1.33
Never	0.31	0.12	0.79
Diet			
As healthy as it could be	1.00		
Quite good	0.99	0.66	1.47
Not very healthy	2.09	1.22	3.59
Don't know	1.47	0.45	4.73
Connections with family and friends			
High	1.00		
Low	2.67	1.26	5.68
Access to facilities			
High	1.00		
Medium	1.34	0.79	2.29
Low	1.73	0.96	3.12
Border: high/medium	1.16	0.54	2.48
Border: high/low	1.00	0.43	2.35
Border: medium/low	5.79	2.03	16.53
Indistinguishable	2.06	0.24	17.87
Participation in the local community			
High	1.00		
Low	1.51	1.08	2.11

Note: The first category in each variable is the reference category.

odds of reporting ill-health than poorer people and when incomes exceed £20,000 we see genuine differences between this group and those in the poorest group.

Those reporting diets as 'not very healthy' also report significantly poorer health. They are over twice as likely to report this, compared with those who consider their diet to be healthy. In addition, respondents who say they are never lonely are significantly less likely to report ill-health. Perceived access to facilities is also a significant influence, with those reporting low access (or in a marginal 'medium/low' category) having poorer health. This indicates that one type of area effect plays a role in shaping health outcome.

What components of social capital are important? From Table 10.3, we see that 'participation in the local community', and 'connections with family and friends' are key influences. Results suggest that those who participate less in the local community, or have fewer connections, report poorer health. Our statistical analysis thus suggests that the differences in health status among those living in the four areas are accounted for by a mix of individual-level variables (including material circumstances, loneliness and reported diet) but also by measures of service provision and by dimensions of social capital.

Are these findings illuminated when we examine our two early in-depth interviews? We consider the accounts given by 'Sally', who lives in Weaste, a relatively deprived part of Salford, and 'Laura', who lives on the fringe of the more affluent Torrisholme area in Lancaster. Both women are White, in their forties and living with their husbands and school-age children. Both husbands are in full-time employment and their houses are owner-occupied and semi-detached, with gardens. Neither have very high total household incomes (both under £15,000). Laura works part-time, while Sally is a full-time housewife. Both had replied 'good' to the question on health status (and therefore fall into the same category in the standard health measure used in quantitative studies). In many ways, then, the women are similar; our aim is to see how their experiences and social worlds differ according to the type of area in which they live.

The interviews were largely unstructured and conversational in style and began with the interviewer posing the question 'What is it like to live around here?'. Both Laura and Sally gave lengthy and markedly contrasting accounts about the features, qualities and personal impacts of their areas. In these accounts, there is much which can be interpreted as evidence of high (Laura) and low (Sally) stocks of social capital at the individual level. For example, there is a strong contrast with regard to participation in the local community. Laura, in relatively affluent Torrisholme, participates actively in community networks, assisting in the running of a local organization for young children and involving herself regularly in church events. She also describes a quite extensive local network of friends and family and has the latter nearby: '. . . my mum and dad live in Lancaster and [my husband's] mum and dad live in Torrisholme, so we are equal time for getting to their houses and stuff'. Sally, in Weaste, highlights the relative social isolation of herself and her family. Her wider family network had dissolved as parents died and other relatives moved away and she does not participate to any meaningful extent in other informal or organized community networks. This is not because she does not want to be part of such networks. On the contrary, she expresses the desire to get to know people and participate in some way, but '. . . community wise I can't seem to find anything at all'. She goes on to say 'I find it hard to relate to some people from this area'. She describes in detail the changing social composition of the locality over the last decade, dissociating herself from what she perceives to be a growing 'wayward element' who 'cause trouble' in the neighbourhood. Sally laments the fact that, as old people die, many of the houses stand empty: 'the people who may have steady jobs are not going to buy houses in this area, they have no confidence in the area'.

Sally's account also highlights her lack of social capital along another dimension: feelings of trust and safety. She paints a picture of urban decay and the growth of a hostile environment: 'there is certainly more crime in this area that wouldn't have occurred even five to six years ago . . . car crime, thieving of cars and people abandoning cars and setting fire to them'. Laura, in contrast, describes her area as 'fairly quiet' and identifies speeding traffic as the only threat to personal safety. She feels 'like' the other people around her and the implicit message in her account is that the people in her neighbourhood are, on the whole, trustworthy.

So, there is much in these women's narratives which is strongly suggestive of the importance of dimensions of social capital for their sense of well-being and health chances, but they both draw attention to other features of their areas which lends support to the statistical evidence that 'access to facilities' is also of relevance. Laura paints a favourable picture in this regard: 'we quite like living here in this area because we are sort of in between everything. We are equal distance to Lancaster and Morecambe. Asda is quite local. We have a Spar just round the back, a hairdresser's, newsagent, a post office, so it's handy'. Local facilities of all kinds were also perceived to be of good quality. Sally, on the other hand, describes a steady decline in the number and quality of local facilities: she talks about a relatively recent past when there were busy local shops, schools with high standards of achievement, good sporting facilities, and cultural and entertainment venues. Now, schools are failing, sports facilities are closed and vandalized, and the area is a 'cultural desert'. With her low family income, Sally cannot avail herself of better facilities further afield. She does make use of local shops but she travels to these by car rather than walk, partly because she gets tired, but to a large extent because she finds it depressing to walk through the neighbourhood: ' . . . you have got litter, you have got empty properties that are either boarded up or people have tried to break into them and vandalize them, and you have gardens that are not cultivated . . . I find that quite dispiriting'. Sally feels that her community has been neglected by those in authority and that no one seems to care that the local housing stock is in a dire state. These kinds of lived experiences certainly give us insight into the ways in which statistically identified 'area effects' manifest themselves in the lives and psychosocial states of individuals.

Discussion and policy implications

Our statistical work can therefore describe the 'significance' of particular variables but we require qualitative data to uncover their 'meaning'. Our preliminary analysis of such data helps us to understand the complex ramifications of the relationships between area or place, health and sense of well-being. We cannot, of course, draw any direct conclusions from two illustrative examples, but they do begin to suggest ways in which people's accounts can show how the experience of place, whether current or past, is fundamental to the quality and meaning of day-to-day life. Woven into these accounts are: features of social relations with people known and unknown; the past and present of places, made significant because they are bound up with individuals' biographies; the physical fabrics of the locality; and the local geographies of services and facilities.

Such accounts are beginning to suggest that, in combination, features of place can be either sustaining or undermining of psychosocial well-being and health. Sally reports her own health as 'good' now, but what will be the long-term health effects of living in an area which she experiences as in decay, populated by people with whom she cannot identify and pervaded by a sense of hopelessness, abandonment and neglect? However, Sally is not a passive victim of place and circumstance. She is someone who draws on her personal resources to create a home for her family which is a 'haven in a heartless world' and to put into practice the sophisticated knowledge that she has about health-promoting behaviours. An important feature of the qualitative data in our study is that it enables us to understand how people exercise their agency: how they can attempt to resist the undermining effects of health-damaging social environments.

These interviews are beginning to inform our understanding of how living out daily lives in contrasting areas has consequences for health and well-being. Our statistical results suggest that there are differences in self-reported health that cannot be attributed solely to individual factors. The locations of people with respect to services and facilities makes a difference, confirming earlier findings in Glasgow (Macintyre *et al.* 1993). In addition, the social networks existing within the localities appear to play a significant part in shaping reported health outcomes (though further work is needed to confirm that positive stocks of social capital produce good health, rather than poor health limiting social engagement). Socio-spatial context there-

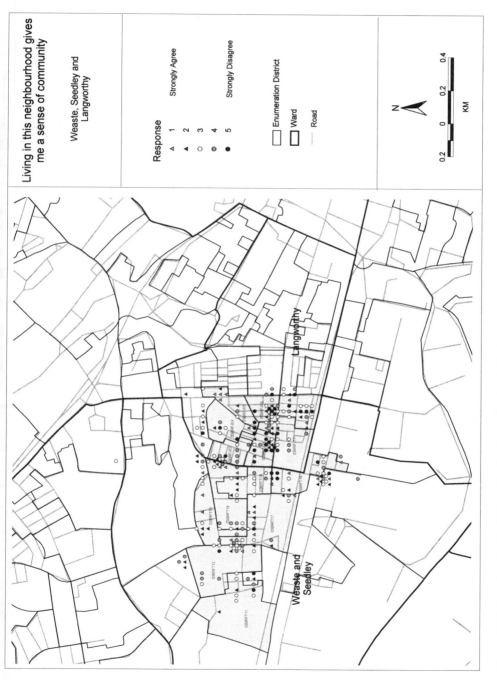

Figure 10.1 Social capital in Weaste/Seedley/Langworthy, Salford

fore has some predictive power, even though we would wish to give more weight to the 'social' as opposed to the 'geographical' space. But we also wish to emphasize that our areas or localities mask considerable local heterogeneity (see Figure 10.1), such that even within a 'deprived' area there are those whose sense of community differs quite dramatically from that of relatively near neighbours.

The kinds of influences that emerge from the two interviews are not so dissimilar to those we have attempted to capture in quantifiable form. We see this mixed quantitative-qualitative approach as a contribution to new structure-agency debates as well as illuminating the broadly-based notion of social capital. But this is an interim statement. In the meantime we agree with Bartley *et al.* (1998: 8) that 'future research may well set out to discover how action is shaped by the narratives people construct to make sense of their own encounters with inequality'.

What of the policy implications? In her recent review, Whitehead (1995: 24) suggested that policy initiatives to tackle inequalities in health can be classified into those that strengthen individuals and communities, those that improve access to essential services and facilities, and those that encourage macroeconomic and cultural change. In a sense, our work impacts upon all these broad areas of social policy, though it is beginning to suggest that policies that improve local social capital and contribute to 'how people in disadvantaged communities can join together for mutual support and in so doing strengthen the whole community's defence against health hazards' (Whitehead 1995: 25) might bear dividends. Equally, we have produced evidence implicating the variable quality of the local infrastructure in health outcomes.

Interestingly, a focus on social capital is emerging in some of the Health Action Zones established in 1998. For example, North Cumbria emphasizes 'community participation, not just for the few but the many' (North Cumbria Health Authority 1998: 3). The same Health Action Zone implementation plan recognizes that service infrastructure must play a part in reducing inequalities. Our work goes some way towards offering some justification for a continued emphasis on social capital and the resource bases of local communities. But its interim message is that relations within social spaces need close attention, as does the heterogeneity of those small areas which secondary data might portray as uniformly 'deprived'.

Acknowledgements

This chapter draws on research funded by the ESRC (L128251020) under the Health Variations Programme. We are grateful to Professor Sally Macintyre (MRC Social and Public Health Sciences Unit, University of Glasgow) for generous use of her questionnaire. The background information in Figure 10.1 is from the Ordnance Survey and is Crown Copyright.

References

Bartley, M., Blane, D. and Davey Smith, G. (1998) Introduction: beyond the Black Report, in M. Bartley, D. Blane and G. Davey Smith (eds) *The Sociology of Health Inequalities*. Oxford: Blackwell.

Bullen, P. and Onyx, J. (1998) Measuring social capital in five communities in New South Wales, Working paper 41. Sydney: Centre for Australian Community Organizations and Management, University of Technology. Overview available at: *http: //www.mapl.com.au/A2.htm*.

Campbell, C. (1999) *Social Capital and Health*. London: Health Education Authority.

Cooper, H., Arber, S., Fee, L. and Ginn, J. (1999) *The Influence of Social Support and Capital on Health*. London: Health Education Authority.

Cornwell, J. (1984) *Hard-Earned Lives: Accounts of Health and Illness from East London*. London: Tavistock.

Curtis, S. and Jones, I.R. (1998) Is there a place for geography in the analysis of health inequality? in M. Bartley, D. Blane and G. Davey Smith (eds) *The Sociology of Health Inequalities*. Oxford: Blackwell.

Elstad, J.I. (1998) The psycho-social perspective on social inequalities in health, in M. Bartley, D. Blane and G. Davey Smith (eds) *The Sociology of Health Inequalities*. Oxford: Blackwell.

Macintyre, S., MacIver, S. and Sooman, A. (1993) Area, class and health: should we be focusing on places or people? *Journal of Social Policy*, 22: 213–34.

North Cumbria Health Authority (1998) *North Cumbria Health Action Zone*. Carlisle: North Cumbria Health Authority.

Phillimore, P. (1993) How do places shape health? Rethinking locality and lifestyle in north-east England, in S. Platt, H. Thomas, S. Scott and G. Williams (eds) *Locating Health: Sociological and Historical Explorations*. Aldershot: Avebury Press.

Popay, J., Williams, G., Thomas, C. and Gatrell, A. (1998) Theorising inequalities in health: the place of lay knowledge, in M. Bartley, D. Blane and G. Davey Smith (eds) *The Sociology of Health Inequalities*. Oxford: Blackwell.

Putnam, R.D., Leonardi, R. and Nanetti, R.Y. (1993) *Making Democracy Work: Civic Traditions in Modern Italy*. Princeton, NJ: Princeton University Press.

Sooman, A. and Macintyre, S. (1995) Health and perceptions of the local environment in socially contrasting neighbourhoods in Glasgow, *Health and Place*, 1: 15–26.

Stanley, L. and Wise, S. (1990) Method, methodology and epistemology in feminist research processes, in L. Stanley (ed.) *Feminist Praxis: Research, Theory and Epistemology in Feminist Sociology*. London: Routledge.

Whitehead, M. (1995) Tackling inequalities: a review of policy initiatives, in M. Benzeval, K. Judge and M. Whitehead (eds) *Tackling Inequalities in Health*. London: King's Fund.

Wilkinson, R.G. (1996) *Unhealthy Societies: The Afflictions of Inequality*. London: Routledge.

Individual deprivation, neighbourhood and recovery from illness

Elspeth Graham, Malcolm MacLeod, Marie Johnston, Chris Dibben, Irene Morgan and Sylvie Briscoe

Introduction

> What we need for policy formation is more information on the *mechanisms* by which social class or area of residence might influence health in positive or negative ways.
>
> (Macintyre *et al.* 1993: 232)

The social inequalities in health in Britain are now well-known. Geographical variations in life expectancy and morbidity persist, with some researchers identifying a North/South divide (Dorling 1997; Wiggins and Mitchell 1998), while others find urban/rural differences (Phillimore and Reading 1992; Congdon 1994) or pockets of especially high mortality and morbidity in coalfield areas (Higgs *et al.* 1998; Wiggins and Mitchell 1998). What is not yet clear, however, is whether these spatial patterns result simply from the geographical distribution of various social groups in Britain (that is, from the social *composition* of areas) or whether there is an additional effect of *context* such that, for example, living in Scotland might constitute a health risk independently of the socio-economic characteristics of individuals living there (see Chapters 1, 9, 10 and 12).

Much of the empirical evidence used to examine these compositional and contextual factors comes from large-scale studies using all-cause mortality data or census data on limiting long-term illness. Such studies have two important and related limitations. First, the conclusions drawn are inevitably general due to the health measures used; second, the suggested explanations of the spatial patterns of health inequality are largely speculative because little attention is given to the mechanisms which might explain the statistical associations identified. The aim of our research is to move beyond these limitations by explicitly investigating the causal pathways which link the socio-economic characteristics of individuals and areas to one particular health outcome: recovery from first acute myocardial infarction (MI) (heart attack).

Deprivation and recovery from myocardial infarction

More than a quarter of all deaths in Scotland are caused by coronary heart disease (CHD), which is the most common cause of death. There are also marked geographical variations and social inequalities in CHD mortality rates within Scotland and a recent study has demonstrated that socio-economic deprivation is associated with reduced access to certain types of treatment (MacLeod *et al.* 1999). The socio-economic gradient in CHD mortality is also reflected in age-standardized first acute MI admission rates for both males and females under 65 years of age (McLaren and Bain 1998). Less is known about the process of recovery itself and whether those who are more deprived in society, and thus at higher risk of suffering an acute MI, also show poorer rates of recovery. Further, if they do, how is it that deprivation impacts on recovery? There are a number of possible explanations. For example, the more deprived tend to have more severe MIs and to be at greater risk from health-related behaviours such as smoking. In addition, those who are less well-off may suffer from greater anxiety and depression, and from lower self-esteem, all of which could affect recovery.

Our particular interest is in whether or not social comparison processes are implicated in these relationships. Could it be, for example, that high levels of depression and anxiety, or low self-esteem, are themselves the outcome of a process in which deprived individuals compare themselves unfavourably with others around them? Could this explain the socio-economic *gradient* in health, where being only a little less well-off than the least deprived still incurs a comparative health deficit? Some support for this idea comes from studies which suggest that *relative* wealth, rather than absolute level of income, predicts levels of health in developed societies. According to Wilkinson (1996), socio-economic differences in health are not reducible to the most obvious causes, such as differences in medical care, behavioural choices, social mobility and genetics. Rather, it is the more egalitarian societies, with greater social cohesion, that enjoy higher standards of physical health and longevity. Thus social relativities play a key role in health outcomes. Social inequality, at least at the national scale, is bad for health and recent evidence suggests that such associations are not simply statistical artefacts (Wolfson *et al.* 1999). The key questions we want to address are whether *local* social relativities are also bad for the health of *individuals* and what mechanisms might account for any association found.

Our study is based on interview data collected from a sample of 200 patients recruited at the Coronary Care Unit, Ninewells Hospital, Dundee, Scotland. This dataset includes detailed information on local environment, housing, income, family and social comparisons, as well as a range of established psychological measures designed to quantify, for example, levels of anxiety (Hospital Anxiety and Depression Scale – HADS) or self-esteem (Rosenberg Self-esteem Scale) (see Johnston *et al.* 1995). Patients are interviewed in their own homes at around 5 weeks (time 1), and again at 15 weeks (time 2), post-MI. The extent of their recovery is estimated by comparing measured scores at first interview with those at second interview. For the purposes of this chapter, we will use scores derived from the Functional Limitation Profile (FLP) (Johnston *et al.* 1995) to estimate recovery over a two-month period. The short timescale and its relationship to the date of first MI should be noted. It was chosen because it provides a controlled window through which to examine the effects of psychological factors at a stage in the recovery trajectory when greater changes are occurring.

All of the patients in the sample were diagnosed on admission to hospital as suffering from first acute MI. The sample itself cannot claim to be representative of all first MI patients as it excludes those who died, those who declined to be interviewed and those who were too ill or for other reasons could not complete the long interviews. Thus it is likely that the sample misses some of the most deprived patients. We are still conducting interviews and any biases in our final sample will be investigated after completing the data collection. It should be remembered, however, that our major concern is with the effects of *relative* deprivation on health outcome and thus with differences across the socio-economic spectrum. Currently 150 patients have completed both interviews and the results reported in this chapter are from a preliminary analysis of these 150 cases. Despite restricted numbers, this subset of the final sample is not homogeneous in terms of wealth: annual income for the highest quartile of the distribution is twice that for the lowest quartile (see Figure 11.1).

The measure of income we use is equivalized individual net income which takes into account the structure of the household (McClements 1978) and is thus comparable between individuals. The mean equivalized individual income for the 141 patients who provided income details is £11,954 per annum. The modal income is £7500, indicating that the sample tends to be weighted towards the lower end of the income spectrum.

Ninewells is a large teaching hospital located in the City of Dundee but serving a much wider area of Tayside, Fife and Perth, and Kinross. The patients in our sample are dispersed throughout this area. Many live in small towns or rural communities but 62 per cent live in Dundee itself. The social geography of the area is equally varied with pockets of high deprivation,

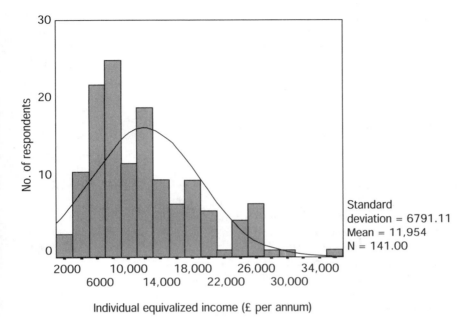

No. of respondents

Standard
deviation = 6791.11
Mean = 11,954
N = 141.00

Individual equivalized income (£ per annum)

Figure 11.1 Individual equivalized net income

especially in the city, but also pockets of considerable affluence. This is reflected in the income distribution within our respondent group. Previous ecological research, examining areas rather than individuals, has shown that levels of deprivation and levels of illness in the population are positively associated (Carstairs and Morris 1991). Our initial expectation was therefore that income, as a measure of an individual's material resources, would also be correlated with recovery from illness.

Does income predict recovery from first MI for this group of patients? The answer cannot be unequivocal. On the one hand, no statistically significant association was found between individual income and the extent of overall recovery from MI.[1] On the other hand, the FLP which we are using to measure recovery has two subscales, allowing us to distinguish between physical and psychosocial aspects of recovery. For all recovery measures, higher values denote better recovery. Interestingly, individual income is a significant predictor of physical recovery, but accounts for only 3.2 per cent of the variance ($r = .197$, adjusted $R^2 = .032$, $p < .05$). Thus those with lower incomes also appear to suffer poorer physical recovery than others in the sample, but not necessarily poorer overall recovery. This suggests both that an individual's material resources alone are not a major influence on physical recovery and that factors other than an individual's wealth are determining overall recovery between 5 and 15 weeks post-MI. The causal pathways linking deprivation with this particular health outcome are thus likely to be both complex and multiple. To give explicit recognition to this, the discussion will focus first on one possible pathway which might link material deprivation and physical recovery.

A multi-variate model of physical recovery

If income only contributes a small amount to the prediction of physical recovery, two questions arise. First, what other factors might combine with income to improve the predictive power of the model? Second, is it possible that psychosocial processes and/or psychological states might act as mediators or intervening variables? International comparisons of levels of wealth and health have been used to argue that income distribution is a more important influence on health than absolute levels of income (Wilkinson 1996). Moreover, income inequality may also have an adverse effect on health at a much more local level. Ben-Shlomo *et al.* (1996), for example, found that mortality rates in England were positively associated with the degree of socio-economic variation within small geographic areas.

Our own research has revealed a more complex picture of how local social geographies impact on health, with different spatial patterns of social inequality being positively and negatively related to morbidity. Using data from the 1991 census, we found that levels of limiting long-term illness in small census areas were significantly related to deprivation levels in these areas. However, they were also related, positively, to social mix and, negatively, to deprivation levels in surrounding areas (Graham *et al.* 1999). This suggests that relative deprivation may also have an influential spatial dimension. Of course, such studies can only identify ecological associations between area measures of health and spatial variations in deprivation. They do not tell us which individuals are most affected by socio-economic heterogeneity nor do they explain how *relative* deprivation might adversely affect the health of individuals even in circumstances of general improvements in income. Nevertheless, they do suggest a hypothesis which can be tested by extending our simple model relating income to recovery.

We can hypothesize that physical recovery from first MI is significantly related not only to the income of our individual patients but also to three further variables:

- their wealth *relative* to the wealth of others in their area of residence;
- the social mix in their area of residence;
- the level of general morbidity in their area of residence.

The latter is included to allow us to explore the possibility that comparing one's health, as well as one's wealth, with that of others might influence recovery from first MI. Since our interest is in the scope people have for making comparisons, we adopted a simple measure of morbidity (the percentage of population in an individual's neighbourhood reporting limiting long-term illness) for our preliminary analysis.

To our knowledge, no study to date has investigated the impact of socio-economic relativities between individuals and those in their local neighbourhood on any health outcome. Thus testing the hypothesis is not straightforward because there are no established measures of relative wealth which could be used. One immediate problem is that individual income (based on interview data) and area deprivation (based on census variables) are measured in different ways, although the measures are related ($r = -.338$, $p < .01$) as might be expected since individuals will tend to live in areas where they can afford housing. We have thus devised a measure to use in this preliminary analysis which we call 'wealth difference' and which allows for the relationship between income and area deprivation. Essentially, this formalizes the general relationship between the equivalized income of individual patients and a measure of deprivation for the neighbourhood in which they live; it then measures the extent to which individuals depart from the general relationship. The size of a neighbourhood is allowed to vary between individuals according to features of local social geography.[2] Thus we can interpret this measure as indicating when an individual is living in an area less, or more, deprived than could be 'bought' with their given level of income. Despite the imperfections of such a measure, its inclusion in our model produces an important result (see Table 11.1).

The model presented in Table 11.1 was fitted to a sample of 140 patients (10 patients for whom data were missing were excluded from our subset of 150). The overall model predicts nearly 15 per cent of the variance in physical recovery (adjusted $R^2 = .148$, $p < .001$). Given the absence of other important variables (for example, measures of the seriousness of the heart attack), to account for even this percentage of the variance must be seen as notable and the model is clearly an improvement on the bi-variate analysis using income alone. Moreover, as the standardized beta values reveal, it is not an individual's income but rather the difference in wealth between an individual and their neighbourhood which contributes most to the prediction. Specifically, those patients living in areas more deprived than expected given their equivalized incomes show relatively poor recovery. This is consistent with one of the results from our analysis of census areas in which we found similar 'pull-down' and 'pull-up' effects (Graham *et al.* 1999).

The third variable in Table 11.1 assesses the extent to which a patient's neighbourhood is socially homogeneous. It is also significantly associated with physical recovery from first MI: greater social homogeneity appears to be related to poorer recovery. This is the reverse of what we expected but is partly explained by our measure which we intend to refine further. At present it mainly reflects the proportion of 'low income' people in an area and is thus picking up the deprivation of the patient's neighbourhood. In general, what this model indicates is that, although lower incomes are associated with poorer recovery, when an individual lives in an area with a higher number of deprived people than their income predicts, they suffer an additional health disadvantage. The impact of social mix in a neighbourhood requires further investigation but these preliminary results do tend to confirm the importance of social and spatial relativities to health outcomes.

The fourth variable, the level of morbidity in the neighbourhood in which an individual resides, is also significantly related to physical recovery. In fact, it contributes more to the overall model than either individual income or social mix. Why should it be that those living in areas characterized by higher levels of morbidity show *better* recovery than expected given their other material circumstances? Clearly the measure of area morbidity is not operating here as a surrogate for area deprivation with which it is correlated ($r = .722$, $p < .01$). The deprivation score for the neighbourhood in which an individual lives is predictive of physical recovery from first MI ($r = -.169$, adjusted $R^2 = .022$, $p < .05$), but the association is a negative one such that those who live in more deprived areas also show poorer recovery. However, in the model (see Table 11.1), area morbidity is *positively* associated with recovery once the material circumstances of individuals are taken into account. Living in an area with higher numbers of ill neighbours appears to confer a relative health benefit, other things being equal. The apparent paradox is not easily explained but it does emphasize the complexity of the relationships between material deprivation and health outcome, and the possibility of multiple pathways linking the two. The model also opens up

Table 11.1 Fitted model for physical recovery from first MI (n = 140)

Model variables	Unstandardized coefficients B	Std. error	Standardized coefficients Beta
Constant	−1.135*	.458	
Individual income	4.191	.000	.280***
Wealth difference (between individual and neighbourhood)	−.397	.117	−.382***
Social mix (social homogeneity in neighbourhood)	−.016	.006	−.221*
Level of morbidity (limiting long-term illness in neighbourhood)	.076	.027	.335**
		Adjusted $R^2 = 0.148$***	

Notes: ***p < .001; **p < .01; *p < .05.

the possibility that social comparison processes are implicated in these pathways since the 'wealth difference' variable is plausibly interpreted as indicative of the scope that individuals have for comparing their own wealth with that of those around them. Equally, the number of ill people surrounding an individual may have an impact on recovery through a comparison process in which those living in areas with low levels of morbidity (usually the less deprived areas) perceive their own health to be worse than that of others and show poorer recovery as a result. Before we can assess the validity of these ideas, we need to look more closely at some of the relationships involved.

Social comparison processes

If we are correct in our assessment that relative material deprivation (measured here by income and wealth difference) is an important predictor of health status and recovery, and that the perception of deprivation relative to others is an important component of this relationship, it would seem plausible that psychological factors (for example, self-esteem, depression) and health-related behaviours (for example, exercise, smoking) might also be implicated. One possibility is that such factors may be intervening variables in the relationship between deprivation and health (see Figure 11.2). We could posit, for example, that those who are more deprived in society will, because of their position relative to others, experience more depression and anxiety which, in turn, may be associated with lower levels of well-being

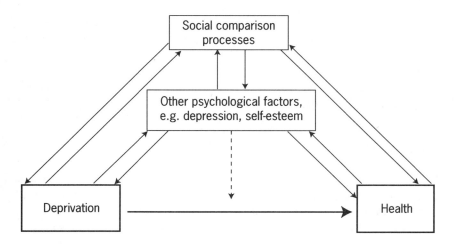

Figure 11.2 Summary of possible relationships between social comparisons, other psychological factors, deprivation and health

and poorer health. Additionally, we could argue that such psychological factors might be viewed as the product of other more fundamental psychological processes.

One of the basic psychological processes in which we engage is the process of comparing ourselves with other people. Psychologists have long recognized that comparisons with other people represent an important source of information for how we evaluate ourselves (Festinger 1954; Schachter 1959), how we may achieve self-improvement (Wilson and Brenner 1971) and as a means of restoring our self-esteem (Wills 1981). Thus, we are currently examining two possible pathways by which relative deprivation might affect health – namely via (a) wealth comparisons, and (b) health comparisons, both of which are suggested by the model in Table 11.1.

The following discussion outlines some of our preliminary results but these must be seen as provisional since the full dataset is not yet complete and there are important aspects of the analysis which have yet to be pursued. For example, other research has demonstrated that the classic social gradient in mortality from acute MI across Carstairs deprivation categories is evident only for the under 65-year age group and is largely absent for the age group 65 years and over (McLaren and Bain 1998). We have tested our model on the 80 patients who were under 65 years of age at the time of the first interview and found that, although the overall percentage of variance predicted increases (adjusted R^2 = .205, p < .001), the variable measuring social mix in an individual's neighbourhood ceases to be significant. The patient's age is not a significant predictor of physical recovery within this age group, whereas for those aged 65 years and over (n = 64) age alone predicts over 15 per cent of the variance in recovery (r = −.412, adjusted R^2 = .156, p < .01). Clearly these differences require further investigation but for the purposes of the present discussion they are ignored and the results reported are based on data for all 150 patients whose ages range from 32 to 85 years, with a mean age of 60.5 years.

Data on social comparisons can be difficult to elicit from respondents, especially if making comparisons is seen as socially undesirable. Despite this, many of the patients in our sample did compare their own material circumstances to those of others when asked a general question about whether there were any occasions recently when they had made such comparisons. Unsurprisingly in the context of their recent MI, more of our respondents made spontaneous health comparisons. However, in order to secure sufficient data for our analysis we also included questions later in the interview which required respondents to compare their own wealth and health with that of others.[3] It is these forced-choice comparisons that are used in our preliminary analysis and caution must be exercised when interpreting the results since they do not distinguish between individuals who generally do make such comparisons spontaneously and those who do not. Nevertheless, we found that forced-choice wealth comparisons are not significantly related to our wealth difference measure, contrary to what we hypothesized, but are related to individual income such that people with higher incomes perceive themselves as being better off than others around them (r = .377, adjusted R^2 = .135, p < .001). Individual income also significantly predicts self-esteem, such that people with higher incomes in our sample reported higher levels of self-esteem (r = −.333, adjusted R^2 = .104, p < .001), whereas our measure of wealth difference does not. Neither measure of wealth is significantly related to anxiety at five weeks post-MI. However, forced-choice wealth comparisons do significantly predict self-esteem – that is, the more wealthy you think you are relative to others around you, the more likely you are to have high self-esteem (r = −.344, adjusted R^2 = .111, p < .001). These results do not entirely accord with our expectations but they do indicate some possible pathways between material deprivation and health outcome.

The second hypothesis derived from our model (Table 11.1) is that those who live in areas with few long-term ill neighbours are more likely to perceive their own health as worse than that of others, have lower self-esteem and heightened anxiety, and thus make a poorer recovery. When we tested these relationships, we found that, as expected, the level of morbidity in a respondent's neighbourhood does not, on its own, predict recovery from first MI, but it also fails to predict either self-esteem or anxiety as measured at first interview. Nor does it predict forced-choice health comparisons, which is unsurprising as other factors are likely to be involved. For example, how ill a person was at five weeks post-MI (time 1) could be expected to be related to how ill they thought they were in relation to others. This was confirmed by our analysis which found that the level of overall functional limitation (FLP total score) at time 1 significantly predicts forced-choice health comparisons so that the more ill a respondent is, the more likely they are to say that they are more ill than friends and neighbours (r = −.420, adjusted R^2 = .170, p < .001). Further, forced-choice health comparisons significantly predict self-esteem to the extent that those who think themselves more ill than others are more likely to have lower self-esteem (r = −.299, adjusted R^2 = .082, p < .001). Importantly, forced-choice health comparisons also significantly predict anxiety (that is, the more ill respondents perceive themselves to be relative to others, the more anxious they are; r = −.409, adjusted R^2 = .161, p < .001). Thus we have identified a relationship between perceived relative health and our measures of self-esteem and anxiety which may form part of a pathway linking psychological factors to recovery from first MI. What is less clear is whether there is a relationship between material deprivation and perceived relative health.

Forced-choice health comparisons appear to be related to the level of functional limitation experienced by a respondent at five weeks post-MI rather than to the social or material circumstances of the individual. It could be, however, that more deprived individuals also experienced greater functional limitation at time 1. We found that individual income does significantly predict functional limitation (FLP total score) at five weeks post-MI but the percentage of variance explained is low ($r = -.171$, adjusted $R^2 = .022$, $p < .05$). None of the other measures of deprivation in our general model of physical recovery was found to be significantly related to functional limitation at time 1. This suggests that material deprivation is not a major predictor of the impact of MI, although the relationship will be explored in more detail once the full dataset is complete. Nevertheless, we found that overall functional limitation at time 1 and forced-choice money comparisons, together, are both significantly related to perceived relative health and predict 24 per cent of the variance (adjusted $R^2 = .240$, $p < .001$). Thus once functional limitation at time 1 is taken into consideration, those who perceive themselves as being materially better off than others are more likely also to perceive their health as better than that of those around them. These results are far from conclusive but they do indicate that both wealth and health comparisons may be implicated in complex ways in the relationships between the relative deprivation of individuals and their recovery from first MI.

This preliminary analysis gives some support to the idea that socio-economic relativities are important to health outcome, but it also leaves a puzzle which requires further research. On the one hand, our measures of individual income, wealth difference and social mix appear to predict physical recovery from first MI. On the other hand, perceptions of relative wealth appear to predict self-esteem and thus may be linked to recovery. Yet we have only been able to show that perceiving oneself as relatively wealthy (or deprived) is related to individual income. It appears that local socio-economic relativities, despite their relationship to physical recovery for our sample of respondents, are not related to how these same respondents perceive their own relative wealth. In sum, we have yet to find any mechanisms which might link the geography of relative deprivation and the psychological factors and processes implicated in recovery from first acute MI.

Future analysis and policy implications

The results we have presented are based on a preliminary analysis of a subset of our final sample. A fuller investigation of the larger completed sample using path analysis has yet to be done. This research, we believe, will have implications for health policy but it would be premature to make any detailed recommendations. Nevertheless, it is possible to draw out some general policy implications which are worthy of consideration.

First, there are indications that poverty is associated with poorer recovery but that the pathways linking deprivation and health are likely to be multiple. Others have suggested that improving the standards of living of poor households might prevent ill-health (Independent Inquiry into

Inequalities in Health 1998); our results suggest that it might also serve to reduce the effects of disease. Those on lower incomes are more likely to show poorer physical recovery from first MI and thus may benefit more from cardiac rehabilitation services. There is evidence from work with patients in the same clinical unit that cardiac rehabilitation can enhance recovery (Johnston *et al.* 1999b) and it will be important to ensure that poorer people have good access to it. Perhaps our most important finding to date, however, is that an individual's income plays only a small part in predicting recovery. If this is confirmed by further research, then any general increases in future income are unlikely to have a major impact on recovery from first MI. As Sloggett and Joshi (1998) suggest, it appears that improving material circumstances is not a complete answer to improving health. However, local socio-economic relativities were found to be associated with recovery in our general model (see Table 11.1), suggesting that policies which aim to reduce wealth inequalities might be more successful in reducing health inequalities.

Second, the characteristics of neighbourhoods do appear to influence an individual's health outcome but in quite complex ways. The implication here is that those most at risk of making a poor recovery are not necessarily the most deprived individuals living in the most deprived areas. Targeting interventions (such as cardiac rehabilitation programmes) at such a group of patients may miss some who could benefit most. Equally, simply concentrating healthcare provision in the most deprived areas may not be the most efficient way of reducing health inequalities.

As these two examples suggest, the policy implications of our findings are not straightforward and it is important to avoid hasty conclusions. The model presented here also indicates that levels of morbidity in a neighbourhood (together with other socio-economic measures) are predictive of physical recovery: patients make a relatively better recovery if surrounded by a community suffering poorer health rather than better health. We do not yet have an explanation for this finding and it would be quite inappropriate to suppose that cardiac patients derive direct benefit from being surrounded by ill neighbours. Indeed, since the relationship does not appear to be due to psychological factors (social comparisons, self-esteem or anxiety), it may be due to the more intensive or skilled provision of health services. Alternatively, individuals from high morbidity (usually more deprived) areas suffering milder health deficits may have experienced less serious MIs. A third possibility is that there may be a stronger expectation or need to resume normal activities in a community where others have more limitations and are less able to provide practical social support. Our data do not allow us to choose between these possible explanations.

Finally, our preliminary findings suggest that social comparison processes predict psychological states such as anxiety and self-esteem. We have yet to examine the relationships between these psychological factors and recovery from first MI. However, we would expect such relationships to be consistent with other data showing that negative affective states predict poor survival in, for example, MI (Frasure-Smith *et al.* 1993) and motor neurone disease (Johnston *et al.* 1999a). Our data suggest that these affective states may be influenced by psychological processes of comparison with other people and that both health and wealth comparisons count. Support or therapeutic intervention for individual MI patients can reduce anxiety (Johnston *et al.* 1999b) and is likely to enhance self-esteem, and it is important to identify those most at risk if such interventions are to be targeted effectively.

The information we are collecting for the 200 patients in our final sample will provide a rich dataset with which to test the ideas and hypotheses we have outlined. Much analysis remains to be done and the implications for health policy must depend on our preliminary findings being replicated. Our results to date lend some support to the claim that policies to reduce wealth inequalities will make a significant contribution to reducing inequalities in health, and may result in some improvement in recovery rates for those who suffer an acute MI. Yet the scope for policy interventions in terms of cardiac rehabilitation services, community social support following MI, and individual counselling and rehabilitation would seem to be considerable. Most importantly, however, a better understanding of the mechanisms by which socio-economic deprivation might influence recovery from MI is a prerequisite for the development of effective policies and strategies to reduce inequalities in outcome. It is our hope that the results of this research will inform the development of such policies and, ultimately, contribute to enhancing recovery from acute MI.

Notes

1 *Recovery:* the recovery measure is the standardized residual resulting from a regression model that attempts to predict an individual's score on the FLP at time 2 from their score at time 1. It measures the extent to which their score at time 2 differs from that expected (in terms of the study sample) given their score at time 1. Scoring was reversed so that a positive score implies better than expected recovery. Three measures of recovery can be derived from the FLP: (a) overall recovery using the total FLP scores; (b) physical recovery using scores from the physical dimension of the FLP only; (c) psychosocial recovery using scores from the psychosocial dimension of the FLP only.

2 *Neighbourhood:* the 'neighbourhood' dataset was constructed using a geographical information system. Each patient was located on a map of output areas (the smallest level of census geography in Scotland). The 'neighbourhood' was then defined as including any output area that intersected a circle, with a radius of 250 metres, drawn around and centring on the patient. Rates were calculated using the variables of interest from the 1991 census Small Area Statistics dataset for all the selected output areas in a 'neighbourhood'.

Area deprivation: defined as the proportion of residents in an area living in a condition indicative of long-term low income: that is, in non-permanent accommodation; local authority, housing association or Scottish Homes accommodation; owner-occupied housing, with a shared bathroom and/or no central heating; and privately rented accommodation, where the household does not own a car. We used this measure in preference to established measures such as the Townsend or Carstairs indexes because of its greater comparability with measures of individual income.

Wealth difference: this variable is the standardized residual (that is, the actual value of the dependent variable minus the value predicted by the regression equation) resulting from a regression model that attempts to predict an individual's neighbourhood deprivation score from their equivalized income. It measures the extent to which the neighbourhood deprivation score differs from that expected (in terms of the study sample) given a specific level of equivalized income. A positive score implies a level of area deprivation higher than expected.

Social mix: this variable measures the ratio of those in a neighbourhood classified as 'deprived' against those who are not, with a highly mixed neighbourhood having 50 per cent of its population classified as deprived. A more homogenous neighbourhood is defined as having, increasingly, *either* less than *or* more than 50 per cent of its population in the 'deprived' category. A low score indicates a mixed neighbourhood, a high score a more homogenous neighbourhood. We are currently seeking to refine this measure.

3 *Social comparisons:* we have collected detailed information on people's spontaneous, prompted and forced-choice comparisons in relation to their perceived wealth, health and quality of living environment. In the present chapter, however, because we are conducting analysis on a subset of our final sample, we chose to employ only our forced-choice comparison data in order to ensure sufficient power for our statistical analyses. Patients were asked about how they perceived themselves in relation to other people (for example, family members and neighbours). A mean score of these comparison judgements was then calculated as an index of the extent to which they perceived themselves as being wealthy or healthy relative to others.

Acknowledgements

This chapter draws on research funded by the ESRC (L128251011) under the Health Variations Programme. Our thanks go to the staff and patients at the Coronary Care Unit, Ninewells Hospital, Dundee, Scotland, without whose help and cooperation this research would have been impossible.

References

Ben-Shlomo, Y., White, I.R. and Marmot, M. (1996) Does variation in the socio-economic characteristics of an area affect mortality? *British Medical Journal*, 312: 1013–14.

Carstairs, V. and Morris, R. (1991) *Deprivation and Health in Scotland*. Aberdeen: Aberdeen University Press.

Congdon, P. (1994) The impact of area context on long term illness and premature mortality: an illustration of multi-level analysis, *Regional Studies*, 29(4): 327–44.

Dorling, D. (1997) *Death in Britain: How Local Mortality Rates Have Changed: 1950s to 1990s*. York: Joseph Rowntree Foundation.

Festinger, L. (1954) A theory of social comparison processes, *Human Relations*, 7: 117–40.

Frasure-Smith, N., Lesperance, F. and Talajic, N. (1993) Depression following myocardial infarction: impact on 6 month survival, *Journal of the American Medical Association*, 270: 1819–25.

Graham, E., Dibben, C. and MacLeod, M. (1999) Geographies of limiting long-term illness: is there a 'neighbourhood' effect? Paper presented to the Royal Geographical Society–Institute of British Geographers Annual Conference, Leicester, 4–7 January.

Higgs, G., Senior, M.L. and Williams, H.C.W.L. (1998) Spatial and temporal variation of mortality and deprivation 1: widening health inequalities, *Environment and Planning A*, 30: 1661–82.

Independent Inquiry into Inequalities in Health (1998) *Independent Inquiry into Inequalities in Health Report* (The Acheson Report). London: The Stationery Office.

Johnston, M., Wright, S. and Weinman, J. (1995) *Measures in Health Psychology: A User's Portfolio*. Windsor: NFER.

Johnston, M., Earll, L. and Giles, M. *et al.* (1999a) Mood as a predictor of disability and survival in patients newly diagnosed with ALS/MND, *British Journal of Health Psychology*, 4: 127–36.

Johnston, M., Foulkes, J., Johnston, D.W., Pollard, B. and Gudmunsdottir, H. (1999b) Impact on patients and partners of inpatient and extended cardiac counselling and rehabilitation: a controlled trial, *Psychosomatic Medicine*, 61: 225–33.

McClements, L. (1978) *The Economics of Social Security*. London: Heinemann.

Macintyre, S., MacIver, S. and Sooman, A. (1993) Area, class and health: should we be focusing on places or people? *Journal of Social Policy*, 22: 213–34.

McLaren, G. and Bain, M. (1998) *Deprivation and Health in Scotland: Insights from NHS Data*. Edinburgh: Information and Statistics Division, National Health Service in Scotland.

MacLeod, M.C.M., Finlayson, A.R., Pell, J.P. and Findlay, I.N. (1999) Geographic, demographic and socioeconomic variations in the investigation and management of coronary heart disease in Scotland, *Heart*, 81: 252–6.

Phillimore, P. and Reading, R. (1992) A rural advantage? Urban-rural health differences in Northern England, *Journal of Public Health Medicine*, 14: 290–9.

Schachter, S. (1959) *The Psychology of Affiliation*. Stanford, CA: Stanford University Press.

Sloggett, A. and Joshi, H. (1998) Indicators of deprivation in people and places: longitudinal perspectives, *Environment and Planning A*, 30: 1055–76.

Wiggins, D. and Mitchell, R. (1998) Car ownership, housing tenure and locality as predictors of long-standing illness in men and women: a 3-level analysis of the

ONS Longitudinal Study of England and Wales, *Risk Decision and Policy*, 3: 181–98.

Wilkinson, R. (1996) *Unequal Societies: The Afflictions of Inequality*. London: Routledge.

Wills, T.A. (1981) Downward comparison principles in social psychology, *Psychological Bulletin*, 90: 245–71.

Wilson, E.S.R. and Brenner, L.A. (1971) The effects of self-esteem and situation upon comparison choices during ability evaluation. *Sociometry*, 34: 381–97.

Wolfson, M., Kaplan, G., Lynch, J., Ross, N. and Backlund, E. (1999) Relation between income inequality and mortality: empirical demonstration, *British Medical Journal*, 319: 953–6.

12 | Housing wealth and community health: exploring the role of migration

Danny Dorling, Mary Shaw and Nicola Brimblecombe

Introduction

Britain has long been scarred by geographical inequalities in health. Differences in mortality rates between rural and urban areas have been reported, with the latter usually experiencing higher rates (Watt *et al.* 1994). Similarly, it is consistently reported that mortality rates are highest in the North and in Scotland and lowest in the South. Recently, researchers have also reported a geographical *polarization* of life chances in Britain (Dorling 1997; Raleigh and Kiri 1997; Shaw *et al.* 1999a). Areas which already had the lowest death rates have experienced the greatest reductions in mortality, whereas areas with the highest death rates have experienced negligible improvements in life chances. Our research looked at the changing geography of health (using mortality as an indicator of the health of a population) in Britain since the 1950s.

We begin the chapter by presenting the latest available evidence which describes the continued spatial polarization of mortality in Britain at the end of the twentieth century. We then go on to briefly review possible explanations for this geographical inequality in mortality before considering one explanation which has to date received relatively little attention: the role of migration. We present evidence, from both national and local data, to suggest that differential migration may play a part in producing the spatial patterning and polarization of mortality in contemporary Britain. In particular, we point to the interaction of the housing market and housing wealth in the spatial distribution and migration of the population and consequently in geographical health inequality. The implications of these research findings for housing policy – and social and economic policies more generally – are then discussed.

The spatial polarization of mortality in Britain

In order to look at the geography of health over time, comparative measures are needed. Geographical boundaries, which frequently change for administrative and political reasons, need to be frozen in order to compare areas over time. This limits the amount of data that is available (see Dorling 1995a for more details). Before 1981 (at least in England and Wales) mortality statistics were only available in printed form and these were only published for particular areas used by the registrar general in the government's decennial supplement on mortality. There were 292 of these areas in Britain and they consisted largely of London boroughs, metropolitan boroughs, the urban districts of counties, the rural remainders of counties, Scottish burghs, islands and Scottish counties for which data were available. The boundaries of these areas were all defined prior to the 1974 reorganization of local government. We have assigned individual postcoded mortality records for 1981–95 to these areas, so that comparisons can be made over time (this process is described in more detail in Dorling 1997).

Table 12.1 shows standardized mortality ratios (SMR) for deaths under the age of 65 from the early 1950s to the late 1990s for these areas of Britain. We focus on deaths under 65 as these are generally considered to be premature. SMRs, or more precisely, age-sex standardized mortality ratios, refer to the ratio of the number of deaths observed in the study group or population to the number that would be expected if the study population had the same age-sex-specific rates as the standard population, multiplied by 100. The standard population is the population of England and Wales for each time period. Rather than listing individual areas, we have divided them into deciles of population, ranked by SMR. Decile 1 contains the 10 per cent of the population living in areas with the highest SMRs, or with the greatest chances of dying prematurely, and decile 10 contains the 10 per cent of the population living in areas with the lowest SMRs. This technique allows us to make a comparison between the worst and best areas (in terms of health) over four decades.

Table 12.1 shows that, in general, inequalities in mortality have increased over the last 20 years, but that this has not always been the case. Most importantly, inequalities in mortality decreased between 1963 and 1969. Since then, they have increased but only rapidly since 1981 (we do not have the data needed to be able to say exactly when this increase began but it was at some point between 1977 and 1981). Geographical inequalities in mortality now stand at the highest levels ever recorded. The gap is such that,

Table 12.1 Age-sex SMR for deaths under 65 in Britain by deciles of population (grouped by old county borough and ranked by SMR), 1950–95

Decile	1950–3	1959–63	1969–73	1981–5	1986–9	1990–2	1993–5	1996–8
1	131.0	135.5	131.2	135.0	139.2	142.3	147.4	150.3
2	118.1	123.0	115.6	118.6	120.9	121.4	120.9	122.4
3	112.1	116.5	112.0	114.2	113.9	111.3	112.7	114.3
4	107.0	110.7	108.1	109.8	106.9	104.9	106.7	108.0
5	102.5	104.5	103.0	102.1	102.2	99.0	98.5	99.2
6	98.6	97.4	96.9	95.7	95.6	93.5	94.6	95.5
7	93.1	90.9	91.8	91.6	91.9	90.9	91.7	92.5
8	88.7	87.6	88.9	89.3	89.1	86.5	86.6	87.8
9	85.7	83.1	87.0	84.3	83.0	80.4	80.2	80.0
10	81.8	77.1	83.0	79.2	78.1	76.2	74.5	74.7
Ratio								
10: 1	1.60	1.75	1.58	1.70	1.78	1.87	1.98	**2.01**

compared to the national average, people living in the worst mortality deciles (of historically comparable areas) between 1996 and 1998 were 50 per cent more likely to die in any year before the age of 65.

Explanations of the geography of ill-health

Various explanations have been proposed for the geographical patterning of premature mortality in Britain. A significant debate surrounds the issue of whether these differences are due to 'people' or 'places', or in other words the relative contribution of compositional and contextual factors (Mac-Intyre *et al.* 1993). For instance, does an area have a relatively high premature mortality rate because the individuals who live there are relatively deprived? Conversely, does living in a deprived area have an additional effect over and above the socio-economic characteristics of individuals? A number of studies have considered questions related to this and report what is termed a residual 'area effect' (for example, Shouls *et al.* 1996; Wiggins *et al.* 1998). The analyses conducted to date give most weight to compositional effects, but they also lend some (secondary) support to the contextual argument: that health is not only a product of the sum of individual characteristics but is also to some extent determined by the context in which a person lives (see Chapter 9). However, while area effects have been identified and areas have been classified into 'types' associated with high and low mortality, little progress has been made in terms of fathoming either what these area types mean or the processes by which they promote or impair the health of the population in those areas (Mitchell *et al.* forthcoming). This chapter seeks to shed light on these processes.

The polarization of mortality in Britain also encourages us to look beyond explanations based solely on 'people' or 'places'. For example, if we consider how we might go about explaining the spatial polarization of mortality, such as that observed in Table 12.1, we must think about whether people in the areas with high and rising SMRs are becoming more deprived (and vice versa for areas with low SMRs), and/or whether area effects are becoming more potent.

There is certainly a great deal of evidence to suggest that the spatial polarization of mortality which has occurred since the late 1970s in Britain was preceded by a social and spatial polarization of material well-being as indicated by income and wealth (Shaw *et al.* 1999a). As discussed in Chapter 1, there has been a sharp increase in poverty since the late 1970s. Taking the measure of poverty/income inequality currently favoured by the government (households with incomes below half the national average), through the 1960s and 1970s, around 10 per cent of households were poor. However, since that time poverty has increased, with the greatest increase occurring in the early and mid-1980s, to reach 25 per cent in the early 1990s. The rate remained high and virtually unchanged throughout the decade. Thus, at the same time that spatial inequalities in health grew, so too did inequalities in income.

Alongside this increase in income inequality, there has been an increase in 'work rich' and 'work poor' households and increases in the proportion of households living in poverty and of children living in poverty. These trends, discussed in more detail in Chapter 1, have reached such a level that nearly 20 per cent of children in Britain live in workless households and over 30 per cent now live in poor households (HM Treasury 1999).

The role of migration

These increases in socio-economic inequality are almost certainly the primary driving force behind the increased spatial polarization of mortality. Polarization of unemployment and economic expansion are strongly spatially patterned. However, this is not the whole picture and we should also pay attention to the role played by migration.

Figure 12.1 shows that many of the areas that experienced population decline also had increasing SMRs between the early 1980s and early 1990s. The fact that population change since the 1970s is so clearly related to mortality change in the 1980s suggests that people in Britain (in aggregate) recognize when the time is right to leave areas if they are able. People react to economic decline: those people who can leave are less likely to be living in poverty than those who remain. They are more likely to be in higher social classes (Champion and Ford 1998), more likely to have a job (Dorling and

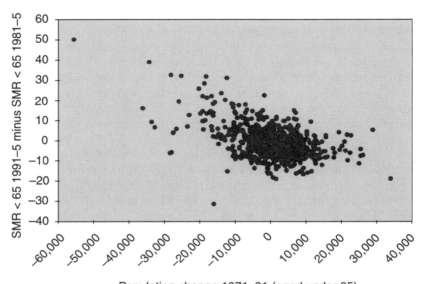

Figure 12.1 Population change (aged under 65) between 1971 and 1991 and absolute change in SMRs for deaths under 65 (1991–5 – 1981–5) for British constituencies
Source: Davey Smith *et al.* (1998).

Woodward 1996) and these are the people who are more likely to live longer (Bethune 1997; Hattersley 1999).

So can migration explain geographical inequalities in health? One study that has considered the role of migration in producing such inequalities is reported in a paper by Strachan *et al.* (1995). They found that geographical patterns in mortality for cardiovascular disease (CVD) at the regional level in England and Wales could *not* be explained by migration between areas. As part of our project, we re-examined this using an alternative data source, the British Household Panel Survey (BHPS). The BHPS is a representative sample of over 10,000 British residents who have been surveyed annually between 1991 and 1996 (see Chapter 6 and Buck *et al.* 1994 for more details). We have analysed the 527 deaths of participants in the BHPS to investigate the effects of lifetime migration on mortality patterns for all of Britain. Our results (presented in full in Brimblecombe *et al.* 1999a) show a remarkable degree of similarity with Strachan *et al.*'s (1995) findings, given that the BHPS allows us to consider all causes of deaths and migration since birth, rather than since 1939, allowing for the fact that we have included Scotland and given that we are considering deaths in a later time period (1991 to 1996). Our results show that selective migration has had no impact on the regional geography of mortality in Britain when measured in this way.

However, as most migration occurs not at the regional level but on a smaller spatial scale (Dorling 1995b; Dorling and Woodward 1996), we turned our attention to that smaller spatial scale. The BHPS codes data at a more detailed geographical scale than standard region, using sample of anonymized records (SAR) districts. These are local government districts, sometimes amalgamated so that no area has a population of less than 120,000. SAR district of both place of birth and of place of residence in 1991 (and subsequently) is recorded for BHPS respondents, so we can consider the effects of selective migration, in effect, between towns. If we divide the country into areas of high and low mortality using the 1991 mortality ratios of SAR districts rather than regions, the spatial divide between rich and poor areas in terms of mortality disappears entirely when migration is reversed. For that sample and at that spatial scale, therefore, migration is all important. These results should be interpreted with caution, however, as due to the relatively small number of deaths of BHPS sample members, the confidence intervals are wide. The results do suggest though that, at the local level, selective migration over the whole lifecourse has an important role to play in explaining spatial inequalities in health in the long term.

Housing and health

The socio-economic polarization seen in Britain through the 1980s and 1990s mentioned above is also visible in terms of housing tenure and housing wealth (see also Chapter 1). Home ownership in Britain increased from 57 per cent in 1981 to 68 per cent in 1991 (Dorling 1995a). However, the number of households in insecure housing tenures has also risen, reflected in increases in the number of mortgage repossessions and households in temporary accommodation, the number of which rose from over 10,000 in 1982 to over 67,000 in 1992 (Wadsworth 1996). There has also been a rise in the number of households applying to local authorities as homeless (Victor 1997).

The connection between housing and health has been known for many decades. Those who live in better housing conditions have better health in terms of morbidity (both physical and mental health) and also in terms of mortality (see Chapter 8). Various studies have reported an association between housing tenure and health, such that those who own their own homes have the lowest mortality rates, followed by those in privately rented accommodation. Residents of local authority housing experience the worst health outcomes (Filakti and Fox 1995). There is also evidence to suggest that homeless people have particularly poor health outcomes (Bines 1994; Hibbs et al. 1994; Victor 1997).

The category of home ownership, however, now contains over two thirds of the population. In order to consider the relationship between housing status and life chances more fully, we developed an alternative measure of the relative social position of people in terms of housing by referring to the price that people are willing or able to pay for it (see Shaw *et al.* 1999b for more details). This is not available at the individual level but at the ecological level for very small areas which can be derived from building societies' and census data. Here, for the time period for which we have suitable data (1981–9) we have calculated average housing wealth at the ward level. National mortality data for the same period, which is also available at the ward level, allows us to calculate average life expectancies for groups of wards. Figure 12.2 amalgamates these data on life expectancy by housing wealth with life expectancies for rough sleepers, hostel users and bed and breakfast residents.

The X axis of Figure 12.2 indicates cumulative population in order of ascending housing wealth while the Y axis shows years of life expectancy (males and females). While the data are not strictly directly comparable, as the housing wealth data dates from 1981–9, the hostel and bed and breakfast mortality data from 1981–92 and the rough sleeper mortality data from 1995–6, we can nonetheless for the first time compare the life expectancy of a full range of tenure groups. A linear gradient between housing wealth and life expectancy is clear, but this has to be extended on a log-linear scale to include the homeless and other vulnerably housed groups.

Figure 12.2 shows that, as ward level housing wealth rises, so does life expectancy, but that above £60,000 of housing wealth there is little additional life expectancy benefit. The biggest gains in life expectancy are between the categories of £5000–£9999 and £10,000–£14,999, because these are the categories that distinguish living in poverty from low living standards. Escaping from poverty improves health most quickly and hence redistribution of wealth makes purely health economic (and moral) sense.

Housing, health and migration

Having established the possible role of migration in producing geographical inequalities in health through the quantitative research presented above, we turned our attention to the *processes* through which this might occur. We focused in particular on investigating the interaction of the housing market and individual housing and migration histories in two case study areas (Oxford and Brighton). We thus collected individual housing histories with people living in different tenures: owner occupation, social housing and those we term the 'vulnerably housed' (people living in hostels for the homeless, bed and breakfast accommodation and on the streets). Interviews were based on the lifegrid method developed by Blane (1996) and discussed in Chapter 5. Interviews were also conducted with local key informants working in housing-related fields. The findings of this case study work are

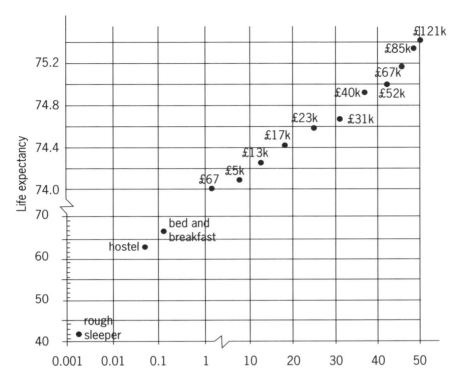

Figure 12.2 Life expectancy by housing wealth, England and Wales 1981–9
Source: Shaw *et al.* (1999b).

presented in detail in Brimblecombe (1998), Brimblecombe *et al.* (1999b), Shaw (1998) and Shaw *et al.* (1999b).

Not surprisingly owner-occupiers were, on aggregate, the tenure group with the greatest financial resources, in terms of both wealth and income. To gain access to this tenure category, and thus to live in the types of areas where this tenure is concentrated, requires sufficient capital and/or income. For many of the owner-occupiers interviewed, inherited wealth had been a key to their ability to access this tenure. Inherited wealth has become increasingly important as house prices rose (crashed and recovered) during the 1980s and 1990s. As property values rose, certain areas became more and more desirable for this tenure group, with concern over school catchment areas playing a part in this. Thus, while this tenure category has grown, it is also the case that it has polarized. It now includes those with high levels of housing wealth living in the most desirable areas located near

good services and facilities and in the most salubrious and pleasant surroundings. It also includes those who are just able to financially qualify for
this tenure, who are barely able to afford repayments and who live in the less
desirable areas in homes which they cannot always afford to maintain. It is
the wealthier group (who are also on average the healthiest), with the safety
net of accumulated wealth and high incomes, who have the most choice
about their migratory moves and thus about where they live. Thus the
changes in the housing market in the past two decades have had the effect of
spatially filtering people, with the result that wealth and location are now
somewhat more closely related.

Social housing is still the most spatially concentrated housing tenure, as
many local authority properties are located within estates. Under the 'Right
to Buy' policy of the Thatcher governments (1979–83, 1983–7), many of the
more desirable homes (especially those which were sturdily built, had three
or more bedrooms and had gardens) in this tenure category were sold off.
This left a diminished housing stock in terms both of quality and supply.
There were thus fewer properties available, but increasing demand from
those who were unable to afford the rising rents in the privately rented
sector, driven by the rise in property prices. As a result, the qualifying criteria for this tenure category became more stringent and it became increasingly populated by those deemed to be in greatest housing need: those out of
work, lone parents, those with very low incomes and the long-term sick or
disabled. This is also the tenure group that is least mobile in geographic
terms (except during brief periods of house price falls). Their socio-economic circumstances mean that they have less choice about where to live in
the first place and, once in social housing, they have little choice about
moving, unless their economic circumstances improve.

A group which is particularly mobile are those who fall outside of the
usual tenure categories – those who are homeless and vulnerably housed.
This group is mobile for many reasons: they may literally be forced to be
mobile, as they have nowhere to live and have to move on, or they may be
on the run from the police or others. Alternatively, they may be looking for
work, which is often of a seasonal nature (such as in the tourist industry or
agricultural work). They may also be drawn to particular areas for the
opportunities for begging or for services provided (such as hostels, day centres and drug rehabilitation), or to areas which they perceive to be particularly tolerant towards the 'socially excluded' and less conventional in
society. While this is a relatively small group, research shows that they have
such elevated morbidity and mortality rates compared to the general population (Bines 1994; Shaw and Dorling 1998) that their health problems and
their spatial location and migration cannot be ignored.

Figure 12.3 shows the last address of a sample of people using an Oxford
hostel and indicates the extent of mobility among homeless people. It shows
that people have come into Oxford from many places throughout England,

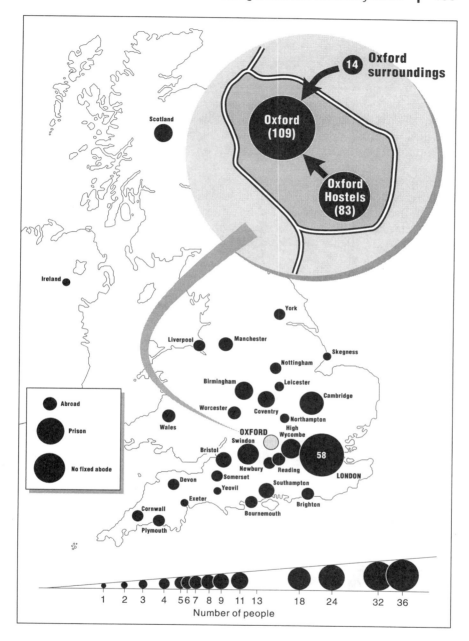

Figure 12.3 Last address of a sample of Oxford hostel residents
Source: Brimblecombe (1998).

as well as from Scotland, Ireland and Wales. Some have come from prisons in the Oxfordshire area and further afield. (It is estimated that, of the approximately 100,000 prisoners released each year nationally, 40 per cent of them are recorded as having on release no fixed abode – Paylor 1992.) Others have come from the rural areas that surround Oxford, where there may not be the necessary services and accommodation, or from Oxford itself. There is also a significant movement between hostels within Oxford.

Thus, in considering the geography of health over the 1980s and 1990s, we should not overlook the role of migration. Those who are most well-off in society have the most choice about where they live. As this group has become wealthier, it follows that certain areas will have become more exclusive, only to be populated by those with access to the most resources. Facilities such as good schools, shops, health centres and leisure facilities will increasingly concentrate in the wealthier areas, further increasing their desirability and exclusivity. Concurrently, as poverty rates have increased, the poorest in society have less choice about where they can live, with the result that some areas become increasingly populated by the worst-off in society, in terms of both wealth and health. The ability to be spatially mobile is thus related to the distribution of wealth and income in a population and the housing market is an integral part of this process.

Conclusion: mortality and social policy

If fiscal policies continue to lead to increased income inequality, we can expect to see the spatial polarization of mortality continuing. Wealthy areas will get wealthier and healthier, and poor people (with poor health) will be left behind in those areas which are considered undesirable and where opportunities are sparse. Without major changes in tax and benefit policy, economic inequality will continue, as will the spatial polarization of both wealth and mortality. Policies that redress such extreme inequalities are therefore urgently needed. In addition, housing policy which would increase both the quantity and quality of social housing would lead to greater opportunities for the homeless and others in housing need, less concentration of the worst-off in social housing and a better quality of housing for all those who do live there. A second strand to housing policy would be to improve the quality and regulate the cost of privately-rented accommodation. However, people are not, by choice, going to stay in an area with poor facilities and little chance of employment and therefore locally-based policies to redress low job supply are also needed.

The New Labour government, elected in 1997, has instituted policies designed to tackle poverty and housing need and to reduce health inequalities (DoH 1999; DSS 1999). These initiatives include the Working Families Tax Credit, the New Deal for Communities, investments in social housing, regulation of the privately rented housing sector and the Rough Sleepers Initiative.

Chapter 6 discusses the impact of policies designed to tackle unemployment and low pay while the concluding chapter reviews the broader impact of welfare policies on socio-economic and health inequalities. The evidence to date suggests that, while the current range of initiatives are important parts of a strategy to tackle health inequalities, their scope and scale is unlikely to be sufficient to reverse the current widening of the health gap. Furthermore, many of these policies have yet to be implemented and depend on budget commitments for the next parliament. What concerns us most on policy is that the current administration reneged on its pre-election promise to implement the major recommendations of the Black Report (DHSS 1980) which are still very pertinent today. Here, we lack the space to explain why we think they did this and what effects this decision will have. For that, more complex, story see Shaw *et al.* (1999a).

Acknowledgements

This chapter draws on research funded by the ESRC (L128251009) under the Health Variations Programme.

References

Bethune, A. (1997) Unemployment and mortality, in F. Drever and M. Whitehead (eds) *Health Inequalities* (Series DS No.15). London: The Stationery Office.

Bines, W. (1994) *The Health of Single Homeless People.* York: Centre for Housing Policy, University of York.

Blane, D.B. (1996) Collecting retrospective data: development of a reliable method and a pilot study of its use, *Social Science and Medicine*, 42(5): 751–7.

Brimblecombe, N. (1998) *Living and Dying in Oxford: The Spatial Polarisation of Life Chances.* Bristol: University of Bristol.

Brimblecombe, N., Dorling, D. and Shaw, M. (1999a) Mortality and migration in Britain – first results from the British Household Panel Survey, *Social Science and Medicine*, 49(7): 981–8.

Brimblecombe, N., Dorling, D. and Shaw, M. (1999b) Where the poor die in a rich city: the case of Oxford, *Health and Place*, 5(4): 287–300.

Buck, N., Gershuny, J., Rose, D. and Scott, J. (eds) (1994) *Changing Households. The British Household Panel Survey 1990–1992.* Colchester: ESRC Centre for Micro-Social Change.

Champion, T. and Ford, T. (1998) *The Social Selectivity of Migration Flows Affecting Britain's Larger Conurbations: An Analysis of the Regional Migration Tables of the 1981 and 1991 Censuses.* Newcastle: University of Newcastle.

Davey Smith, G., Shaw, M. and Dorling, D. (1998) Shrinking areas and mortality, *Lancet*, 352: 1139–40.

DHSS (Department of Health and Social Security) (1980) *Inequalities in Health: Report of a Working Group* (the Black Report). London: DHSS.

DoH (Department of Health) (1999) *Reducing Health Inequalities: An Action Report*. London: The Stationery Office.

Dorling, D. (1995a) *A New Social Atlas of Britain*. Chichester: Wiley.

Dorling, D. (1995b) The visualization of local urban change across Britain, *Environment and Planning B*, 22: 269–90.

Dorling, D. (1997) *Death in Britain: How Local Mortality Rates Have Changed: 1950s–1990s*. York: Joseph Rowntree Foundation.

Dorling, D. and Woodward, R. (1996) *Social polarisation 1971–1991: a micro-geographical analysis of Britain*. Monograph in the *Progress in Planning* series 45: 1–67.

DSS (Department of Social Security) (1999) *Opportunity for All: Tackling Poverty and Social Exclusion*, Cm 4445. London: The Stationery Office.

Filakti, H. and Fox, J. (1995) Differences in mortality by housing tenure and by car access from the OPCS Longitudinal Study, *Population Trends*, 81: 27–30.

Hattersley, L. (1999) Trends in life expectancy by social class – an update, *Health Statistics Quarterly*, 2: 16–24.

Hibbs, J.R., Benner, L. and Klugman, L. *et al.* (1994) Mortality in a cohort of homeless adults in Philadelphia, *New England Journal of Medicine*, 331: 304–9.

HM Treasury (1999) *The Modernisation of Britain's Tax and Benefit System, Number Four: Tackling Poverty and Extending Opportunity*. London: HM Treasury.

MacIntyre, S., MacIver, S. and Soomans, A. (1993) Area, class and health: should we be focusing on places or people? *Journal of Social Policy*, 22(2): 213–34.

Mitchell, R., Bartley, M. and Shaw, M. (forthcoming) Combining the social and the spatial: improving the geography of health inequalities, in P. Boyle, S. Curtis, A. Gatrell, E. Graham and E. Moore (eds) *The Geography of Health Inequalities in the Developed World*.

Paylor, I. (1992) *Homelessness and Ex-offenders: A Case for Reform?* Norwich: University of East Anglia.

Raleigh, V.S. and Kiri, V.A. (1997) Life expectancy in England: variations and trends by gender, health authority, and level of deprivation, *Journal of Epidemiology and Community Health*, 51: 649–58.

Shaw, M. (1998) *A Place Apart: The Spatial Polarization of Mortality in Brighton*. Bristol: University of Bristol.

Shaw, M. and Dorling, D. (1998) Mortality among street sleeping youth in the UK, *Lancet*, 352(9129): 743.

Shaw, M., Gordon, D., Dorling, D. and Davey Smith, G. (1999a) *The Widening Gap: health inequalities and policy in Britain*. Bristol: The Policy Press.

Shaw, M., Dorling, D. and Brimblecombe, N. (1999b) Life chances in Britain by housing wealth and for the homeless and vulnerably housed, *Environment and Planning A*, 31: 2239–48.

Shouls, S., Congdon, P. and Curtis, S. (1996) Modelling inequality in reported long term illness in the UK: combining individual and area characteristics, *Journal of Epidemiology and Community Health*, 50: 366–76.

Strachan, D.P., Leon, D.A. and Dodgeon, B. (1995) Mortality from cardiovascular disease among interregional migrants in England and Wales, *British Medical Journal*, 310: 423–7.

Victor, C.R. (1997) The health of homeless people in Britain: A review, *European Journal of Public Health*, 7: 398–404.

Wadsworth, M. (1996) Family and education as determinants of health, in D. Blane, E. Brunner and R. Wilkinson (eds) *Health and Social Organization: Towards a Health Policy for the 21st Century*. London: Routledge.

Watt, I.S., Franks, A.J. and Sheldon, T.A. (1994) Health and health care of rural populations in the UK: is it better or worse? *Journal of Epidemiology and Community Health*, 48: 16–21.

Wiggins, R., Bartley, M., Gleave, S. *et al.* (1998) Limiting long-term illness: a question of where you live or who you are? A multilevel analysis of the 1971–1991 ONS Longitudinal Study, *Risk Decision and Policy*, 3(3): 181–98.

Part 4
Assessing policy impact

Researching the impact of public policy on inequalities in health

Margaret Whitehead, Finn Diderichsen and Bo Burström

The need for health impact assessment

Research on health inequalities has entered a challenging phase. On the one hand, there is increasing political commitment to tackle inequalities in health. Furthermore, as earlier chapters have shown, many of the major determinants of health inequalities lie outside the health sector, and therefore policies beyond this sector are required. On the other hand, there is growing acknowledgement that the effectiveness of many of the broader interventions has not been evaluated and, indeed, the tools and methodologies to do so are underdeveloped.

In the UK, this kind of research is being driven by a number of policy imperatives. The government has responded to the evidence of a growing health divide by making the reduction of inequalities in health a duty of public agencies at all levels and in all sectors. All government departments, the National Health Service (NHS) centrally and the health and local authorities must assess the health impact of their activities. Initiatives from the Social Exclusion Unit, and under the auspices of Health, Education and Employment Action Zones, are targeted at areas suffering disadvantage and are required to build strategies to tackle health inequalities into their design and evaluation. The 1998 Acheson Report (Independent Inquiry into Inequalities in Health 1998) has gone one step further in making the first of its 39 recommendations a call for health *inequalities* impact assessment of all policies likely to have an impact on inequalities in health. Internationally, the World Health Organization (WHO), the European Union (EU) and the World Bank have all called for health impact assessments of policies and programmes.

Despite this heightened concern, research analysing the health impact of policies is still at an early stage. Too little has been done to evaluate actions to reduce, or ameliorate, the effects of social inequalities in health (Arblaster *et al.* 1995; Gepkens and Gunning-Schepers 1995; Whitehead 1995; Mackenbach and Gunning-Schepers 1997). The project described here is one attempt to respond to this challenge. The chapter is divided into four main sections. The first section raises some of the methodological dilemmas in evaluating wider public policy and describes some pragmatic approaches to deal with them. The second section outlines the conceptual framework developed and the methods used in this project to study the health impact of social position and social policies. The third section illustrates how this framework was used to assess the impact of social welfare policies on the health and socio-economic circumstances of lone mothers in the UK and Sweden. Finally, implications are highlighted from this work for future research and policy development.

Evaluation dilemmas and pragmatic solutions

Evaluation dilemmas

One reason for the lack of policy impact studies is the complexity of the research task. Policy can be considered to be one component of the wider political, cultural, social and economic environment which characterizes a society or a community. Policy operates at this contextual, or aggregate level, but the pathways from social position to exposure to health hazards/risks and on to ill-health operate at the individual level, as do the consequences of ill-health. The task of identifying the impact of policy on the individual pathways to ill-health requires cross-level inferences to be made, from the contextual (aggregate) level to the individual level and vice versa.

The classic research designs typically employed in medical and drug research can only take us a short distance along the road when it comes to policy evaluation. Table 13.1 shows a much quoted 'hierarchy of evidence', with randomized controlled trials as the gold standard at the top and descriptive studies and the opinions of respected authorities at the bottom (Arblaster *et al.* 1995). However, the limitations of concentrating on this approach to the exclusion of others have been amply set out by Black in relation to health services research. As Black suggests, even in this specific field, there are many situations when a randomized trial is 'unnecessary, inappropriate, impossible, or inadequate' (1996: 1215).

For policy beyond healthcare, the problems are even greater. If randomized controlled trials are used for evaluation, then the focus may, of necessity, have to be on relatively small-scale interventions where such an experimental design can be set up. Most policy initiatives concerned with promoting equity in health, however, take place in situations where people, or more often whole populations, cannot be randomized, where 'controls' cannot be shielded from the influences intended exclusively for the experimental groups and where external factors may act differentially on subgroups within the population. The fiscal measures in tobacco control policies illustrate these dilemmas well. What is possible in relation to relatively small-scale local policies becomes increasingly difficult and inappropriate as the scale shifts to regional, national and even international levels.

There is a real danger that overemphasis on these controlled experimental research designs may result in a narrow conception of what the policy options are, leading to neglect of the most important aspects of healthy public policy. A good example comes from recent reviews of the evidence on interventions to reduce social inequalities in health. In 1995, the Department of Health commissioned a review of the evidence restricted to studies with experimental and quasi-experimental designs – that is, categories I and II-1 in Table 13.1, and explicitly excluding observational studies (Arblaster *et al.* 1995). The Dutch government commissioned a review on the same issue, and although it did include observational studies and the so-called 'grey' literature, it was limited by its reliance on medical literature databases (Gepkens and Gunning-Schepers 1995). As a result, the studies identified by both reviews were predominantly rather small-scale interventions, overwhelmingly involving personal health education or improving access to healthcare. Although the scientific quality of the reviews was excellent, in the end they had very little to say about modification of structural factors and wider policy initiatives which could reasonably be expected to have a significant influence on the major causes of the health divide. In fact, the authors of both reviews acknowledged this limitation and called for wider analysis in the future.

Table 13.1 Hierarchy of evidence

I	Well-designed randomized controlled trial
II-1	Other types of trials: • Well designed controlled trial without randomization • Quasi-experiments
II-2	Well-designed cohort (prospective) study, preferably from more than one centre
II-3	Well-designed case control (retrospective) study, preferably from several centres
III	Large differences from comparisons between times and/or places with or without the intervention
IV	Opinions of respected authorities based on clinical experience; descriptive studies and reports of expert committees

Source: Adapted from Arblaster *et al.* (1995) after Woolf *et al.* (1990).

Pragmatic solutions

The above discussion is not an argument for the abandonment of experimental designs, but rather a reminder that they are only *one* aspect of what is required in assessing the effectiveness of actions to reduce inequalities in health. Acknowledging some of the complexities of the task, Mackenbach and Gunning-Schepers (1997) have developed a number of guidelines and design recommendations to help in the evaluation of specific interventions (rather than broader policies) to reduce inequalities in health for the Dutch government's programme of inequalities research. They conclude that while randomized controlled trials involving individuals are rarely possible, there are circumstances in which community intervention trials are feasible and then it may be possible to employ the basic rules of the classic study designs. They do, however, point out that such community intervention trials are likely to be complicated and costly. As a consequence, they suggest that there is a need to pool experiences from different countries, to increase the scope for drawing sensible and relevant conclusions.

The Dutch guidelines for evaluating specific community interventions, however, still rarely cater for the assessment of broader policy. Increasingly in these situations, pragmatic solutions are being adopted, including identifying 'natural experiments'. These take advantage of situations that arise where variations in policy occur and effects of exposure can be investigated, for example:

- studying a cross-section of localities in which different levels of policy on a specific issue are in operation;
- studying changes over time in one country when policy on a specific issue has fluctuated;
- studying the period before and after the introduction of a new policy in several countries.

In making comparisons of the situation in two or more places over time, many factors have to be taken into account, as many different policy inputs and influences are going on concurrently with the policy under review. It is not sufficient to find an association between two variables and draw conclusions about cause and effect. A broad understanding needs to be gained of the context in which the policy is being played out and an inventory taken of possible linked events and influencing factors. Some, though not all, of these factors can then be controlled for, but awareness of them all is needed to improve the interpretation of results. One way of reducing (while not eliminating) such methodological problems is to combine macro- and micro-level data (Morgenstern 1995), which might reveal some of the mechanisms operating between contextual and individual factors that are influenced by differences in policy.

In the messy world of policy analysis, Chapman conjures up the imagery of unravelling the delicate threads of gossamer with boxing gloves to describe the task of sorting out cause and effect 'when there is interplay of continuous, uncontrolled, unmeasured, and sometimes unmeasurable variables' (Chapman 1993: 429). He was referring specifically to interventions on a single risk factor – smoking. The level of complexity goes up several notches when multi-stranded policy programmes are under review, for example when there is a more diffuse aim of improving health in disadvantaged communities.

Awareness is also growing that the same policy may have a differential effect on different subgroups within the population: beneficial effects for some, but little or even negative effects for others. Concentration solely on the overall health impact may miss serious shortcomings of the policy, and the measurement of the distributional effects needs to be a standard part of the evaluation process. This includes assessment of how policies are experienced by people themselves in their differing circumstances. From an equity point of view, one of the most important questions to ask is: what is the impact of this policy on the health of the most vulnerable sections of the population?

Moreover, policies are not always what they seem; the policy as implemented on the ground may bear little resemblance to the official statements of intention or the wording of regulations. There is scope for the various components of a policy to be implemented in different combinations or for the emphasis to vary from one locality to another. A vital component of any evaluation, therefore, is an assessment of how a policy has been interpreted and how, if at all, it is being enforced (Pawson and Tilley 1997).

It may be an impossible task to take all these issues into consideration, but we can certainly improve on the limited range of methodologies in common use in the health field. The evaluation of public policy requires the use of combined methods, both quantitative and qualitative, adapted where necessary from a variety of disciplines, to measure multiple outcomes, with a range of subjects – policymakers, practitioners, and different population groups. In the hierarchy of evidence in Table 13.1, evidence from lay expertise is noticeable by its absence, an omission which urgently needs to be remedied (Popay and Williams 1994).

Conceptual framework and methods

Taking these dilemmas and possible solutions as a starting point, the aims of the research reported in this chapter were to:

- develop the theory and methodology further for exploiting a 'natural policy experiment' in relation to health;
- use the methodology to investigate the contribution of social welfare polices in addressing social inequalities in health;
- draw out policy implications/policy guidance from the findings.

Specifically, the objectives were to analyse social welfare policies and socio-economic conditions in the UK and Sweden from 1979 to 1995–6 and examine their consequences for the health and social circumstances of lone parents and people at risk of, or experiencing, unemployment.

Conceptual framework

The framework developed by Diderichsen (1998) for mapping the impact of policies on the social pathways to health inequalities was refined and adapted to guide the research (see Figure 13.1). In this framework, the pathways leading to ill-health can be approached from the perspective of the individual or of society. One line of enquiry considers an individual's social position (defined by their gender, occupational class or ethnic origin, for example) and how that position influences their exposure to important health risks such as poverty, nutritional deficiencies, dangerous working conditions, health damaging behaviours and so on. Different social positions may carry very different probabilities of being exposed to specific health hazards or risk conditions, leading to differential exposure (mechanism I). In addition, a specific exposure may or may not lead to ill-health or disease for an individual, depending on whether other contributory risk factors or risk conditions are present (mechanism II: differential vulnerability). In relation to lone mothers, for example, the effect of poverty on health may be dependent on the absence of social support. Since lone mothers will often be exposed to risk factors of this type, these may *interact* to produce a higher vulnerability to the health-damaging effects of poverty among lone than among couple mothers (Hallqvist *et al.* 1996).

The social and economic consequences of illness are not only dependent on the health problem suffered by the person, but also on the effects of the illness on their ability to stay employed, live independently and participate in their community. These effects may vary according to the social position of the individual (mechanism III: differential consequences of disease). The social consequences of illness might also feed back into the etiological process and influence social stratification and context (mechanism IV). Since the social consequences of illness are differential across social groups, they might play an important role in aggravating social inequalities in health. This is an area where healthcare and sickness insurance policies might play a significant role.

The societal perspective focuses on how the prevailing social context interacts with and influences the pathways from social position to ill-health. As part of the social context, policy may have an influence on the pathways between social position and health consequences at four distinct points represented in Figure 13.1:

- *Policy may influence the social position individuals occupy in society (entry point A).* The education system and family policies, for example,

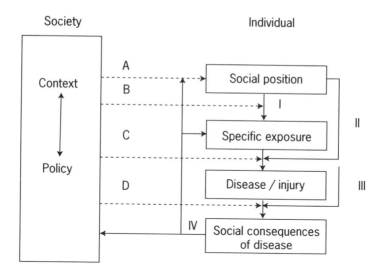

Figure 13.1 Framework for researching policy impact on health inequalities
Notes:
(I)   The impact of social position on health through differential exposure
(II) Differential vulnerability
(III) Differential consequences of disease
(IV) Consequences of disease might feed back into a causal pathway
(A)   The modifying effect of social context and policy on social stratification
(B)   Policies influencing differential exposure
(C)   Policies influencing differential vulnerability
(D)   Policies influencing differential social consequences of disease
Source: Diderichsen (1998).

may influence the opportunities people have to move up the social scale, and indeed, can influence how wide the gulf is between people in different social positions.

- *Policy may influence exposure to health hazards faced by people in different social positions (entry point B).* Most health policies that have been implemented so far to combat inequalities in health have been aimed at preventing people in disadvantaged positions from being exposed to poverty, unhealthy housing, dangerous working conditions, nutritional deficiencies and so on. These policies will often be designed to have a greater impact on some groups than others.
- *Policy may influence the effect of being exposed to a hazardous factor (entry point C).* As noted under mechanism II, the size of the effect of a certain risk factor or risk condition will often be dependent on the presence of other contributory causes. For example, the impact on health of being poor or unemployed may be different in different societies or even

in different communities or time periods within the same country. Local or national policies may be in place, for instance, which not only influence the risk of being poor (as in entry point B) but also either soften or reinforce the effects of being poor.

- *Policies may influence the impact of being ill (entry point D).* A number of policies, most prominently those concerned with the effectiveness and equity of healthcare services, may have a direct impact on morbidity and its consequences in terms of survival, disability and daily living. The social consequences of being ill in a specific society may vary, and will partly depend on the way chronic illness interacts with a number of factors related to social context (for example, what state the local labour market is in and what policies are in place encouraging or discouraging people with disabilities or chronic conditions to have paid employment).

By selecting two countries with contrasting social and policy contexts – the UK and Sweden – we used this conceptual framework to study some of the society and health relationships at different points in these pathways.

Methods

The study employed both quantitative and qualitative methods, carried out by British and Swedish researchers in a collaborative, jointly-funded initiative. A careful comparative analysis was carried out using the conceptual framework, drawing on official policy documents, on routinely collected statistics, on empirical analysis of household survey data and on reviews of the research literature in both countries relating to each element in the framework. As part of the review process, literature searches (both electronic and manual) were carried out on cross-country comparative social welfare policy studies published in the English and Swedish languages. We also followed up references and work in progress with key researchers and interest groups in this field.

For empirical analysis of household survey data, the General Household Survey (GHS) of Great Britain and the Swedish Survey of Living Conditions (ULF) were employed. Both datasets have 17 years of data, from 1979 to 1995. At the start of the project, great care was taken to find and create comparable variables for analysis. To obtain sufficient statistical power for some of the subgroup analyses, several years of data were pooled to create four main time periods: 1979–83, 1984–7, 1988–1991 and 1992–5.

For the social and health variables, simple prevalence rates and age-specific prevalence rates were calculated, together with the relative differences between population groups expressed as odds ratios (ORs). In this chapter, the ORs express the chance of lone mothers being in ill-health compared to couple mothers, taking into account differences in age structure and other relevant characteristics between the lone and couple groups. In

Table 13.2 Odds ratios (ORs) with 95% confidence intervals (CIs) of prevalence of fair/poor health and limiting long-standing illness for lone compared to couple mothers adjusted for age and ethnicity, Britain and Sweden, ages 16–64, 1979–95

	Britain Lone:Couple mothers OR (95% CI)	Sweden Lone:Couple mothers OR (95% CI)
Fair/poor health		
1979–83	1.62 (1.33–1.97)	1.56 (1.32–1.85)
1984–7	1.61 (1.45–1.78)	1.65 (1.31–2.10)
1988–91	1.69 (1.53–1.87)	1.92 (1.53–2.40)
1992–5	1.74 (1.58–1.90)	1.62 (1.31–1.99)
Limiting illness		
1979–83	1.58 (1.22–2.03)	1.44 (1.21–1.72)
1984–7	1.64 (1.43–1.87)	1.39 (1.10–1.77)
1988–91	1.58 (1.38–1.80)	1.42 (1.13–1.80)
1992–5	1.43 (1.27–1.62)	1.44 (1.15–1.80)

Source: Whitehead *et al.* (2000); authors' own analyses of GHS and ULF datasets.

addition European Standardized Rates (ESRs) of fair/poor health and limiting long-standing illness were calculated using the WHOs European Standard Population (Armitage and Colton 1998). The ESRs allowed us to adjust for:

- differences in age between lone and couple mothers;
- differences in age structure of the populations in the two countries; and
- changes in age structure in both over time.

While the ORs show only the relative differences, the ESRs have the added advantage of showing absolute changes in prevalence of ill-health over time.

Case study: lone mothers in the UK and Sweden: how do they fare in different policy contexts?

One set of studies carried out within this project examined social welfare policies and their impact on the health disadvantage of lone versus couple mothers (see Whitehead *et al.* 2000 for a full presentation of findings). First, the results show that the health of lone mothers is poor relative to couple mothers in Sweden as well as in the UK, most notably that the magnitude of the differential (measured by ORs) between lone and couple mothers is of a similar order in the two countries, as shown in Table 13.2.

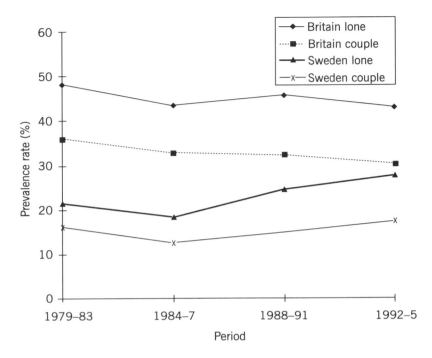

Figure 13.2 European standardized prevalence rates of less than good health, lone and couple mothers in Britain and in Sweden, ages 16–64, 1979–95
Source: Adapted from Whitehead *et al.* (2000); GHS and ULF datasets.

The ORs tell only part of the story, though. From Figure 13.2 – which gives absolute rates of fair/poor health (ESRs) – it can be seen that the two countries exhibited very different health trends for lone and couple mothers over the period from 1979 to 1995. In particular, there was an increase in the prevalence of fair/poor health for both groups in Sweden (more pronounced for younger lone mothers), coinciding with changes in social policies and more difficult times on the labour market, especially for parents (Burström *et al.* 1999; Shouls *et al.* 1999).

In addition, our results show that the pathways leading to the observed health disadvantage of lone mothers appear to be very different in the two countries in relation to the identified policy entry points. Taking the various pathways set out in the conceptual framework in Figure 13.1 in turn, at policy entry point A the most striking difference between the two countries is that the UK has a much higher proportion of young lone mothers – 16 per cent compared to 6 per cent in Sweden. As being a young mother can limit a person's ability to complete education and gain well-paid employment in the future, the high rate of young lone motherhood in the UK is of concern, with its potentially long-term consequences on the life chances and hence health of the young women (and of their children). The policy comparison at this entry point indicated two main policy levers. One was the development of more comprehensively available contraceptive services and sex education programmes for young people, as is already the case in Sweden and other countries with low teenage pregnancy rates. The second was to draw on the conclusions of the Economic and Social Research Council (ESRC) Social and Economic Life Initiative, which highlighted the need to improve the employment opportunities for young women from poor backgrounds, so that they could foresee a more rewarding role for themselves in the future than the low-paid, low-status work currently available to them. The Social Exclusion Unit (1999) has since come to similar policy conclusions in its analysis of how to reduce teenage pregnancy and support vulnerable teenage parents.

At entry point B in Figure 13.1, there are major differences between Sweden and the UK in lone mothers' risk of exposure to the health hazards of poverty and joblessness. British lone mothers are at an exceedingly high, and increasing, risk of poverty. This is partly because 58 per cent were not employed, and of those nearly all were poor. In contrast, even in the recession of the 1990s, only 10 per cent of Swedish lone mothers were poor. A high proportion (74 per cent) were in employment, but being without work did not automatically carry the high risk of poverty found in the UK: a quarter of Swedish lone mothers who were not in employment were poor, leaving three quarters who were not poor. The policy comparison reveals major contrasts in social policies in the two countries, which have had a direct bearing on the socio-economic circumstances of lone mothers and, indeed of women in general. Specific policies, which have helped protect Swedish lone mothers from exposure to poverty and joblessness and given them autonomy, have included extensive and high quality, affordable daycare for children, family-friendly employment policies and social security support adequate to meet the needs of families with children. In addition, there has been a workable child maintenance system that guarantees income to lone parents, whether or not the state can then get the payment back from the other parent. Policies which have led to the contrasting pattern in the UK have included the inadequate uprating of social security benefits to meet the need of families with children, inadequate provision of affordable childcare services and underdevelopment of employment policies which allow parents to combine paid work with their caring role. Clearly there is much that could be done.

Turning to policies influencing pathway C in Figure 13.1, the outcome of being exposed to poverty and joblessness differs somewhat in the two countries, though the picture is complex. There is some indication from our further studies that the health impact on all mothers (whether lone or couple) of being exposed to poverty may be stronger in the UK than in

Sweden. The policy implication is that there may be factors which have made the experience of poverty worse in the UK than in Sweden. From the policy comparison, candidates for these factors include the increasing concentration of British families living in the deepest poverty into geographically isolated social housing; cold, damp housing, with fuel poverty due to energy inefficient homes in the UK; and lower level of provision of goods and services, such as affordable childcare services, which may provide emotional as well as financial support for both lone and couple parents. The possibility that lone mothers may be more vulnerable, or susceptible, than couple mothers to the health-damaging effects of poverty and joblessness (mechanism II in Figure 13.1), appears to play a minor role in both countries, at least when tested against broad outcomes such as general self-rated health and limiting long-standing illness. There are theoretical reasons why interactions are more difficult to detect when using outcomes where many different causal pathways converge, compared to more narrowly defined health outcomes with fewer pathways.

Our results from multi-variate analyses show that overall in the UK around 50 per cent of the health disadvantage of lone mothers is accounted for by the mediating factors of poverty and joblessness, whereas in Sweden these factors only account for between 3 and 13 per cent of the health gap (see Table 13.3). This serves to re-emphasize the differences in mechanisms between the two countries.

In another study in this project (not described in detail here), we are investigating mechanism III and policy entry point D in Figure 13.1. This compared the social class gradient in the socio-economic consequences of limiting long-standing illness in the two countries where one has a more deregulated labour market than the other. Much higher rates and steeper social gradients in exclusion from employment were found among people with limiting illness in the more deregulated British labour market (Burström *et al.* in press).

Implications for research strategy and policy development

The findings of the above case study support the thrust of policy recommendations advocated in recent years in the UK to tackle the poor socio-economic circumstances of lone mothers, including removing barriers to work for those who wish to do so. The Swedish results, however, add new facets to the policy debate not only within the country itself, but also in the UK and elsewhere. What may be striking, particularly to British observers, is that many of the policies being advocated currently in the UK to improve the life chances and health of lone mothers – including recommendations of the Acheson Report (Independent Inquiry into Inequalities in Health 1998) – have been in place in Sweden for many years. Our findings should not be interpreted as

Table 13.3 Proportion of the health disadvantage of lone mothers explained by poverty and joblessness in Britain and Sweden; OR with 95% confidence intervals (CIs) and the 'explained fraction' 1984–95

BRITAIN *Fair/poor health*	1984–7 OR 95% CI	1988–91 OR 95% CI	1992–5 OR 95% CI
Model 1*	1.59 (1.44–1.76)	1.76 (1.59–1.94)	1.78 (1.63–1.95)
Model 2**	1.26 (1.13–1.41)	1.39 (1.25–1.55)	1.45 (1.31–1.61)
Explained fraction§	56%	49%	42%
Limiting long-standing illness			
Model 1*	1.61 (1.41–1.83)	1.56 (1.36–1.78)	1.45 (1.28–1.64)
Model 2**	1.28 (1.11–1.48)	1.26 (1.05–1.43)	1.19 (1.04–1.37)
Explained fraction§	52%	54%	58%
SWEDEN *Fair/poor health*	1984–7 OR 95% CI	1988–91 OR 95% CI	1992–5 OR 95% CI
Model 1*	1.64 (1.29–2.08)	1.93 (1.54–2.42)	1.62 (1.31–2.00)
Model 2**	1.62 (1.27–2.06)	1.88 (1.50–2.36)	1.59 (1.28–1.96)
Explained fraction§	3%	5%	5%
Limiting long-standing illness			
Model 1*	1.39 (1.10–1.76)	1.43 (1.13–1.80)	1.45 (1.16–1.82)
Model 2**	1.36 (1.07–1.73)	1.40 (1.10–1.78)	1.39 (1.11–1.74)
Explained fraction§	8%	7%	13%

Notes:
* Model 1 controls for age and for ethnicity (Britain) or being born outside the country (Sweden).
** Model 2 in addition controls for poverty and working status
§ Explained fraction shows percent reduction of OR lone/couple mothers with model 2, compared to model 1.
Source: Whitehead *et al.* (2000), authors' own analyses of GHS and ULF datasets.

casting doubt on the value of these Swedish policies: it is clear that they have had social and economic benefits for lone and couple mothers in Sweden. Rather, we interpret our study findings as an indication that, even if such policies are a necessary prerequisite, they may not be sufficient in themselves to have a beneficial health impact on the health indicators we use, or there may be strong influences working in the opposite direction (Whitehead *et al.* 2000). We plan to investigate other hypotheses about the underlying causes of the health disadvantage of Swedish lone mothers. These include the possibility that lone mothers in Sweden suffer from time poverty, if not financial poverty, to a greater degree than couple mothers; the possibility that they may have weaker, more insecure positions in the labour market; or that they have lower access to social support compared to couple mothers.

At a more general level, there are some lessons in terms of methodology for policy evaluation that can be drawn from this study so far:

- While this chapter emphasizes that macro-level policies cannot normally be subjected to controlled experiments, there is no reason why they should not be subjected to observational evaluation. This study illustrates, however, that limiting the analysis to descriptive comparisons of the magnitude of the health differentials across societies might lead to the wrong conclusions. In this case, the similarity of the health gap between lone and couple mothers in two countries with contrasting policies might erroneously have been interpreted as indicating that policies do not matter for the health disadvantage of lone mothers. By combining macro- and micro-level analyses, however, we could see that social policies had great impact on the mechanisms underlying the health inequalities.
- We found the theoretical framework developed for this research programme, depicted in Figure 13.1, helpful both in terms of pointing out distinct and empirically testable mechanisms generating inequalities in health, and also in distinguishing between several entry points where policy might potentially have an impact. The framework's applicability is not limited to the example of lone mothers, but could be used for other types of health inequalities and other types of specific exposures. As it points to the key mechanisms, it can, in combination with adequate individual level data on exposure levels and distributions and so on, be used for health *inequality* impact analysis.

Finally, researchers still tend, empirically, to treat populations as 'a collection of independent individuals' rather than 'population systems' (see Chapter 1). As earlier chapters have also emphasized, there is a great need to develop a better understanding of what social context actually is. This encompasses questions of patterns of exposure, outcomes and how the relationships between individuals work. It also includes investigations into how institutional arrangements developed by policy actually work, and what psychosocial effects these might have in terms of cohesion, trust and solidarity within a society.

Acknowledgements

We thank Susanna Shouls for extracting the original GHS data files and preparing the variables for comparative purposes. This research was jointly funded by the

ESRC (L1282251029) under the Health Variations Programme, the Swedish National Institute of Public Health, and Stockholm County Council. Data from the GHS were made available through the Office for National Statistics and the ESRC data archive. The authors alone bear the responsibility for the analyses and interpretations presented here.

References

Arblaster, L., Entwistle, V. and Lambert, M. *et al.* (1995) *Review of the Research on the Effectiveness of Health Service Interventions to Reduce Variations in Health*, CRD Report 3. York: York University NHS Centre for Reviews and Dissemination.

Armitage, P. and Colton, T. (eds) (1998) *Encyclopedia of Biostatistics.* Chichester: Wiley.

Black, N. (1996) Why we need observational studies to evaluate the effectiveness of health care, *British Medical Journal*, 312: 1215–18.

Burström, B., Diderichsen, F., Shouls, S. and Whitehead, M. (1999) Lone mothers in Sweden: trends in health and socio-economic circumstances 1979–1995, *Journal of Epidemiology and Community Health*, 53: 750–56.

Burström, B., Whitehead, M., Lindholm, C. and Diderichsen, F. (in press) Inequality in the social consequences of illness: how well do people with long-term illness fare on the labour markets of Britain and Sweden? *International Journal of Health Services.*

Chapman, S. (1993) Unravelling gossamer with boxing gloves: problems in explaining the decline in smoking, *British Medical Journal*, 307: 429–32.

Diderichsen, F. (1998) Understanding health equity in populations – some theoretical and methodological considerations, in *Promoting Research on Inequalities in Health: Proceedings from an International Expert Meeting.* Stockholm: Swedish Council for Social Research.

Gepkens, A. and Gunning-Schepers, L. (1995) Interventions to reduce socio-economic health differences: an evaluation of Dutch and foreign interventions aimed to reduce socio-economic health differences. Amsterdam: Institute of Social Medicine, University of Amsterdam.

Hallqvist, J., Ahlbom, A., Diderichsen, F. and Reuterwall, C. (1996) How to evaluate interaction between causes: A review of practices in cardiovascular epidemiology, *Journal of Internal Medicine*, 239: 377–82.

Independent Inquiry into Inequalities in Health (1998) *Independent Inquiry into Inequalities in Health Report* (The Acheson Report). London: The Stationery Office.

Mackenbach, J. and Gunning-Schepers, L. (1997) How should interventions to reduce inequalities in health be evaluated? *Journal of Epidemiology and Community Health*, 51: 359–64.

Morgenstern, H. (1995) Ecological studies in epidemiology, *Annual Review of Public Health*, 16: 61–81.

Pawson, R. and Tilley, N. (1997) *Realistic Evaluation.* London: Sage.

Popay, J. and Williams, G. (eds) (1994) *Researching the people's health.* London: Routledge.

Shouls, S., Burström, B., Diderichsen, F. and Whitehead, M. (1999) Lone mothers in Britain – trends in health and social circumstances, *Population Trends, 95*: 41–6.

Social Exclusion Unit (1999) *Teenage Pregnancy*, Cm 4342. London: The Stationery Office.

Whitehead, M. (1995) Tackling inequalities: a review of policy initiatives, in M. Benzeval, K. Judge and M. Whitehead (eds) *Tackling Inequalities in Health: An Agenda for Action*. London: King's Fund.

Whitehead, M., Burström, B. and Diderichsen, F. (2000) Social policies and the pathways to inequalities in health: a comparative analysis of lone mothers in Britain and Sweden, *Social and Science Medicine*, 50(2): 255–70.

Woolf, S., Battista, R. and Anderson, G. *et al.* (1990) Assessing the clinical effectiveness of preventive manoeuvres: analytic principles and systematic methods in reviewing evidence and developing clinical practice recommendations, *Journal of Clinical Epidemiology*, 43: 891–905.

Glossary

Key surveys

BCS70   1970 British Birth Cohort Study. A longitudinal study of individuals born in 1970 with information collected at birth and at the ages of 5, 10, 16 and 26.

BHPS   British Household Panel Survey. A national longitudinal survey of household members aged 16 and over interviewed annually since then.

Census   Census of the UK population carried out every ten years. The last census, in 1991, included a question on health status (limiting long-term illness) for the first time.

FNS   Fourth National Survey of Ethnic Minorities. A survey of ethnic minority and White people carried out in England and Wales in 1993/4.

GHS   General Household Survey. A survey of households in Britain, carried out annually from 1971.

HALS   Health and Lifestyle Survey. A survey carried out in 1984 in England, Scotland and Wales. Two thirds of the sample were re-interviewed in 1991.

HSFE   Health Survey for England. An annual survey instituted in 1991 to monitor trends in the nation's health.

LFS	Labour Force Survey. A survey of adults in Britain, started in 1993, carried out on a continuous basis.
NCDS	National Child Development Study. A longitudinal survey of individuals born in 1958 in England, Scotland and Wales, with information collected at birth and at the ages of 7, 11, 16, 23 and 33.
ONS-LS	Office for National Statistics Longitudinal Study. A study based on a 1 per cent sample of those enumerated in England and Wales, with data on this sample added from the 1981 and 1991 censuses and from vital registration records (births, cancers, deaths).

Other key terms

absolute poverty	An income too low to secure basic necessities.
Acheson Report	The Report of the Independent Inquiry into Inequalities in Health, established in 1997, after the election of the Labour government. Chaired by Sir Donald Acheson, the Independent Inquiry produced its published report in 1998.
Black Report	The Report of the Working Group on Inequalities in Health, known as the Black report because its Chairperson was Sir Douglas Black, formerly Chief Scientist at the Department of Health. It was submitted to the Secretary of State for Social Services in 1980 and subsequently published, in a slightly slimmed down version, in 1982.
BMI	Body mass index. Weight in kilograms divided by the square of height in metres. If the resulting value is between 25.0 and 30.0, the person is defined as 'overweight'. If it exceeds 30.0, she or he is defined as 'obese'.
CHD	Coronary heart disease.
FEV1	Forced expiratory volume. The amount of air (in litres) that a person, after having breathed in fully, breathes out of his or her lungs during the first second of an expiration with maximum effort.
FVC	The forced vital capacity is the total volume of air (measured in litres) that an individual can

	breathe out of their lungs after having breathed in fully.
housing tenure	Refers to whether those living in a household rent or own (outright or through a mortgage) their home.
lifecourse	A term used to describe the period from birth to death. It is often broken down into lifecourse stages, like childhood, adolescence and early adulthood, to identify the influence on current health of experiences from earlier periods of an individual's life.
LLTI	Limiting long-term illness. Also called limiting long-standing illness.
MI	Myocardial infarction. Heart attack.
poverty line	Usually measured by household income. Households with incomes below half the average for all households, adjusted for size and composition, are deemed to be poor. This is a *relative poverty* line.
regression (linear, logistic)	A statistical procedure used to investigate the independent effects of two or more factors (e.g. SES and ethnic group) on an outcome variable (e.g. health status).
relative poverty	Having an income substantially below the average for that society and too low to secure a standard of living regarded as decent and acceptable by the society in which one lives.
SES	Socio-economic status. In the UK this has traditionally been based on occupation, with women living with men classified on the basis of their partner's occupation. Own occupation is increasingly used for both men and women, with education, income, housing tenure and car ownership providing additional or alternative measures.
SMR	Standardized mortality ratio. A measure which allows us to compare the relative risks of death between different groups in the population: for example, between social classes, between regions, between areas. An SMR of 100 means that the odds of dying are the same in that social class (region, area) as in the country as a whole. An SMR below 100 means that the chances of death are lower; one above means that the individuals in that group have a higher mortality than the population as a whole.

Index

Page numbers in *italics* refer to figures and tables, *g* indicates a glossary definition.

occupation-based measures of socioeconomic status
and mortality rates, 6–8
patterns and trends, 9–13
research challenges, 13–18
and women's health, 70, *71*
sports participation, *161*
women, *68*
standardized mortality ratios (SMRs), 221*g*
in UK, 7, 8–9, 129–30, 187, *188*, 189
standard of living, 30
stroke rates and ethnicity, 35
Sure Start, 108
Sweden and UK, lone mothers, 210, 211–16
Swedish Survey of Living Conditions (ULF), 210

trust and safety, *160*
see also protection

unemployment, *see* joblessness
'unreflective ethnicity', 54
'un-theorized' ethnicity, 38, 39

vulnerably housed people, 194–6

'wealth difference', *see* income distribution
WFTC, *see* Working Families Tax Credit
Whitehead, M., 167–8
women
area comparisons, 164–6
area versus individual factors, 147
dimensions of inequality, 58–62
of ethnic minorities, 26–7, 30, 31
hazard exposure, 84, *85*, 86, 87, 89
income, 108
measuring inequality, 62–3
social class assignment, 5, 26–7, 83
pathways from social to health inequality, 68–72
work, lifestyle and health, 64–8, *69*
see also lone mothers
'work control', 61, 67–8, *69*
Working Families Tax Credit (WFTC), 107, 108, 196–7